The Arnold and Caroline Rose Monograph Series
of the American Sociological Association

Undocumented Mexicans
in the United States

For other titles in this series, turn to p. 233

Undocumented Mexicans in the United States

David M. Heer

Population Research Laboratory
University of Southern California

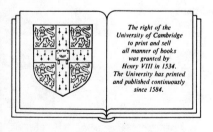

The right of the
University of Cambridge
to print and sell
all manner of books
was granted by
Henry VIII in 1534.
The University has printed
and published continuously
since 1584.

Cambridge University Press
Cambridge
New York   Port Chester   Melbourne   Sydney

Published by the Press Syndicate of the University of Cambridge
The Pitt Building, Trumpington Street, Cambridge CB2 1RP
40 West 20th Street, New York, NY 10011, USA
10 Stamford Road, Oakleigh, Melbourne 3166, Australia

First published 1990

Printed in the United States of America

Library of Congress Cataloging-in-Publication Data
Heer, David M.
Undocumented Mexicans in the United States / David M.
Heer.
    p.   cm. – (The Arnold and Caroline Rose monograph series of
the American Sociological Association)
ISBN 0–521–38247–5
1. Mexicans – United States – Social conditions.   2. Mexican
Americans – Social conditions.   3. Aliens, Illegal – United States –
Social conditions.   4. Immigrants – United States – Social
conditions.   5. Mexico – Emigration and immigration.   6. United
States – Emigration and immigration.   I. Title.   II. Series.
E184.M5H376   1990
305.8'6872073–dc20   89-49074
                                                              CIP

British Library Cataloguing in Publication Data
Heer, David M.
Undocumented Mexicans in the United States.–
(The Arnold and Caroline Rose monograph series of the
American Sociological Association)
1. United States. Mexican immigrants. Social conditions
I. Title   II. Series
305.86872073

ISBN 0–521–38247–5 hardback

Contents

Acknowledgments *page* ix

1 Introduction 1
    My interest in the topic 1
    The value of this book 2

2 Mexican immigration to the United States: determinants and
  trends 7
    A theory concerning determinants of the volume of
    migration 8
    U.S. immigration law as it has affected immigration from
    Mexico 11
    Mechanisms for the enforcement of U.S. immigration law 16
    Illegal immigration as an aid to legal immigration 22
    Numbers and settlement patterns 24
    Decennial increase in the number of persons born in Mexico
    in relation to the number of legal immigrants 25
    Mexican immigrants as proportions of the U.S. and Mexican
    populations 30
    Trends in the geographic distribution of Mexican
    immigrants 31

3 Undocumented Mexican immigrants: numbers, geographic
  distribution, and social consequences 34
    Attempts to estimate the stock and flow 34
    The geographic concentration of undocumented Mexican
    immigrants 53
    Social consequences of undocumented immigration 61

4 Alternative ways of surveying the undocumented and some
  results   72
  Alternative methods for surveying the undocumented *n*   72
  Some important results from the existing surveys   79

5 How the Los Angeles County Parents data were obtained   88
  The proposed research design and its genesis   88
  Modifications made to meet human-subjects' constraints   90
  Details of the data collection   92

6 The validity of data on legal status   98
  Categorizing legal status of the immigrants   98
  Assessing the validity of the responses   100

7 A comparison of the social characteristics of undocumented
  immigrants, legal immigrants, and U.S. natives of Mexican
  origin   106
  Methodological notes   106
  Births   108
  Age   112
  Marital and family status   112
  Immigration history   117
  Educational attainment   120
  Geographic distribution of residence   125
  Fertility   133
  School enrollment and relative progress in school   140

8 A comparison of the economic characteristics of undocu-
  mented immigrants, legal immigrants, and U.S. natives of
  Mexican origin   143
  Employment status and weeks worked in 1979   144
  Occupation, industry, and class of worker   146
  Income   154
  Participation in entitlement programs   156
  Taxation   166

9   Characteristics of one individual compared to characteristics
    of another family member   169
        Legal status of the individual compared to legal status of the
        spouse   169
        Legal status of the individual compared to legal status of the
        sibling   171
        Difference between husband's and wife's length of stay by
        own legal status   172

10 A multivariate analysis of the impact of legal status on the
    hourly wage, hours worked per year, and annual earnings   175
        Details of the methodology   176
        Results   178
        Discussion   184

11 Policy options and their likely consequences   187
        The values at stake   187
        Brief historical overview of proposals for legislative change 195
        Evaluation of specific provisions enacted or proposed   196
        Personal policy preference   205
        Specific proposals   206

Notes   213

Index   229

Acknowledgments

I have many persons to thank for helping me with the preparation of this book and with the carrying out of the Los Angeles County Parents Survey.

In developing plans for the Los Angeles County Parents Survey, I am indebted to David Fox, Leo Estrada, Martin Donabedian, Beth Berkov, Joan Moore, and the students who were enrolled in Sociology 522 at the University of Southern California in the spring of 1979.

I wish to thank Robert García for his assistance in generating community support for the Los Angeles County Parents Survey. I am thankful to Robert García, John Long, Robert Castro, and all of the staff of the Chicano Pinto Research Project, Inc. (now known as Community Systems Research, Inc.) for their efforts, which resulted in the successful completion of the interviewing. I also wish to express my appreciation to the 903 persons who agreed to be interviewed. In addition, I wish to thank Joan Moore, Marta Seoane, and Dee Falasco for their several contributions during the period in which the interviews were conducted.

I am very much indebted to Dee Falasco for her competence in conducting much of the computer programming. Others to whom I owe thanks for their programming assistance are Leo Schuerman, John Brennan, Chyong-fang Ko, and Ichi Tanioka. For help in analyzing the data, I wish to thank Dee Falasco, Paula Hancock, Paul Fast, Anita Jackson, and Walter Fogel.

I am grateful to the National Institutes of Health for the grant that made the Los Angeles County Parents Survey possible and to the Hoover Institution on War, Revolution, and Peace for providing me with a stipend to write this book. For their specific efforts in providing institutional support, I wish to acknowledge the invaluable contributions of Earl Huyck, Maurice D. Van Arsdol, Jr., Henry Birnbaum, Kingsley Davis, Peter Duignan, and Richard Staar.

I am indebted to Ricardo Anzaldua for providing bibliographic assistance and to Stephanie Ventura for making available to me unpublished tabulations. I wish to thank Philip García and Manuel García y Griego for conversations that stimulated my thinking. For help in mastering the intricacies of various word-processing systems and otherwise assisting in the preparation of the manuscript, I am grateful to Gloria Watson, Nina Barnes, and Amentha Dymally. I am especially appreciative of the contribution of Dudley Kirk, who read the entire manuscript and made many valuable suggestions for its improvement.

I wish to thank Ernest Campbell and Teresa Sullivan, successive editors of the Arnold and Caroline Rose Monograph Series, and the anonymous referees for the Series, who guided me toward a more concise and readable manuscript. I am also thankful to Terri Leclercq, who, on behalf of the Arnold and Caroline Rose Monograph Series, made valuable suggestions for improving the clarity of the final manuscript. I am grateful to Margo Koss for her competent preparation of the index.

Finally, I am indebted to my wife, Kaye, for valuable editorial suggestions with respect to this book, and, of course, her patience in enduring my moods for the entire period during which this research took place.

1. Introduction

My interest in the topic

As a demographer my lifetime interest has been the study of fertility. Why did I become absorbed by the topic of undocumented Mexican immigrants? The reason is simple. During the 1970s, the neighborhood around my office at the University of Southern California, some three miles southwest of downtown Los Angeles, was changing rapidly. What had been a typical inner-city black area was being transformed. The new residents were brown-skinned rather than black, and they spoke Spanish rather than English. I wondered: Could these newcomers be undocumented Mexican immigrants?

My office at the university's Population Research Laboratory is southeast of the main campus. It is in a largely industrial district in which there are numerous small factories, many of them manufacturing apparel. Scattered among these small factories there is tenement housing. Today the casual observer can note that almost all the residents speak Spanish and are Mexican.

To the northeast of the university, beyond the enclave in which a largely student population resides, the neighborhoods are entirely residential. Here too the inhabitants are now almost all Mexican. To the west and south of the university the neighborhoods are also completely residential. They are still largely black, but there is now also a substantial Mexican population.

A comparison of 1970 and 1980 Census figures for the sixteen census tracts including and surrounding the University of Southern California quantifies the changes that occurred.[1] The total population of these tracts increased from 60,362 to 73,060. The proportion of the total population that was black decreased from 65 percent to 45 percent. The proportion that was Hispanic increased from 15 percent to 38 percent. For all of the sixteen census tracts, the total population increased 21 percent, the black population declined 18 percent, but the Hispanic population increased by 213 percent.

In the six census tracts to the east of the university, the proportion of the total population of Hispanic origin increased from 27 to 56 percent, and the proportion black decreased from 49 to 24 percent. In the nine census tracts located to the

1

west or south of the university, the proportion of the population of Hispanic origin increased from 8 to 28 percent whereas the proportion black declined from 79 to 62 percent.

Based on data (Chapter 7), I believe the large majority of the adults among the Hispanic population in these sixteen census tracts were undocumented Mexican immigrants.

The value of this book

My book offers two contributions. The first is to understand, within a sociological perspective, the conditions of life among a group of individuals who hold a very special legal status in our nation. The second is to provide facts that can help persons devising policy concerning the presence in the United States of these individuals.

All human societies have differentiated status in terms of legally recognized rights and responsibilities. The illegal, or undocumented, immigrant represents one legally distinct status.

All societies make legal distinctions according to age; children are not granted the same status as adults. All societies also differentiate privileges and responsibilities according to sex. Finally, because reproduction is a key societal concern, all societies have granted differential rights and privileges according to marital status.

In almost all societies other criteria have also been used to distinguish types of legal status. For example, in ancient Greece and Rome the differentiation between slave and free person was profound. Moreover, among free persons an important distinction was made between citizen and noncitizen. Political rights were reserved for the former. As an immigrant to Athens, the famous philosopher, Aristotle, could never be an Athenian citizen.[2]

Many legal status systems are explicitly designed to differentiate sharply members of the society with respect to rights and privileges. Nevertheless, almost all legal status systems recognize the legitimate presence in the society of persons holding each type of legal status, even the lowest. What is unique about the status of the undocumented immigrant in America currently is that such a person has no legal right to remain in the society at all. Attempts to avoid deportation while entering the United States sometimes lead to tragic consequences. For example, on July 2, 1987, near El Paso, Texas, eighteen undocumented Mexican men died by suffocation in a closed railroad boxcar in which the temperature reached 130 degrees Fahrenheit.[3]

The undocumented immigrant who remains in the United States does so only because the legal authorities have not been able to force departure. In turn, depar-

ture has not been forced for the very important reason that elements within the
nation have welcomed the illegal presence of undocumented immigrants. Thus
lack of unanimous support of the laws governing who may legitimately reside in
the United States has allowed substantial numbers of undocumented aliens to
remain within the society.

The status of the undocumented is not merely defined by their having no legal
rights to be present in the United States. In common with legal aliens, they lack
the voting and other political rights of the citizen. In contrast to all other status
groups, they lack access to the many entitlement programs that have become so
important with the advent of the welfare state. Because the undocumented have
almost no legally recognized rights, we may very rightly term them a legal
underclass.

Sociologists commonly use the term *underclass* to denote persons who persist-
ently live in poverty and who have inherited low status from their parents and are
likely to hand it on to their children. In my use of the term *legal underclass,* I do
not necessarily imply either of these characteristics, nor do I presume that an
undocumented immigrant will continue in that status for all of a remaining lifetime. Many undocumented persons in the United States will no doubt succeed in
changing their status to legal immigrant, and some will become naturalized citizens. Many others will leave the United States and return to their country of birth,
where they will resume the status of native citizen. Furthermore, at least in the
United States, the status of being undocumented cannot be transmitted to one's
future children. According to the U.S. Constitution, children born in the United
States of undocumented immigrants are always U.S. citizens.

Societies frequently change the ways in which they define legal status or the
ways in which persons are assigned to a particular status. For example, consider
the changes in legal status in the history of the United States. At the beginning,
20 percent of the total population were slaves. Almost all of the remaining population were citizens, but only a minority of these (adult males) had the right to
vote. No laws restricted immigration, but aliens from abroad could become naturalized citizens only if their race was white.

Just before the outbreak of the Civil War, in 1857, the U.S. Supreme Court, in
the famous *Dred Scott v. Sanford* decision, made an important pronouncement
concerning the nature of citizenship. Chief Justice Taney proclaimed the court's
judgment that no black person, not even a free one, could ever be a U.S. citizen.
Following the Civil War and the abolition of slavery, Americans ratified the Fourteenth Amendment to the Constitution. In reversing the *Dred Scott* decision, this
amendment stated simply, "All persons born or naturalized in the United States,
and subject to the jurisdiction thereof, are citizens of the United States and of the
State wherein they reside." With the Fourteenth Amendment, the United States

thus embraced a rule for citizenship, *jus soli,* very different from that of the major European nations, where citizenship depended (and still depends) on *jus sanguinis,* a rule decreeing that the native-born children of aliens are also aliens.[4] Henceforth all children born in the United States of undocumented persons would themselves be native-born citizens.

However, when the Fourteenth Amendment was added to our Constitution in 1868, the United States had no illegal aliens. The very concept of an illegal alien is impossible unless laws restrict the numbers and characteristics of immigrants; until 1875 the United States had no such laws. Although the United States has undoubtedly had some illegal aliens ever since 1875, their existence was not considered a major social problem until the early 1970s. In 1974 the commissioner of the U.S. Immigration and Naturalization Service (INS) set the probable number of undocumented immigrants in the United States as from 6 to 8 million persons. He later characterized the inflow as a "silent invasion of the United States."[5] These statements received wide publicity.

In my opinion, the numbers represented gross exaggeration. Two demographers, one from the U.S. Bureau of the Census and the other from the INS, later carefully executed a study of the number of undocumented persons counted in the 1980 Census. They determined that 2.1 million undocumented persons had been counted by the census. Of these, 1.1 million were from Mexico; no other nation provided as many as 60,000.[6] Nevertheless, the number of undocumented persons counted in the 1980 Census, a minimum estimate of the number actually present, was sufficiently large to indicate, even to the most skeptical, that undocumented individuals constituted an important component of the U.S. population.

In an effort to solve the problems of undocumented persons in the United States, the federal government enacted the Immigration Reform and Control Act of 1986. This law allowed undocumented persons to legalize their status if they had resided continuously in the United States since January 1, 1982, or were seasonal agricultural workers in 1986. The law made it unlawful for employers knowingly to hire undocumented persons. In theory, the law would solve the problem of undocumented immigration by eliminating the presence of the undocumented in the United States. Around 50 percent of them would be legalized. The rest, unable to secure jobs, would leave either voluntarily or by compulsion. As of November 2, 1989, almost 3.1 million persons had applied to legalize their status, including almost 2.3 million from Mexico. Among the Mexican applicants, more than 1.0 million had applied as seasonal agricultural workers and more than 1.2 million as having lived continuously in the United States since 1982.[7]

It is still too early to determine whether in practice the law will work the way its proponents have assumed. The law is unlikely to eliminate the presence of undocumented persons. Many Americans, particularly employers who hire them, benefit by the presence of the undocumented in our midst. Moreover, the Act did not establish a foolproof national identity card. Accordingly, many undocumented workers will secure employment by presenting false documents that make them appear to be legal residents when they are not. Thus, many undocumented persons will continue to live and work in the United States. If this is so, it is important for Americans to have some understanding of their conditions of life and the extent to which these conditions are caused simply by their undocumented status.

The second purpose of this book is to provide facts helpful in devising policy. If the Immigration and Reform Control Act of 1986 will not eliminate the presence of undocumented individuals in the United States, it follows that passage of that law has been but a prologue to what will be a long policy debate. Policies are derived both from values and from presumptions about facts. If the facts are incorrectly presumed, the policy will not advance the values it is supposed to embody. Accordingly, policies are often adopted that have unintended consequences. Some of these consequences may be beneficial, but many others may be harmful. We should all like to minimize the extent to which legislation concerning undocumented individuals has unintended consequences. This limiting can be done if policymakers have access to the most complete data available concerning their numbers, their reasons for coming to the United States, the consequences of their presence for other Americans, and the differences in socioeconomic status between the undocumented and Americans with other legal status.

Thus the two goals of this book are to aid sociological understanding of the conditions of life among undocumented Mexican immigrants to the United States, and to summarize all facts about them that should be of relevance to policy-making.

To support these two goals, the book analyzes data gathered by other social scientists as well as data collected in a survey I directed that allowed a direct comparison of the characteristics of undocumented Mexican immigrants with the characteristics of legal Mexican immigrants and of U.S.-born citizens of Mexican descent. The organization of this book follows the dichotomy defined by these two types of data. Chapters 2–4 are concerned with data gathered by others and Chapters 5–10 with my own data.

In my survey, interviews were conducted with the parents of 903 babies born in Los Angeles County for whom either the mother or the father was reported on the birth certificate to be of Mexican descent. From the survey, an explicit comparison can be made among four groups of Mexican Americans: undocumented immigrants, legal immigrants, naturalized citizens, and citizens born in the United States of Mexican descent. Although a nationwide survey might have provided data somewhat more relevant to policy, it is highly significant that Los Angeles County was the home of 44 percent of all undocumented Mexican aliens in the United States who were counted in the 1980 Census. These persons constituted 6.7 percent of that county's entire population.[8]

Apart from the specific questions on type of legal status, the questions on the Los Angeles County Parents Survey were largely identical to those of the 1980 Census of Population. The questions concerned the baby's mother, the baby's father, an unmarried adult brother of the respondent living in Los Angeles County, and a childless adult sister of the respondent also living in Los Angeles County. The information gathered was meant to cover in aggregate all adults of reproductive age and of Mexican origin in Los Angeles County.

The survey allows a researcher to answer two types of questions concerning undocumented Mexican immigrants. The first is simple: How do the undocumented differ from either legal Mexican immigrants or the native-born of Mexican descent? The second question is more complex: Were the differences the result of selection or were they caused by the very fact of difference in legal status? For example, if a difference in the average wage between undocumented and legal immigrants was found, it could have been caused by the fact that undocumented immigrants had been in the United States for a shorter time than legal immigrants (a selection factor). Alternatively, it could have occurred because lack of access to entitlement programs gave the undocumented less choice to refuse low-wage offers (a direct effect of legal status).

I must admit that the survey has two drawbacks. First, it describes the situation of undocumented Mexicans in 1980–81, prior to the passage of the Immigration Reform and Control Act of 1986. The imposition of employer sanctions under that Act may have significantly changed the socioeconomic position of undocumented persons in the United States. Second, the survey relates only to Los Angeles and not to the United States as a whole; inferences from the former do not necessarily hold for the latter.

2. Mexican immigration to the United States: determinants and trends

A large and growing proportion of all legal immigrants to the United States have come from Mexico. Between 1971 and 1980 about 14 percent of all legal immigrants came from that nation. From 1951 through 1970 that percentage was only marginally lower. Prior to 1950 the proportion of all legal immigrants from Mexico was substantially less. In the decade of the 1940s, the proportion was about 6 percent and during the 1930s only 4 percent. Although during the 1920s it was 11 percent, from 1901 to 1910, a decade of large-scale European immigration, less than 1 percent of all legal immigrants came from Mexico. Moreover, in recent decades the absolute number of legal immigrants from Mexico has been increasing at an even higher rate than the proportion: from 61,000 during the 1941–50 decade to 637,000 during the 1971–80 decade.[1]

The figures with regard to legal immigrants do not tell the whole story, of course. There has also been widespread illegal, or undocumented, immigration. As a result, the 1980 Census, which included undocumented as well as legal immigrants, showed 1,270,000 persons residing in the United States who had been born in Mexico and had immigrated to the United States since January 1, 1970. This figure is double the number of persons legally immigrating from Mexico during that decade and represents 22.8 percent of all U.S. residents who had been born abroad and had immigrated to the United States during this period.[2]

This chapter first describes generally some causes of migratory behavior and then discusses the specific case of Mexican migration to the United States. One factor determining the volume of immigration is so important that its components are discussed separately; that factor is U.S. immigration law and its enforcement. The chapter also reviews the ways in which prior illegal immigration aids future legal immigration. It then discusses in detail (1) how many legal immigrants have come in each time period, (2) the relation between the number of legal immigrants in each decade and the decennial increase in the Mexican-born population in the corresponding decade, (3) the relationships between the Mexican-born population of the United States in each time period and the populations of the United States and Mexico, and (4) the settlement patterns of immigrants from Mexico in terms of the states and Metropolitan Statistical Areas in which they have resided.

7

A theory concerning determinants of the volume of migration

Demographers analyze the determinants of the volume of migration into two components. The first concerns the propensity of a given individual to migrate. The second concerns the number of individuals who are at risk of migration at each level of propensity. The volume of migration can be calculated as the sum over all levels of propensity of the products obtained by multiplying each separate propensity to migrate by the number of individuals with that propensity.

A conceptual scheme for determining individual propensity to migrate

One much used conceptual scheme for discussing the determinants of the propensity to migrate is that of Everett Lee.[3] He summarized the factors entering into the decision to migrate as follows:

1. factors associated with the area of origin,
2. factors associated with the area of destination,
3. intervening obstacles, and
4. personal factors.

A second conceptual scheme, which I had developed previously, cuts up the pie in a somewhat different way.[4] It follows a scheme developed by Joseph J. Spengler for the analysis of the determinants of decisions with respect to fertility. In it, I classified the factors affecting the decision to migrate into factors affecting a preference system, a price system, and the total amount of resources in time and money available for all goals. I shall use this second conceptual scheme to discuss the determinants of the individual propensity of Mexicans to emmigrate to the United States. First, however, the concepts must be defined.

The preference system describes the relative attractiveness of various places as goals for the potential migrant compared to other goals that his resources would allow him to pursue. An area's attractiveness is the balance between the positive and negative values that it offers.

The price system describes the expenditure of resources that is both a precondition to and a concomitant of migration. For many migrants the price of migration is in large part simply the monetary expense of moving. Because the cost of migration generally varies in direct proportion to the distance traveled, the number of migrants to a given place tends to vary inversely with the distance.

The total resources in time and money available for all goals also affects the decision to migrate. If the only drawback to migration is the expense of the move, then an increase in monetary income should increase the probability of migration.

Determinants of the propensity of Mexicans to emigrate to the United States

To apply this conceptual scheme, let us begin with factors associated with the preference system. Among the positive values generated by migration, perhaps the most important is the prospect of a better job. This value is particularly important with respect to immigration to the United States from Mexico because of the tremendous disparities in per capita income between the two nations. For example, in 1983 Mexican per capita income was only about $2,240. In contrast, U.S. per capita income was $14,090,[5] more than six times greater than in Mexico. Nevertheless, unless employers in the United States were willing to hire them, differences in the standards of living between Mexico and the United States would not be sufficient to induce Mexicans to believe that they could get a better job in the United States. For immigrants to the United States from Mexico the 1980 unemployment rate was only marginally higher than for the total native population.[6] Employers in the United States were indeed willing to hire such immigrants.

Migration also creates negative values. One of the most important is disruption of interpersonal relationships with kin and old friends. The greater the distance the greater this disruption, because return visits and contacts become more costly. To mitigate against this disruption, many migrants travel to the same towns or city neighborhoods to which relatives or other people from their towns of origin have previously migrated.

In addition, the volume of migration from one locale to another tends to rise once a small nucleus of persons from the place of origin has established itself in the place of destination. The increasing volume of the migratory stream, once a nucleus of persons related in some way has been established, has been termed "chain migration."[7] With respect to migration from Mexico to the southwestern states, patterns of chain migration have probably been in existence since the accession of this territory from Mexico in 1848. Nevertheless, it is also probable that over time these chains have strengthened, particularly for places outside the southwestern states. The important aspect of chain migration is that once it has begun, the negative values associated with disruption of interpersonal relationships markedly decline.

Migration may also cause deprivation because of the necessity to adapt to a new culture including a new language. All Mexican immigrants are forced to cope with a new language following immigration to the United States (although some already know English). However, the Spanish language being closely connected to English, learning the new language is less of a barrier for Mexican immigrants than it would be for potential immigrants from many other parts of the world.

Religion is another important component of the culture that may differ between the immigrant's country of origin and new country of destination. Because the predominant religion of Mexico is Roman Catholic, a religion that is well established in the United States, the barrier of religious difference is much less for immigrants to the United States from Mexico than for potential immigrants from most parts of Asia or Africa.

Laws restricting the number of legal entrants to the United States are of course a major negative value for those immigrants who enter the United States without legal permit. Such persons live in fear of being discovered and sent back to their native land. As a result of their illegal status, they will be deprived of entitlement programs available to legal immigrants. Their lack of legal status will also be a hindrance to their attaining the wage or salary level they might otherwise have attained.

Let us now consider how the price system may have affected Mexican immigration to the United States. The most salient fact is the availability of very cheap international transportation. Of course, the price of transportation to the United States varies markedly from one part of Mexico to another. Nevertheless, in international perspective, there can be no doubt that the transportation price for legal immigration to the United States from Mexico is one of the lowest for any nation.

Another aspect of the price system is the price for obtaining knowledge about opportunities in the United States. It is fair to assume that, because of improvements in educational level in Mexico and the advent of mass communications, this price has declined consistently over the past several decades.

However, restrictive legislation with respect to legal immigration also has a major effect on the price system. The undocumented immigrant who succeeds in reaching the United States must often pay for forged documents and for the services of a *coyote,* a guide who will lead him safely through the barriers imposed by the U.S. Border Patrol.

Finally, the decision to migrate is a positive function of the total resources in time and money available for all goals. A salient fact about Mexico is that per capita income in that nation is apparently now much higher, in constant pesos, than it was in earlier decades. However, per capita income in constant pesos cannot be easily measured. Therefore, as evidence for this contention, we will examine change in per capita energy consumption, a close correlate of per capita income. In Mexico, per capita energy consumption more than tripled from 1950 to 1980. Of course, this large increase in per capita energy consumption in Mexico may also have affected the relative status of Mexico vis-à-vis the United States with respect to this variable. If per capita consumption of energy in Mexico increased more rapidly than in the United States, a change in the preference system would have ensued, causing a reduction in the attractiveness to Mexicans of immigrating to the United States. In fact, per capita energy consumption in Mexico relative to that in the

United States did increase from 8 percent in 1950 to 17 percent in 1980.[8] Thus we must assume that the attractiveness of immigration to the United States was diminished during this period.

Mexican population size as a determinant of immigration volume

Collectively, the preference system, the price system, and total resources of time and money determine the propensity of any given Mexican to immigrate to the United States. The total volume of immigration from Mexico to the United States can be calculated as the product of the average propensity of Mexicans to immigrate and the total population of Mexico. A very strong influence on the rapid increase in total volume of Mexican immigration to the United States is thus Mexico's population growth, which has been among the most rapid in the world.

In 1950 the population of Mexico was only about 26 million. By 1980 its population had reached around 67 million.[9] In this 30-year period Mexico's average annual population growth rate was 3.2 percent. Clearly the potential demand of Mexicans for immigration to the United States has substantially increased. It is fitting to see how American immigration legislation has responded. As we have seen, restrictive legislation can both reduce the attractiveness of immigration and increase its price.

U.S. immigration law as it has affected immigration from Mexico

Early legislation

Until the second half of the nineteenth century, the United States had no laws restricting immigration. In 1875 the U.S. government passed a law prohibiting the immigration of convicts and prostitutes; in 1882 a second law was enacted also prohibiting idiots, lunatics, and paupers[10] and imposing a head tax of $0.50.[11] A law enacted in 1885 prohibited labor contracts in which an employer would pay for the transportation costs of an immigrant and later deduct such costs from the immigrant's wage. The Immigration Act of 1917 decreed that henceforth immigrants to the United States must pay a head tax of $8 and that all adult immigrants must pass a literacy test. However, this act also provided for the admission of temporary workers otherwise excludable if the secretary of labor deemed it necessary.[12] This last provision of the Act of 1917 was to have special bearing on immigration from Mexico.

✦ Legislation in the 1920s

The immigration acts of 1921 and 1924 drastically reduced immigration from Eastern Hemisphere nations. Although Congress had debated the issue, the resulting laws contained no quotas for Western Hemisphere nations. The provisions of the Act of 1924 that did affect Mexican immigration had to do with a change in administrative procedure for the legal admittance of immigrants. Prospective immigrants to the United States were required to obtain a visa from a consular official of the U.S. Department of State in their own homeland. The fee of $10 demanded for the visa was in addition to the $8 head tax.[13]

In 1925 the U.S. Congress passed additional legislation establishing the U.S. border patrol to forestall illegal immigration into the United States from Mexico or Canada.[14] Another important change, not in the immigration law itself but in its interpretation, came about in 1929. In that year the U.S. Department of State introduced its version of a catch-22. It ruled that if an applicant claimed to have an American job offer, his or her admittance should be denied on the basis of a violation of the Alien Contract Labor Law of 1885. On the other hand, without such a job offer, the applicant should usually be denied admission on the basis of the likelihood of his or her becoming a public charge, a contingency that had disallowed the issuance of a visa since the Immigration Act of 1882 but had not previously been so strictly interpreted.[15]

✦ Legislation from 1952 through 1980

The Immigration Act of 1924 continued in effect until the passage of the Immigration Act of 1952. This act made only minor changes with respect to immigration from Mexico. The most important was the so-called Texas proviso, which clearly stated that the act of employing an illegal alien was not to be considered an unlawful practice.[16] Major changes with respect to immigration from Mexico came only with passage of the Immigration Act of 1965.

According to the 1965 legislation, a quota of 120,000 persons per year would be allowed to enter the United States from Western Hemisphere nations beginning in 1968. Within the quota, visas were issued on a first-come, first-served basis. However, applicants intending to be gainfully employed (other than parents, spouses, and minor children of permanent resident aliens, or parents of minor U.S. citizens) had to obtain labor certification from the secretary of labor. Labor certification was to be granted only if there were not sufficient qualified and available workers to fill the particular job in the particular locality which the applicant sought. In addition, unless the prospective worker were a professional, certification could not be granted unless the applicant had an actual job offer. It was very significant, however, that parents of minor U.S. citizens were exempt from the need for labor certification. For a period of time undocumented immigrants who had given birth in the United States gained a significant advantage over other applicants for admission to the United States as permanent legal residents. The immediate relatives of U.S. citizens were exempt from these numerical quotas established for Western Hemisphere applicants. These included spouses, unmarried children under 21 years of age of U.S. citizens, and the parents of U.S. citizens 21 years of age or older.

Additional important legislation enacted in the fall of 1976 went into effect on January 1, 1977. This new legislation established a maximum quota of 20,000 annual entrants for each Western Hemisphere nation. The major effect of this change was to reduce drastically the number of Mexicans who could legally enter the United States. In addition, the 1976 legislation decreed that applicants from the Western Hemisphere for admission under the quota were to be admitted according to a preference system (identical for applicants from both the Eastern and the Western Hemisphere). Seven ranked preference categories were established in addition to a residual, nonpreference category.

With respect to admission under the third and sixth preference categories (professional and skilled and unskilled workers) and with respect to admissions in the nonpreference category, no visas could be granted unless the secretary of labor granted labor certification, which was now modified to require a job offer for applicants in the third preference category as well as the sixth preference and nonpreference categories. Moreover, in a very important provision for Mexican visa applicants, the previous labor-certification exemption for the parents of minor U.S. citizens was repealed.

Additional changes in the immigration laws have been made since the Immigration Act of 1976. Effective October 1978, a single worldwide quota of 290,000 persons was established in place of separate hemisphere quotas. Effective October 1979, this worldwide quota was reduced to 280,000 persons. Finally, the Refugee Act of 1980 abolished the refugee category as a separate category and redistributed the 6 percent quota for refugees to the second preference category. The Refugee Act also decreed that beginning in 1981 the worldwide numerical quota for nonrefugees would be reduced to 270,000. Table 2.1 outlines the quotas authorized for each of the six preference categories according to the Refugee Act of 1980.

The Immigration Reform and Control Act of 1986

The major features of the 1986 Act are briefly discussed in Chapter 1. A comprehensive exposition of this legislation is presented in Chapter 11.

Table 2.1. *The preference system created under the Refugee Act of 1980*

Preference	Category	Maximum proportion of total admitted
First	Unmarried sons and daughters of U.S. citizens	20 percent
Second	Spouses and unmarried sons and daughters of aliens lawfully admitted for permanent residence	26 percent plus any not required by first preference
Third	Members of the professions, or persons of exceptional ability in the sciences and arts	10 percent
Fourth	Married sons and daughters of U.S. citizens	10 percent plus any not required by first and third preferences
Fifth	Brothers and sisters of U.S. citizens, 21 years of age and older	24 percent plus any not required by first, second, and fourth preferences
Sixth	Skilled and unskilled workers in occupations for which labor is in short supply	10 percent
Nonpreference	Any applicant	Numbers not used by preceding categories

The bracero *program and the Silva decision*

Before ending this discussion of U.S. immigration law as it has affected immigration from Mexico, two further matters should be discussed. The first is the history of the Mexican Labor (*bracero*) Program. Participants in the *bracero* program, in effect from 1942 through 1964, were not considered to be immigrants to the United States. However, they were allowed entrance to the United States as temporary workers in agriculture and were afforded certain protections with respect to housing, transportation, food, medical needs, and wages. In each year from 1951 through 1964 the number of workers admitted was more than 100,000. Between 1956 and 1959 the annual number of workers admitted was always at least 400,000. Nevertheless, there were always many more applicants to the program than could be admitted.[17] The program was ended in 1964 because of the objections of the American labor unions.

The second matter that merits discussion is a 1978 decision of the U.S. Supreme Court, *Silva v. Levi*, which declared that the U.S. government had illegally deprived 145,000 visa applicants from Western Hemisphere nations of a right to enter the

United States. According to the court's decision, the U.S. government should not have reduced the Western Hemisphere quotas to allow for the admission of Cuban refugees. The court ruled that to qualify for admission as a U.S. immigrant under the *Silva* case, an alien must have met both of the following conditions: (1) have registered with a U.S. consulate before January 1, 1977, for a permanent resident visa and be a parent, spouse, or child of a U.S. citizen or lawful permanent resident, or have registered for a visa as an alien with a labor certification, and (2) have maintained continuous presence in the United States since an entry prior to March 11, 1977.[18] In effect, the court's decision allowed undocumented persons, particularly those with a child who was born in the United States, a chance to enter the United States as legal immigrants.

Following this decision by the court, the U.S. Immigration and Naturalization Service (INS) issued letters to 250,000 persons, nearly all of whom were Mexicans living illegally in the southwestern part of the United States. These letters provided temporary protection from deportation while the U.S. government decided exactly which persons would be given the newly created 145,000 visas. Eventually, 145,000 of the letter holders were given immigrant visas. However, at least 100,000 letter holders, of whom some 60,000 were estimated to be living in Southern California, were left out. The INS granted these persons an additional temporary reprieve from deportation until February 1, 1983. Since that time, the INS has mounted no formal effort to deport the letter holders, but some have been deported under the usual enforcement activities of the Service.[19]

Summary of impact

Over a long period extending through 1976 the restrictions with respect to immigration from Mexico were gradually tightened. Perhaps the most significant action was the legislation of 1976 that not only restricted immigration from Mexico under the quota to 20,000 persons a year but also removed the immigration advantage given to parents of a minor born in the United States. The high demand of Mexicans to immigrate to the United States, coupled with severe restrictions on immigration imposed by the United States, resulted in a very large backlog of visa applications from Mexican nationals, more than from any other nation in the world. As of January 1, 1982, this backlog was 271,582, a figure equal to 23 percent of the backlog among all nations.[20]

Prior to 1968, but not thereafter, the law was bendable to reflect the need for Mexican labor in the United States. The Immigration Act of 1917 had allowed the secretary of labor to admit temporary Mexican laborers whether or not they might otherwise be excludable. This flexibility allowed the United States to expand the import of Mexican laborers during World War I, when labor was needed, and to limit it, by means of administrative restrictions on visa applicants in 1929 at the advent of the Great Depression. Finally, the *bracero* program was begun in World War II to permit migration of laborers and was greatly expanded during the period of the Korean conflict, both periods of severe labor shortage in the United States.

The growing presence in the United States of undocumented Mexican immigrants has created pressures both toward their legalization and toward their expulsion. The pressure for legalization was registered first in the *Silva* decision and later in the legalization program of the Immigration Reform and Control Act of 1986. The pressure for expulsion was reflected in the employer sanctions of the Act.

Mechanisms for the enforcement of U.S. immigration law

Descriptive accounts

In recent years a number of excellent books have been published in the United States detailing the work of the Immigration and Naturalization Service in enforcing the immigration law or the ways in which undocumented persons have succeeded in entering the United States.[21] Two deserve special mention. John Crewdson's *The Tarnished Door,* was awarded the Pulitzer Prize in 1983. This book concerns what happens when prospective undocumented immigrants encounter the efforts of the INS to keep them out of the United States. It highlights anecdotal accounts of INS beatings of apprehendees, of rock-throwing at INS agents by Mexicans from their side of the border, and of border crossers being assailed by gangs that rob them of carefully saved dollars. It devotes many pages to describing instances of INS staff corruption and bribe taking. *Pablo Cruz and the American Dream,* an oral history compiled by Eugene Nelson, is a fascinating autobiography of an undocumented immigrant and his many experiences in illegally crossing the border before finally legalizing his status.

Number of deportable aliens located

Table 2.2 presents data on the number of deportable (illegal) aliens located by the INS from fiscal year 1925 through fiscal year 1988, the latest period for which final data are available. From 1964 to 1977 the number of located deportable aliens rose very rapidly: from 87,000 to 1,033,000.[22] In each year since 1977, at least 800,000 located deportable aliens were from Mexico.[23] In fiscal 1988 the INS located 1,008,000 such persons, of whom 950,000 were from Mexico.

The beginning of this period of rapid rise in located deportable aliens coincided with the ending of the *bracero* program. It is impossible to ascertain as yet what long-term effect the Immigration Reform and Control Act of 1986 will have on

Table 2.2. *Deportable aliens located, 1925–88 (numbers in thousands)*

Period	Number	Period	Number
1925–30	128	1959	45
1931	22	1960	71
1932	23	1961	89
1933	21	1962	93
1934	10	1963	89
1935	11	1964	87
1936	12	1965	110
1937	13	1966	139
1938	13	1967	162
1939	12	1968	212
1940	10	1969	284
1941	11	1970	345
1942	12	1971	420
1943	11	1972	506
1944	31	1973	656
1945	69	1974	788
1946	100	1975	759
1947	194	1976	866
1948	193	1977	1,033
1949	288	1978	1,048
1950	468	1979	1,069
1951	509	1980	910
1952	529	1981	976
1953	886	1982	970
1954	1,090	1983	1,251
1955	254	1984	1,247
1956	88	1985	1,349
1957	60	1986	1,767
1958	53	1987	1,190
		1988	1,008

Sources: For 1977 and earlier years, *Annual Report: Immigration and Naturalization Service* (Washington D.C.: Government Printing Office); for 1978 through 1988, *Statistical Yearbook of the U.S. Immigration and Naturalization Service* (Washington D.C.: INS).

the number of located deportable aliens. However, the number for 1987 was substantially less than that for the preceding year.

It is important to be aware of what is being counted when the INS gives figures concerning deportable aliens located. The figures refer to the total number of events in which a deportable alien has been located; the figures do not refer to the total number of persons located. Thus if an illegal alien makes five successive unsuccessful attempts to cross the border, each of these attempts will be counted as a deportable alien located.

Organization of enforcement efforts

Within the INS, the responsibility for locating (apprehending) deportable aliens is divided between the border patrol, which has jurisdictions only over areas that are on or adjacent to the Mexican or Canadian border, and the various district offices of the INS, which collectively cover the entire territory of the United States. The preponderance of deportable aliens has consistently been located by the border patrol. In fiscal 1987 the border patrol located 1,158,000 deportable aliens, of whom 1,124,000 were from Mexico. The investigations branches of the various district offices located only 32,000, of whom 16,000 were Mexicans.[24]

There is a difference between the types of deportable aliens located by the two enforcement branches within INS. The border patrol tends to locate persons who have been in the United States only a short time, whereas the investigation branches of the district offices tend to locate persons who have been in the United States for a longer time. For example, in fiscal 1981, the latest year for which such data are available, 81 percent of all deportable aliens located by the border patrol were located within 72 hours of entry and only 3 percent had been in the United States over one year. In contrast, among the 128,135 deportable aliens located by the district offices, only 6 percent had been found within 72 hours of entry and 38 percent had been in the United States more than one year.[25]

The data on duration of illegal stay in the United States have important implications for the probability that an illegal alien will be apprehended provided he has been in the United States for at least 72 hours: the chance of being caught by the INS is smaller than might appear from the gross figures on apprehensions. Altogether, in fiscal 1980 only 254,000 deportable aliens were located with a duration of stay in the United States of more than 72 hours.[26] This figure is only 12 percent of the 2,057,000 undocumented persons estimated to have been here and counted in the 1980 Census.[27] Moreover, the geographic concentration of undocumented persons counted in the 1980 Census appears to have been much greater than that of located deportable aliens with duration of stay of more than 72 hours. In fact this meant that Los Angeles County was a far safer place for the undocumented than was the country as a whole. Passel has shown that 658,000 undocumented aliens living in Los Angeles County were counted in the 1980 Census, a figure equal to 32 percent of all undocumented persons in the nation.[28] In contrast, the maximum number of located deportable aliens in Los Angeles County in fiscal 1980 (the number reported by the Chula Vista sector of the border patrol plus the number reported by the Los Angeles district office) was only 30,000,[29] a figure equal to only 5 percent of the undocumented persons in Los Angeles County counted in the 1980 Census.

Where undocumented persons are found

The majority of deportable aliens are caught right at the border. Members of a second large segment are found close to the border. Many of this second group are discovered at highway checkpoints, of which the most famous is that at San Clemente, California, halfway between San Diego and Los Angeles; others are found at bus and train stations, usually in cities at or near the border.

Two Mexican social scientists, Zazueta and Zazueta, who interviewed apprehended Mexicans immediately upon their return across the Mexican border, observed interestingly that a high number of undocumented persons were apprehended at bus stations enroute back to Mexico. According to them, the practice was particularly common in Sacramento, California, and in Del Rio, Texas, a small Texas city right on the Mexican border. These apprehensions, of course, did not reduce the number of undocumented persons working in the United States but did serve to meet the arrest quotas of the INS agents.[30]

Another sizable proportion of deportable aliens have been found by means of farm and ranch checks. It is significant that, prior to the 1986 Immigration Reform and Control Act, the INS could make farm and ranch checks without first securing a warrant. A warrant, on the other hand, has been necessary before the INS could raid a factory or an urban business place without the owner's consent. Warrants are not usually obtained unless a citizen or legal resident has reported to the INS that one or more persons at a particular place of business are undocumented.[31]

Processing of deportables

Once the INS has located an undocumented person, the Service proceeds with one of two actions: deportation or required departure. Deportation occurs only after an immigration judge has ruled that the petitioner (the alleged illegal alien) has no legal right to remain in the United States. Required departure occurs if the alleged illegal alien has waived the right to a deportation hearing. In the vast majority of cases the apprehendee waives this legal right. Of 1,611,000 illegal aliens forced to leave the United States in fiscal 1986, 1,589,000 were required to depart; only 23,000 were expelled following a deportation hearing.[32]

With respect to undocumented aliens, the waiving of a right to a deportation hearing is of advantage both to the U.S. government and to the apprehendee. The government saves the cost of the hearing and the even greater cost of maintaining the apprehendee in detention before a hearing. The undocumented alien saves himself or herself from serving time in a detention facility.[33]

In the very large majority of cases, the Mexican deportable alien is simply sent back to the nearest Mexican border city. For the deportable alien found in Los Angeles this is Tijuana, situated only 136 miles away. For the very large number of Mexicans apprehended right at the border, the required trip to the Mexican port of entry will probably be less than 10 miles. As a consequence, it is likely that the actual number of *persons* who have been expelled from the United States during a given year is very much less than the officially reported figure for aliens expelled. In other words, many persons are apprehended and expelled *several* times before they finally succeed in entering that part of the United States beyond the immediate border area.

Before 1971 the INS had a different policy.[34] Then the deportable alien was sent back to the place in Mexico which he reported as his home. However, according to Samora, many apprehended persons did not tell the truth to INS agents about where they came from and falsely claimed that they came from the nearest border city. That way, if they wanted to make another attempt to enter the United States, they could do so with ease. Even among those who were placed on buses departing for a city in the Mexican interior, many were able to bribe the bus driver to let them out of the bus shortly after departure.[35] For these reasons, and because the cost to the U.S. government for the trips was substantial, the INS discontinued the policy.

How to avoid the INS

To discover how undocumented immigrants succeed in entering the United States we must rely heavily on lengthy unstructured interviews conducted with undocumented persons. A person who wishes to enter the United States illegally must first decide whether he wishes to make the attempt on his own or with the assistance of a coyote, the guide who demands a payment for his services. This payment is variable and depends not only on the services proffered but also on the reputation of the vendor. First-time entrants probably find the services of a coyote more valuable than those who have entered the United States illegally many times.

Another decision, related to the first, is whether the attempt to cross the border should be made at an official point of entry or otherwise. Payments made by the prospective illegal entrant to the coyote may be used to bribe an inspector at the port of entry. According to Zazueta and Zazueta, if this alternative is chosen, the prospective entrant must normally pay the coyote between $150 and $250. The coyote in turn pays some of the money to bribe the U.S. official but must also reserve some of it to bribe the Mexican border inspector; otherwise the Mexican official will turn the coyote's name over to the U.S. officials.[36]

Alternatively, admittance to the United States through a port of entry may be accomplished through fraudulent use of the border-crossing card, Form I-186. This card allows the holder to enter the United States for visits of not more than 72 hours to places within 25 miles of the border. The card is valid indefinitely. More than a million of such cards have been issued to Mexican nationals.[37] If the prospective entrant does not himself have his own Form I-186, he may borrow one, either for free or for a price, provided the photo on the card is not too dissimilar to the borrower's own appearance. Once safely across the border, most illegals mail the card back to a friend or relative in Mexico so it can be used again and so there will be no evidence of fraudulent use if the holder should be apprehended more than 72 hours after entry. Finally, admittance to the United States through a port of entry can sometimes be secured through use of a counterfeit U.S. birth certificate or a counterfeit Form I-151, a certificate that the holder is a permanent legal resident of the United States.

The successful entrant to the United States at other than an official point of entry must have detailed knowledge of the enforcement practices of the INS border patrol. The services of a coyote are often valuable to inexperienced crossers. Experienced crossers express pride that they no longer need such services.[38] What happens if the attempt to cross into the United States is not successful? An interesting study by Richard Mines shows that entrants who have been forced back to the Mexican border can obtain help there from relatives and friends in order to attempt crossing the border again. Mines conducted a field study in Las Animas, a rural community in the province of Zacatecas. He also interviewed former Animenos (people of the village of Las Animas) now living in California and in Tijuana, the Mexican border city immediately adjacent to the southern boundary of San Diego. He reported that about 40 adult males originally from Las Animas now lived in Tijuana. Migrants enroute from Las Animas and those temporarily deported by the INS commonly stayed with these townsmen while in Tijuana. One former Animeno ran a large boarding house for Animenos seeking to enter the United States.[39] One may also infer from Mines's account that Animenos were also able to choose coyotes who were fellow villagers by origin.

Detecting fraudulent marriages

The INS also makes an effort to be sure that no fraud is involved when a foreign national seeks to legalize his or her status after marrying an American citizen. According to INS officials many marriages are contracted on paper for this purpose. These marriages have never been consummated and are often ones in which the citizen-spouse, usually a female, has been paid a sum of money.[40] However, according to Harwood, under current law the burden of proof is on the INS to show that

Table 2.3. *Number and percentage distribution by class of admission of permanent legal immigrants from Mexico and from the world, 1981 (excluding Silva immigrants and refugees from the percentage distributions*

Class	Mexico			World		
	Number	Total percent	Percent of quota	Number	Total percent	Percent of quota
Total	101,268			596,600		
Silva	50,331			56,682		
Refugees	15			107,573		
Other than refugees or Silva	50,922	100.0		432,345	100.00	
Nonquota	28,829	56.6		158,947	36.8	
Parents of U.S. citizens	1,581	3.1		34,220	7.9	
Spouses of U.S. citizens	18,390	36.1		87,221	20.2	
Minor children of U.S. citizens and orphans	6,546	12.9		25,707	5.9	
Special immigrants	96	0.2		3,255	0.8	
Spouses of U.S. citizens, Act of April 7, 1970	494	1.0		5,211	1.2	
Children born abroad to alien parents	1,631	3.2		3,021	0.7	
Other	82	0.2		312	0.1	
Quota	22,102	43.4	100.0	273,398	63.2	100.0
Relative preference	18,265	35.9	82.6	226,576	52.4	82.9
First	1,689	3.3	7.6	5,721	1.3	2.1
Second	8,654	17.0	39.2	112,664	26.1	41.2
Fourth	3,382	6.6	15.3	15,979	3.7	5.8
Fifth	4,540	8.9	20.5	92,212	21.3	33.7
Nonrelative preference	2,011	3.9	9.1	44,311	10.2	16.2
Third	215	0.4	1.0	18,872	4.4	6.9
Sixth	1,796	3.5	8.1	25,439	5.9	9.3
Nonpreference, private bill, and other	1,826	3.6	8.3	2,511	0.6	0.9

Source: 1981 Statistical Yearbook of the U.S. Immigration and Naturalization Service, Tables 5 and 7.

fraud exists. Consequently, if both bride and groom deny the marriage to be fraudulent, the petition for legal status must usually be granted.[41]

Illegal immigration as an aid to legal immigration

Recent research indicates that a majority of the recently admitted legal immigrants from Mexico are former undocumented immigrants. The earliest evidence came from an article by Charles Hirschman reporting the results of a survey of 822 self-supporting male Mexican immigrants legally admitted to the United States and entering at Laredo or El Paso, Texas, in late 1973 and early 1974.[42] Among these men, 62 percent had previously lived here, 40 percent reported the United States as their last permanent residence, and 31 percent had lived here at least three years. Of the 356 men who gained admission to the United States as husbands of U.S. citizens, 75 percent had previously lived here. Among the 46 men who gained admission as parents of adult U.S. citizens, only 17 percent had previously lived here. Among the 378 quota immigrants, 55 percent had previously lived here.

The latest and most definitive evidence comes from a study conducted by Lisa Kubiske of the U.S. Embassy in Mexico City. Among 1,225 visa applicants surveyed in 1984 who had applied for a visa at the U.S. Embassy in Mexico City, 80 percent had lived illegally in the United States with an average length of illegal stay of seven years.[43]

Table 2.3 shows the number of immigrants by class of admission for Mexico and for the world for fiscal 1981 (the year of the Los Angeles County Parents Survey). The table also provides a percentage distribution for Mexico and for the world of the immigrants who were neither refugees nor Silva immigrants. From the two percentage distributions, one can note the much higher proportion of nonquota immigrants for Mexico than for the world as a whole, 57 percent versus 37 percent. Especially noteworthy is the much higher proportion of all immigrants from Mexico coming in as spouses of U.S. citizens, 36 percent for Mexico and only 20 percent for the world as a whole. Assuming Hirschman's and Kubiskie's results are generalizable, many, if not most, of these Mexicans coming into the United States legally as spouses of American citizens must have been former undocumented residents of the United States.

Another striking fact that differentiates Mexico from the world as a whole in this respect is the sex of the immigrants who come in as spouses of U.S. citizens. For fiscal 1979 (the latest year for which such data have been computed) 66 percent of all such Mexican spouses were husbands. For spouses in the world as a whole, only 42 percent were husbands; a large number were the brides of American servicemen.[44]

Table 2.3 also shows that the proportion of nonpreference, private bill, and other immigrants from Mexico is very much higher (3.6 percent) than for the world as a whole (0.6 percent). Nonpreference immigrants must have labor certification; to get this certification, one must have an actual job offer. It is much easier to get such a job offer if one is already working for the employer who is petitioning for one's admission. Therefore, this difference can most probably be attributed to the greater likelihood that the Mexican applicant is already in the United States and illegally employed.

A great advantage in the eventual chance for legalization of an undocumented immigrant is being parent to an American-born child. Under current law, the child, upon attaining his twenty-first birthday, may petition to have his parents admitted as legal nonquota immigrants. Such a child may also petition to have his undocumented brothers and sisters admitted as legal immigrants under the fifth preference of the quota. Table 2.3 does not show any excess for Mexico in either the category of parent of a U.S. citizen or in the fifth preference category of the quota. However, it is possible that this statistic could change in the future if more of the undocumented immigrants in the United States attained the status of having an American-born child aged 21 or older.

Moreover, from 1965 to 1977 being the parent of an American-born child of any age allowed immigrants to apply for permanent legal residence without labor certification. Thus illegal immigration was a much more important aid to legal immigration during this period than afterward.

Finally, I should like to point out that for many years free legal aid was widely available to undocumented immigrants in the United States seeking to legalize their status. Such aid was begun as part of the War on Poverty initiated in the administration of President Johnson. The One Stop Immigration Center in Los Angeles was one of the largest of such agencies. However, beginning January 1, 1980, a new federal law went into effect severely restricting the amount of such aid. The new law decreed that undocumented immigrants could no longer receive assistance in regularizing their status from any agency that obtained funds from the federal Legal Services Corporation. Before this date, most of the principal legal aid organizations involved in immigration counseling had depended on funding from this agency. The effect of the law was to reduce severely the availability of free legal aid to undocumented persons wishing to legalize their status.[45]

Numbers and settlement patterns

Trends in number of legal immigrants

Table 2.4 shows the number of legal immigrants from Mexico for each decade from 1901 to 1980 and during the eighties. Shown also is the percentage of Mexican immigrants among all legal immigrants to the United States. The major increase in the number of legal immigrants from Mexico in the 1911–20 decade compared to the preceding decade can be attributed in part to the advent of the Mexican Revolution of 1910 but also to the cutoff of European immigration during World War I.

The 1921–30 decade saw another tremendous increase in legal Mexican immigration. The immigration laws of 1921 and 1924 had sharply cut off immigration

Table 2.4. *The Number of legal immigrants to the United States from Mexico and the proportion of all immigrants from Mexico by decade*

Period	Number	Proportion of total
1901–10	49,642	0.6
1911–20	219,004	3.8
1921–30	459,287	11.2
1931–40	22,319	4.2
1941–50	60,589	5.9
1951–60	319,300	12.7
1961–70	443,300	13.3
1971–80	637,200	14.2
1981–88	569,100	12.1

Note: Data for 1951 and later refer to nation of birth. Prior data refer to country of last permanent residence.
Sources: For years prior to 1951 U.S. Bureau of the Census, *Historical Statistics of the United States: Colonial Times to 1970* (Washington, D.C.: Government Printing Office, 1975), Part 1, pp. 107–8; for 1951 through 1987, U.S. Bureau of the Census, *Statistical Abstract of the United States, 1989*, (Washington, D.C.: Government Printing Office, 1989), p. 10; for 1988 *1988 Statistical Yearbook of the Immigration and Naturalization Service*, pp. 6–7.

from Europe but had not affected immigration from the Western Hemisphere. In this period more than 11 percent of all legal immigrants to the United States were from Mexico. The following decade, however, saw a dramatic drop in the number of legal Mexican immigrants, occasioned by the drastic tightening in the issuance of visas to Mexicans beginning in 1929 and perpetuated throughout the Great Depression. The number of legal immigrants rose in the 1941–50 decade but was still very small compared to the numbers admitted from 1921 to 1934. However, the *bracero* program began in this decade, and the average annual number of laborers admitted from 1943 through 1950 was more than 53,000. The following decade, 1951–60, witnessed a tremendous rise in the number of legal Mexican immigrants. The average annual number of legal immigrants continued to rise thereafter despite the tightening of the immigration law in 1976.

Decennial increase in the number of persons born in Mexico in relation to the number of legal immigrants

The reader might suppose that there should be a very close connection between the number of legal immigrants admitted to the United States from Mexico each decade and the increase in the Mexican-born U.S. population during the correspond-

Table 2.5. *Number of persons in the United States born in Mexico, decennial change in the number of such persons, and number of legal immigrants from Mexico in the preceding decade*

Census date	Number born in Mexico	Decennial change in number born in Mexico	Legal immigrants in preceding decade
1850	13,317	—	
1860	27,466	14,149	
1870	42,435	14,969	
1880	68,399	25,964	
1890	77,853	9,454	
1900	103,393	25,540	
1910	221,915	118,522	49,642
1920	486,418	264,503	219,004
1930	641,462	155,044	459,287
1940	377,433[a]	−264,029	22,319
1950	454,417	76,984	60,589
1960	575,902	121,485	319,300
1970	759,711	183,809	443,300
1980	2,199,221	1,439,510	637,200

[a]Whites only. In 1950 white persons born in Mexico numbered 450,562 of a total of 454,417 persons born in Mexico; in 1930 white persons born in Mexico numbered 639,017 and the total persons born in Mexico 641,462.

Sources: For the number of persons born in Mexico in 1970 and earlier years, *Historical Statistics of the United States,* Part 1, pp. 117–18; For the number of persons born in Mexico in 1980, U.S. Bureau of the Census, *1980 Census of Population,* PC-80-D1 (Washington, D.C.: Government Printing Office, 1984), p. 9.

ing period. This supposition is quite false, though a perusal of these data gives us valuable clues about the flow of undocumented immigrants.

Table 2.5 shows the number of persons in the United States who were born in Mexico at each census date from 1850 to 1980. The table also shows the decennial increase in the number of such persons and repeats the data from Table 2.4 on the number of legal immigrants during each decade.

In the absence of undocumented immigrants, one might expect the number of legal immigrants always to be a little higher than the decennial increase. Inspection of the last two columns reveals that the relation between the decennial totals for legal immigration and the decennial increase in the Mexican-born U.S. population does not follow this pattern. For example, from 1911 to 1920 the number of legal immigrants was less than the decennial increase in the Mexican-born population from 1910 to 1920. Moreover, from 1921 to 1930 the number of legal immigrants was several times larger than the decennial increase in the Mexican-born population from 1920 to 1930. From 1931 to 1940 the number of legal immigrants was a small positive figure whereas the decennial change from 1930 to 1940 was a large negative. How can we account for such discrepancies?

To attempt an answer we must first decompose the decennial increase into its component elements. There are ten such elements, and the number of legal immigrants is only one of these ten. The complicated formula below provides the decomposition:

$$DC = LI + UI + RLI - DLI - DUI - DFB - LE - UE - LUI + E.$$

The various terms in this equation are defined as follows:

DC = the decennial change in the population born in Mexico.

LI = legal immigrants, the number of immigrants legally admitted to the United States from Mexico during the decade.

UI = undocumented immigrants, the number of undocumented immigrants who came to the United States from Mexico during the decade.

RLI = returned legal immigrants, the number of persons legally admitted to the United States before the beginning of the decade but living outside the United States at the beginning of the decade who returned to live in the United States during the decade.

DLI = deaths of legal immigrants, the number of deaths in the United States to immigrants legally admitted to the United States from Mexico during the decade who had not been in the United States at the beginning of the decade.

DUI = deaths of undocumented immigrants, the number of deaths in the United States to undocumented immigrants who came to the United States from Mexico during the decade.

DFB = deaths of foreign-born residents, the number of deaths during the decade to the Mexican-born population in the United States at the beginning of the decade.

LE = legal emigrants, the number of legal immigrants from Mexico from any period who emigrated during the decade or never lived in the United States after their legal immigration.

UE = undocumented emigrants, the number of undocumented immigrants from Mexico from any period who emigrated during the decade.

LUI = legalized undocumented immigrants, the number of undocumented immigrants from Mexico from any period who converted their status to that of legal immigrant during the decade, and

E = the error of closure, that is, the difference between the actual census change and the change that would have occurred if both censuses had completeness of coverage.

Because most of the immigrants who come to the United States in a given decade are young, the values of DLI and DUI should be small and can be ignored. This still leaves us with many other variables to consider. Accordingly, any interpretation of which variables are most important during any particular decade must be conjectural.

Note that both for the decade ending in 1910 and for the decade ending in 1920 the decennial change is much larger than the number of legal immigrants.[46] I would interpret the cause of this phenomenon for both decades to be a large influx of undocumented immigrants.

For the decade ending in 1930, on the other hand, the decennial change is much less than the number of legal immigrants. I would interpret this fact as being due to a very large value of LUI, the number of undocumented immigrants from Mexico from any period who converted their status to that of legal immigrant during the decade. After the establishment of the INS border patrol in 1925, undocumented persons who wanted to visit relatives in Mexico would have had a hard time returning to the United States. On the other hand, times were prosperous in the United States and visas were easy to obtain.

For the decade ending in 1940 the decennial change was large and negative and the number of legal immigrants a small positive number. Experts would agree that the other major variables in the equation for this decade were large volumes of emigration (LE or UE) coincident with the beginning of the Great Depression.[47]

According to Abraham Hoffman, from the beginning of the Depression until the middle of 1931 this exodus was almost entirely voluntary. Subsequently, many of the undocumented immigrants departed under more forcible circumstances. Legal aliens, during their first five years of stay, were liable by law to deportation as public charges if they could not support themselves. Undocumented immigrants were always deportable. Hence, many immigrants left only after they had been informed by welfare officials that unless they left on their own they could be officially deported and never be eligible to legalize their status.

In the same period another large portion of the Mexican immigrant population was paid to leave. In a three-year period the Los Angeles County Department of Charities paid the expenses of return to Mexico for 13,332 Mexicans.[48] Because many of the immigrants, both legal and undocumented, who returned to Mexico had American-born children, the years of the Great Depression also witnessed a decline in the U.S.-born population of Mexican descent.

For the decade ending in 1950 the decennial change was somewhat greater than the number of legal immigrants. This can probably be explained by a resurgence of undocumented immigration during World War II when the shortage of labor in the United States was acute.

For the decade ending in 1960 the number of legal immigrants was much larger than the decennial change. It is not easy to account for this difference. Some part of the explanation may come from a somewhat higher number of deaths to the existing population than in earlier decades; the average age of this population in 1950 must certainly have been higher than in earlier decades.

Another part of the explanation may come from a very high number of emigrants among the undocumented population. From 1950 through 1954 the number of deportable aliens located by the INS was invariably at least 400,000. In 1953 it was around 900,000 and in 1954 about 1.1 million.[49] These last two years coincided with Operation Wetback, a concerted attempt by the INS to remove illegal aliens in the southwestern part of the United States. Many of the undocumented Mexicans required to depart as a result of Operation Wetback were, however, almost immediately allowed to return to the United States as part of an enlarged Mexican Labor Program. In 1960, 316,000 Mexicans were admitted to the United States for temporary labor in agriculture under this program.[50] However, as temporary laborers, they were probably not counted in the 1960 Census. It is likely that the number of undocumented immigrants from the previous decade who succeeded in gaining legal status during this decade was also quite high.

If the foregoing factors are not sufficient to explain the low decennial increase for the 1950–60 decade, one would also have to conclude that there was a substantial amount of emigration among legal immigrants. However, this emigration is not likely because the decade was one of general prosperity in the United States.

On the surface, it is also puzzling that the decennial change from 1960 to 1970 was so much less than the number of legal immigrants. A very major consideration here is that apparently there was a severe undercount in the 1970 Census of the population born in Mexico. Data from the 1980 Census show 929,000 Mexican-born persons who had immigrated to the United States in 1969 or earlier;[51] the 1970 Census showed only 760,000 Mexican-born persons.[52] Obviously, some of the persons enumerated in 1970 would have died or emigrated by 1980. It is probable that there would have been at least 1 million Mexican-born persons in the United States in 1970 if the coverage of the census had been complete.

A report by the U.S. Commission on Civil Rights provides reasons why the coverage of the 1970 Census was inadequate for Spanish-speaking persons. Among the facts that it mentions is that the INS conducted raids in Los Angeles in search of illegal aliens at the same time the 1970 Census was being conducted.[53]

If the true decennial increase were only the number recorded, this fact would imply that there was little undocumented immigration during this decade unless there was also a substantial amount of emigration among legal or undocumented immigrants or unless a large number of undocumented immigrants had legalized their status during the decade. That from 1965 through 1976 being the parent of an American-born child allowed one to become a legal immigrant without labor certification suggests that a large number of persons who entered as undocumented immigrants during the 1960–70 decade (or earlier) did legalize their status during the last half of this decade by virtue of becoming the parents of an American-born child. The fact that 1970 was the first year of the 1970–71 aerospace recession, which hit Southern California severely, suggests the possibility that departures among undocumented immigrants just prior to the census date may have been abnormally high.[54]

For the decade ending in 1980 the decennial increase was very much greater than the number of legal immigrants. On their face, these data imply that the net flow of undocumented Mexicans into the United States must have been very high. However, before coming to that conclusion, it will also be important to make some estimate as to the size of the error of closure.

In 1980 the U.S. Bureau of the Census made a special effort to count undocumented persons.[55] As part of this effort the Census Bureau prevailed upon the INS to suspend raids on neighborhoods and workplaces while the census was being conducted. It is my opinion that the percentage underenumeration of the population born in Mexico was very much lower in 1980 than in 1970. However, the absolute size of this population was probably at least twice as large in 1980 as in 1970. Therefore it is likely that the error of closure for the 1970–80 decade was probably somewhere around 0. Assuming an error of closure of 0, the net inflow of undocumented Mexicans during the decade (UI − DUI − UE − LUI) would have been at least equal to 803,000 (1,440,000 minus 637,000) and no doubt considerably higher because one would also have to take into account deaths to the existing foreign-born population (DFB), deaths to legal immigrants (DLI), and emigration of legal immigrants (LE).

Mexican immigrants as proportions of the U.S. and Mexican populations

Let us now consider a different way of looking at the figures from the various censuses on the number of persons in the United States born in Mexico. The purpose is twofold: (1) to examine the impact of Mexican immigration on the United States, and (2) to consider the pressures in Mexico evoking immigration to the United States.

Table 2.6 presents the number of such persons first as a proportion of the total population of the United States and then as a proportion of the total population of Mexico. The results are surprising. Considering first the persons in the United States born in Mexico as a percentage of the U.S. population, we see a rise from 1900 to 1930. There is then a drastic fall in 1940. In 1970 the percentage, 0.37 percent, based on the reported count is also less than it was in 1930. Even if we assume that there really were 1 million Mexican-born persons in the United States in 1970, the percentage, 0.49 percent, would still be less than in 1930. However,

Table 2.6. *Number of persons in the United States born in Mexico as percentage of the U.S. population and as percentage of the population of Mexico*

Year	U.S. population (in thousands)	Persons born in Mexico in the United States as percentage of U.S. Population	Population of Mexico (in thousands)	Persons born in Mexico in the United States as percentage of population of Mexico
1900	75,995	0.14	13,607	0.76
1910	91,972	0.24	15,160	1.46
1920	105,711	0.46	14,150	3.44
1930	122,755	0.52	16,553	3.88
1940	131,669	0.29[a]	19,654	1.92[a]
1950	150,697	0.30	25,791	1.76
1960	179,323	0.32	34,923	1.65
1970	203,302	0.37	48,225	1.58
1970		0.49[b]		2.07[b]
1980	226,546	0.97	66,847	3.29

[a]Numerator is white persons born in Mexico.
[b]Numerator adjusted to assume there were one million persons in the United States in 1970 who were born in Mexico.
Sources: For population of the United States, U.S. Bureau of the Census, *Statistical Abstract of the United States, 1985*, p. 6; for population of Mexico, *Anuario Estadístico de los Estados Unidos Mexicanos, 1980*, p. 59 (Mexico City: Secretaría de Programación, y Presupuesto, 1982); *Censo General de Población y Vivienda, 1980*, Resumen General Abreviado, p. 13, (Mexico City: Secretaría de Programación y Presupuesto, 1984).

by 1980 the percentage reaches its all time high of 0.97 percent, a figure almost double that of 1930.

Now let us consider the persons in the United States born in Mexico as a percentage of the population of Mexico. Again we see a monotonic increase from 1900 through 1930, followed by a drastic decline. A low point is probably reached in 1960. However, the 1980 figure, 3.29 percent, still fails to equal the figure for 1930, 3.88 percent.

Trends in the geographic distribution of Mexican immigrants

Mexican immigrants have clustered in California and Texas, but their relative numbers in each of these two states has varied considerably over time. Table 2.7 presents a historical overview of the geographic distribution of Mexican immigrants in the United States. Shown here is the proportion of all Mexican-born persons living

Table 2.7. *Percentage distribution by state of residence for persons born in Mexico, 1850, 1880, 1900, 1930, 1950, and 1980*

Area	1850	1880	1900	1930	1950	1980
Total	100.00	100.0	100.0	100.0	100.0	100.0
California	48.5	12.6	7.8	31.1	36.0	58.1
Texas	33.5	63.1	68.7	41.5	43.5	22.7
Arizona, New Mexico, and Colorado	10.2	21.5	20.4	12.4	8.9	5.1
Illinois	0.2	0.1	0.2	3.4	2.8	7.6
Other states	7.6	2.7	2.9	11.6	8.8	6.5

Sources: For 1900–70, A.J. Jaffe, Ruth Cullen, and Thomas Boswell, *The Changing Demography of Spanish Americans* (New York: Academic Press, 1980), p. 124; for 1980, U.S. Bureau of the Census, *1980 Census of Population*, Vol. I, Characteristics of the Population, PC80-1-C1 (Washington, D.C.: Government Printing Office, 1983), Table 236.

respectively in California, Texas, the three remaining southwestern states, Illinois, and all other states for 1850, 1880, 1900, 1930, 1950, and 1980. In 1850 almost half of the Mexican immigrants were in California. This concentration can be attributed to the Gold Rush and the fact that experienced miners from Mexico were prominent among those prospecting for gold in California. During the rest of the nineteenth century, Texas gained at the expense of California. By 1900 less than 8 percent of Mexican immigrants lived in California and almost 69 percent in Texas. This change corresponded to the great use of Mexican labor in the expanding agriculture of the lower Rio Grande valley. Thereafter, there was a remarkable switch back to California. By 1980, 58 percent of all immigrants born in Mexico were found in California and only 23 percent in Texas. Noteworthy too are the large declines since 1880 in the percentages for Arizona, New Mexico, and Colorado, and the sharp rise for Illinois since 1900.

Table 2.8 presents the geographic distribution of persons born in Mexico from the 1980 Census in somewhat greater detail. Shown are the figures for each state with 50,000 or more Mexican-born inhabitants, each Standard Metropolitan Statistical Area with population of 250,000 or more, and a Mexican-born population of at least 50,000 and each Standard Consolidated Statistical Area with at least 50,000 Mexican-born inhabitants.

The outstanding statistics of this table concern the very high proportions of the total Mexican-born population in either the Los Angeles–Long Beach SMSA (Los Angeles County), which was almost 32 percent of the total in the nation, or in the Los Angeles–Long Beach–Anaheim SCSA (Los Angeles County and four surrounding counties), which was almost 40 percent of the national total.

Table 2.8. *Number and percentage distribution of persons born in Mexico for selected states, standard metropolitan statistical areas of 250,000 population or more, and standard consolidated statistical areas having Mexican-born population of 50,000 or more*

Area	Number	Percentage distribution
United States	2,199,221	100.0
Arizona	70,952	3.2
California	1,277,969	58.1
Illinois	167,924	7.6
Texas	498,181	22.7
SMSAs by State		
California		
Anaheim–Santa Ana–Garden Grove	86,944	4.0
Los Angeles–Long Beach	697,771	31.7
Riverside–San Bernardino–Ontario	52,772	2.4
San Diego	86,947	4.0
San Francisco–Oakland	56,029	2.5
Illinois		
Chicago	160,729	7.3
Texas		
El Paso	83,093	3.8
Houston	93,718	4.3
McAllen–Pharr–Edinburg	51,007	2.3
SCSAs		
Chicago–Gary–Kenosha, IL–IN–WI	167,968	7.6
Houston–Galveston, TX	96,503	4.4
Los Angeles–Long Branch–Anaheim, CA	872,126	39.7
San Francisco–Oakland–San Jose, CA	101,955	4.6

Sources: For states, U.S. Bureau of the Census *1980 Census of Population* (Washington, D.C., Government Printing Office, 1980) PC80-1-C1, Table 236; for SMSAs: *1980 Census of Population*, PC80-1-D6, Table 195; PC80-1-D15, Table 195; PC80-1-D45, Table 195; for SCSAs: *1980 Census of Population*, PC80-1-D1-C, Table 342.

3. Undocumented Mexican immigrants: numbers, geographic distribution, and social consequences

Since the mid-1970s, growing public concern over what has been perceived as a major influx of undocumented Mexicans into the United States has evoked numerous studies concerning their numbers and rate of flow into the United States, their geographic distribution, and the consequences to the United States of their presence here. The lack of definitive data and the strong passions aroused concerning the desirability of this influx have stirred considerable scholarly controversy.

Attempts to estimate the stock and flow

In the middle of the 1970s, the mass media spotlighted the problem of undocumented aliens in the United States. In part, this attention was caused by the pronouncements of Leonard Chapman, who was commissioner of the Immigration and Naturalization Service from 1974 through 1976 during the administration of President Ford. He asserted that the number of illegal aliens in the United States was very large and that something must be done about it. To quote his words of 1976, "We're facing a vast army that's carrying out a silent invasion of the United States."[1]

There is no doubt that many Americans agreed with Chapman. The reason was their own fear of unemployment and their belief that the further influx of illegal aliens would deprive additional Americans of their jobs. The period of Chapman's directorship of the INS coincided with the severe economic recession occasioned by the sharp rise in the price of oil in 1973 and 1974.

In the annual report of the Immigration and Naturalization Service for 1974, Commissioner Chapman wrote, "It is estimated that the number illegally in the United States totals 6 to 8 million persons and is possibly as great as 10 or 12 million."[2] Early in 1975 Chapman was questioned by a reporter from the *Washington Post* as to how the estimate was derived. Chapman replied that the overall estimate was a composite derived from separate estimates by each of the thirty-two district offices of the INS. Each of these offices used a composite of information sources.[3] But the phenomenon that made Chapman's estimate plausible to many persons was the very rapid rise during the immediately preceding years in the number of located deportable aliens. From 1964 to 1974 the number of illegal aliens apprehended had

34

increased by a factor greater than 9, from 87,000 in the former year to 788,000 in the latter (Table 2.2).

Estimates by Lesko Associates and by Goldberg

Chapman was not content with having only what his critics considered a "gut-level" estimate of the number of undocumented persons. He therefore commissioned Lesko Associates, a private research firm, to prepare "more scientific" estimates of the total number of undocumented persons in the United States. Lesko Associates first prepared an estimate of the number of illegal aliens from Mexico based on a mathematical formula that included the annual number of apprehensions of Mexicans as a crucial variable. Lesko Associates then convened a panel of experts and asked them to reach a consensus, via the so-called Delphi method (one in which the experts approached consensus during a series of consecutive pollings) concerning the total number of undocumented persons in the nation. The use of Lesko Associates' mathematical formula for the number of undocumented Mexicans in the United States resulted in a figure for 1975 of 5,204,000. The use of the Delphi method for estimating the total number of illegal aliens resulted in an average figure of 8.1 million with a range in the estimates from 4.2 millions to 11 million.[4]

Lesko Associates' estimate of the number of undocumented Mexicans in the United States in 1975 rested heavily on an estimate made in 1975 by Howard Goldberg concerning the increase in the number of undocumented Mexican immigrants in the United States between 1960 and 1970.[5] In truth, Goldberg's paper represented the first scholarly attempt to estimate the number of undocumented Mexicans in the United States. His method was based entirely on comparing specific age–sex cohorts in the 1960 Census of Mexico with the same cohorts in the 1970 Census of Mexico. He estimated that the increase in the number of undocumented Mexicans in the United States during this decade was 1.6 million. Lesko Associates assumed that there were no undocumented Mexicans in the United States in 1960 and therefore used Goldberg's estimate of increase to estimate the number in 1970.

They then estimated total entrances into the United States by undocumented Mexicans as a function of a "got-away" ratio and the total number of apprehensions. This ratio was calculated (1) on the basis of the ratio of apprehensions of illegals away from the border to apprehensions at the border and (2) on the basis of the annual increase in the number of undocumented immigrants as earlier calculated by Goldberg. A very crucial element in the formula was the assumption that only 2 percent of the undocumented immigrants who successfully entered the United States each year either legalized their status, voluntarily returned to Mexico, or died during each year they remained in the United States.[6] It is interesting to note Goldberg's own caution regarding the estimate of the number of undocumented Mexicans in the United States in 1975. He said, "One may probably assume that the minimum number of illegal immigrants from Mexico now present in the United States is over two million. The estimates made in this analysis would be put on firmer ground if any of the assumptions made earlier could be verified or any potential sources of error were found not to be of major significance."[7]

The estimates made by Lesko Associates immediately aroused intense controversy. In response to an inquiry from Congressman Herman Badillo of New York, Vincent Barabba, the director of the U.S. Bureau of the Census wrote in December 1975, "we have examined the Lesko study and analyzed the formula used to estimate the current illegal Mexican alien population of the United States. In our opinion the estimates of the current illegal alien population shown in this study are based on weak and untenable assumptions, and add very little to our knowledge of the size of the illegal alien population."[8] The Lesko estimates were also attacked by Professor Jorge Bustamante, one of Mexico's leading demographers and that nation's foremost expert on Mexican immigration to the United States.[9]

Despite opposition, important government officials continued to announce very high figures for the influx of illegal aliens. Although Lesko Associates had estimated that for 1975 the number of Mexican illegal aliens successfully entering the United States was only 968,000, Secretary of Labor Marshall proclaimed in 1977 that probably 2 to 3 million illegal aliens entered the United States each year.[10] During the same year officials of the INS stated that for every alien apprehended two aliens succeed in entering the United States.[11]

My estimates of net flow

At this point I too became convinced that the figures being proclaimed by high Washington officials concerning the current stock of Mexican undocumented immigrants could not possibly be true. As a demographer, I also knew that in almost all cases the gross migratory flow into an area is always much greater than the net flow. It seemed to me that Washington officials were not taking this into account at all. Thus motivated, I began my own work, which resulted in estimates of net flow that, although not small, were considerably below those posited by Lesko Associates.

At the time, Maurice D. Van Arsdol, Jr., my colleague at the Population Research Laboratory, was conducting a study under contract to the U.S. Department of Labor. This study concerned the characteristics of 2,905 immigrants from Latin America, mostly from Mexico, who had come to the One Stop Immigration Center in Los Angeles to seek legal advice on how to legalize their current undocumented status.[12] Thus, I was aware that many undocumented persons wanted to legalize their status.

I decided I would try to make my own estimate of the net flow of undocumented Mexicans into the United States; simultaneously Professor Van Arsdol offered to include me as a consultant to his contract during the summer of 1977 to make the estimates. In examining the yearly totals for the Mexican-origin population in the United States collected each March from the Current Population Survey (CPS) and published annually by the U.S. Bureau of the Census, I had noted that the totals seemed to be increasing at a rate beyond that which could be explained by natural increase or legal immigration alone. Hence, the Current Population Survey did seem to be counting undocumented persons.

In my estimates I used as a base population an average of the Mexican-origin populations from the November 1969 and March 1971 surveys. For later population I averaged the Mexican-origin population from the results of the March 1975 and March 1976 surveys. I also corrected for a change in definition of Mexican origin for children only one of whose parents was of Mexican origin. I did not correct for a change in the CPS's sampling scheme adopted in March 1973 that had served to increase the total Hispanic population by 545,000. I did not make this latter correction because I wanted my estimates of the increase in the undocumented population to be overestimates rather than underestimates. I then estimated the rate of natural increase as 2.1 percent a year (based on the child–woman ratio in the corrected population and a model life table that appeared reasonable).

I then computed seven different estimates of the annual net flow of undocumented immigrants from Mexico. Three of these estimates assumed that the ratio of net legal immigration to gross legal immigration was unity (obviously false but used as a maximum). Within this assumption I made three assumptions concerning undercount of the Mexican-origin population in the CPS: either there was no undercount, the true count was larger than the reported count by 10 percent, or the true count was larger than the reported count by 20 percent. Four of the estimates assumed that the ratio of net legal migration to gross legal migration was only 0.70. This ratio was identical to the ratio that Keely and Kraly had estimated for all immigrants to the United States.[13] In these last four estimates I assumed alternatively that there was no undercount, that the true count was larger than that reported by 10 percent, was larger by 20 percent, or was originally 10 percent and then increased to 20 percent. My seven estimates of the annual net flow of undocumented Mexican immigrants to the United States ranged from 82.3 thousand to 232.4 thousand. My preferred estimate was 116,000. This number was obtained by assuming that the ratio of net legal to gross legal flow was 0.70 and that the true count was larger than the reported count by 10 percent. A very detailed statement of my results and methodology is to be found in our final report to the U.S. Department of Labor.[14] The major assumptions and findings are found in an article published in *Demography* in 1979.[15]

The Lancaster–Scheuren estimates of stock

While I was working on my study, Lancaster and Scheuren, two U.S. government statisticians, published a paper giving the results of their estimate of the total stock (number) of undocumented immigrants in the United States as of 1973.[16] Their estimate made use of a "capture–recapture" technique based on a data set for simulated tax units from the 1973 Current Population Survey that had been matched with data from Internal Revenue Service records concerning whether a federal income tax had been returned and data from the Social Security Administration concerning both whether social security payroll tax had been paid and whether social security benefits had been received. The simulated tax units were also cross-tabulated by sex, by color, and into two age groups according to characteristics of the head of the household. A table with sixty-four cells was thus produced.

A log-linear model was then applied to the data that assumed that certain pairwise associations occurred and that there were no second-order interactions. Lancaster and Scheuren stated that the model applied included a "number of (strong) assumptions." With these assumptions, Lancaster and Scheuren estimated the total number of undocumented immigrants in the population 18 to 44 years of age to be 3,885,000 in 1973. Of these, 2,575,000 were white and 1,310,000 nonwhite. They also concluded that the total number of undocumented immigrants in the United States was only little more than 4 million.

In my chapter in our final report to the U.S. Department of Labor, I discussed the congruence of my own results with those of Lancaster and Scheuren and of Goldberg. "In fact, even given all the difficulty of estimating stock from net flow during the past 15 years, it does appear that Lancaster and Scheuren's estimate of about 2.8 million for the total white undocumented migrant stock is not incongruent with the net flow of 1.6 million undocumented Mexican migrants, estimated by Goldberg for 1960 to 1970 and my own preferred estimate of a net flow of 600,000 undocumented Mexican migrants for the period from 1970 to 1975."[17]

Since 1979 a number of other demographers have attempted to estimate either the stock or net flow of undocumented Mexican immigrants. I shall now describe some of these other works.

The Robinson estimates by the death-rate method

Gregory Robinson of the U.S. Bureau of the Census had noted that in ten states, which one could presume to have a large number of illegal aliens, the death rates for white males aged 20 to 44 appeared to be higher than in the remaining states. Robinson presumed that illegal aliens who died would be classified as being of the white race. In his article in *Demography,* Robinson presented a number of estimates of the deportable white male population aged 20 to 44 based on his method of estimating first excess deaths and then the undocumented population by assuming a set of death rates for that population. For the ten states combined, these estimates of the undocumented population ranged from 577,000 to 4.7 million. For five southwestern states, the data for which could be considered a close proxy of undocumented Mexican immigrants, his numbers for the same age group of white men ranged from 374,000 to 2.5 million.

Robinson also made estimates of the net flow for the 1970–75 period. For the five southwestern states he estimated the annual net flow to be between 62,000 and 357,000.[18] Robinson's estimates have a very wide range. However, his maximum estimate for the five southwestern states was much less than the estimated number of undocumented Mexican immigrants made by Lesko Associates.

Diez-Cañedo's estimates by the remittances method

Juan Diez-Cañedo, in a Ph.D. dissertation submitted to the Massachusetts Institute of Technology, made estimates of the undocumented Mexican population in the United States by collecting data on total remittances of postal or money orders from Spanish-surnamed individuals in the United States to Mexico and comparing them to data, earlier gathered by North and Houstoun, on the amounts of remittances made by apprehended Mexican immigrants. He then made a series of estimates of the undocumented Mexican population of the United States which varied because of differing assumptions about the average remittances sent by legal migrants and by unapprehended illegal migrants. He estimated that the number of undocumented Mexican immigrants in the United States in 1975 ranged from 235,000 to 2.9 million.[19] Diez-Cañedo's estimates also have a very wide range.

García y Griego's estimates by the migration-history method

In a book published in Spanish under the auspices of the Mexican government's Centro Nacional de Información y Estadisticas del Trabajo (CENIET), Manuel García y Griego prepared estimates not only of the stock and net flow of undocumented Mexican immigrants in the United States but also of the gross flow.[20] His estimates were based on several data sources. These included the results gathered from migration histories of expelled Mexicans returned to Mexican border points, the INS statistics on located deportable Mexicans classified by month of detection and length of stay, and data previously collected by Alejandro Portes (mentioned in Chapter

2 in connection with their use by Hirschman) on legal immigrants admitted to the United States from Mexico cross-classified by their length of previous residence in the United States.

García y Griego's basic model assumed that exits following an entrance to the United States could occur either through expulsion, voluntary return, legalization of status, or death. The method assumed not only that the migration histories reported by expelled immigrants were representative of those not apprehended but also that future exits could be predicted by past exits. Various estimates were prepared covering a range of assumptions. The stock of undocumented Mexican immigrants as of January 1977 was estimated to be from 482,000 to 1.22 million. The average annual net flow of undocumented Mexicans during the 1972–76 period was estimated to be between 50,000 and 158,000. Finally, the average annual gross flow into the United States of undocumented Mexican immigrants was estimated to range between 629,000 and 2.04 million.

The work of García y Griego is the first to estimate a gross flow since the unsupported statements concerning this parameter made by Secretary of Labor Marshall and various INS officials in the middle of the 1970s. It is interesting that the highest of his estimates for the gross flow is quite congruent with these earlier statements. What is striking about these estimates is the tremendous difference between the estimated gross flow and the estimated net flow. This difference results in part from the fact that García y Griego assumed the majority of all legal immigrants were prior undocumented immigrants. It also results from the large number of voluntary departures that had been found to have occurred in the migration histories of the expelled immigrants interviewed. In many cases these voluntary departures occur among undocumented immigrants who intended to work in the United States only a part of the year.

Bean et al.'s estimates of stock by the sex-ratio method

The latest attempt to estimate the number of undocumented Mexican immigrants in the United States based on Mexican data is a work by Frank Bean, Allan King, and Jeffrey Passel.[21] Their research reports the results of applying a sex-ratio–based method to estimate the number of undocumented Mexicans residing in the United States in 1980. Their approach compares the hypothetical sex ratio one would expect to find in the Mexican Census in the absence of emigration to the United States to the sex ratio that was in fact reported. Their procedure assumed a range of values for the sex ratio at birth and also for differentials in census coverage by sex. The resulting estimates had a wide range, from a low of 1.5 million undocumented Mexican immigrants in the United States in 1980 to a maximum of 4 million.

Critiques of the estimates

The estimates made by Goldberg, Lesko Associates, and Lancaster and Scheuren, which were the earliest estimates prepared, all provided only a single figure for what they attempted to estimate. All of the later estimates provided a range of figures. Thus these later estimates are less subject to criticism than the earlier ones but are also less useful to policymakers who would prefer a single figure upon which to base policy. The change from single-figure estimates to multiple, alternative estimates was no doubt fostered by the critical reviews that were prepared of the early estimates. Let us now examine these reviews.

Among the first was one by Charles Keely, a well-respected demographer then at Fordham University.[22] He focused his attention on what he considered to be inadequacies in the estimates made by Lesko Associates and also reviewed a preliminary version of the estimate prepared by Lancaster and Scheuren.

A more comprehensive critique of the Lesko Associates estimates was undertaken by Roberts, Conroy, King, and Rizo-Patrón, all of the University of Texas.[23] They performed a sensitivity analysis of the various assumptions made by Lesko Associates and established that the Lesko estimates were extremely dependent on the assumptions that had been made. Specifically, they first demonstrated that the Lesko estimates were sensitive to the base year estimate, which had been taken from the work of Goldberg. They showed that if the base-year estimate were halved, the estimate for 1975 would also be halved if no other assumptions were varied.

They then quoted earlier research done at the U.S. Bureau of the Census that showed that the Goldberg estimate was extremely sensitive to the degree of underenumeration in the Mexican Census in 1960 and 1970. Goldberg had assumed that the absolute magnitude of undercount was identical in both censuses. He made this assumption because the Mexican government had placed the 1960 undercount as 2.3 percent and the 1970 undercount as 2.1 percent. If what the Mexican government had said was true, Goldberg had made the right assumption. On the other hand, the U.S. Census Bureau had pointed out that if Goldberg were to have assumed a 5 percent rate of underenumeration at both censuses, he would have obtained an estimate of only 767,000 undocumented Mexican immigrants in the United States in 1970 instead of 1,597,000. Roberts et al. then revealed that the Lesko Associates' estimates were also somewhat sensitive to the exact assumptions made about the relationship between the gross inflow and interior and border apprehensions. Finally, they showed that the Lesko Associates' estimates were extremely sensitive to the coefficient of annual return migration, legalization, and death. Their estimate of 5.2 million undocumented Mexican immigrants in the United States in 1975 would be reduced to only 1.195 million if they had assumed a coefficient of 0.80 rather than 0.02.

A third review was published in 1980 by Jacob Siegel, Jeffrey Passel, and J. Gregory Robinson, all of the U.S. Bureau of the Census, at the request of the Select Commission on Immigration and Refugee Policy.[24] They discussed the work of Goldberg, of Lancaster and Scheuren, Heer, Robinson, and García y Griego. They also discussed a field investigation, done in a Mexican village by Joshua Reichert and Douglas Massey, that emphasized that the majority of the villagers in that community who worked in the United States did so only seasonally and not permanently.[25] Additionally, they took into consideration the fact that all studies of the Mexican place of origin of undocumented immigrants showed the majority to have come from six states of Mexico, all located in the northwestern half of the Central Plateau: namely Chihuahua, Guanajuato, Jalisco, Michoacán, San Luis Potosí, and Zacatecas. Because of this last fact, Siegel et al. felt that the number of illegal Mexican immigrants must be less than 4 million. With respect to all of the aforementioned studies that had attempted to estimate the stock or flow of undocumented immigrants, they stated, "They characteristically depend on broad, untested assumptions and are subject to other major limitations . . . . Often alternative reasonable assumptions could be employed which could substantially modify the estimates and could produce an impracticably wide range." Despite this skepticism, Siegel, Passel, and Robinson concluded that in 1978 the total number of illegal residents was "almost certainly below 6.0 million, and may be substantially less, possibly only 3.5 to 5.0 million . . . . The Mexican component . . . is almost certainly less than 3.0 million, and may be substantially less, possibly only 1.5 to 2.5 million . . . . Apparently, most of the Mexican nationals who enter the United States illegally in any year return to Mexico to live for a part of the year."

A later review was prepared by Manuel García y Griego and Leobardo Estrada.[26] Their clearly written review provides more detail concerning the cited studies than the review by Siegel, Passel, and Robinson. The studies discussed include those of Goldberg, Lancaster and Scheuren, Heer, Robinson, García y Griego, and Diez-Cañedo. They concluded, not surprisingly in the light of the results of García y Griego's own study, that the number of undocumented Mexican immigrants was considerably less than popularly imagined.

The latest review, very skeptical of all previous work, is by Kenneth Hill.[27] Hill reviews the studies by Goldberg, Lancaster and Scheuren, Heer, Robinson, and García y Griego. To my knowledge his is the only critique of the latter study. Hill is also the only one to review the two studies that are the topic of the next section of this chapter.

The Warren and Passel estimate and the CENIET count

We are now ready to discuss two major studies that finesse the question of how many undocumented Mexicans there are in the United States. The study by Robert Warren of the United States Immigration and Naturalization Service and Jeffrey Passel of the U.S. Bureau of the Census attempted merely to estimate the number of undocumented persons who were counted in the 1980 Census of the United States by nationality, age, and year of arrival.[28] Importantly, it provides a minimum count of the number of undocumented persons in the United States at that time, excluding undocumented persons only temporarily in the United States and, among those maintaining a permanent residence here, those who were not counted in the 1980 Census. A study conducted by the Centro Nacional de Información y Estadísticas del Trabajo (CENIET) of the Mexican government attempted to count the number of habitual residents of Mexico 15 years old and over who were either in the United States at the time of the survey or who had been in the United States working or looking for work for at least one day during the preceding five years.[29] It should be emphasized that the Mexican survey did not attempt to count the number of Mexican nationals who were permanently living in the United States. Hence the CENIET study and the Warren and Passel study provide what should be more or less complementary estimates.

To have a better idea of the degree of complementariness of the two studies, we ought to have a better acquaintance with the rules of the U.S. Bureau of the Census with respect to who is a usual resident of the United States. For the 1980 Census the usual place of residence was "generally construed to mean the place where the person lives and sleeps most of the time." Moreover, "Citizens of foreign countries having their usual residence (legally or illegally) in the United States on Census Day, including those working here (but not living at an embassy, ministry, legation, chancellery, or consulate) and those attending school (but not living at an embassy, etc.), were included in the enumeration, as were members of their families living with them." Finally, "Persons without a usual place of residence, however, were counted where they happened to be staying."[30] It is thus clear that if a person lived in the United States for less than six months and for more than six months in Mexico, that person should not have been counted in the 1980 Census of the United States. However, if that person worked nine months in the United States in only one place, he should have been counted in the 1980 Census even if not present in the United States on census day, April 1. If that person worked nine months in the United States in two or more places and stayed less than six months in any one place, he would have no usual place of residence in the United States. Nevertheless, even without a usual place of residence in the United States, if he were present in the United States on the census day, April 1, such a person should have been enumerated in the United States.

On the other hand, the CENIET survey no doubt considered as habitual residents of Mexico all persons who lived in Mexico at least part of the year, particularly because most of these probably had their wives and children in Mexico. Hence, there is a likelihood that many persons included in the CENIET survey should also, according to the rules of the U.S. Bureau of the Census, have been included in the 1980 Census of the United States.

The 1978–79 CENIET Survey

The CENIET Survey was an area-probability sample of 62,500 dwelling units throughout Mexico. It was conducted between mid-December 1978 and mid-January 1979, a time of year when the number of seasonal workers in the United States would be at a minimum. According to the survey there were 519,301 workers who were habitual Mexican residents but present in the United States at the time of the survey. There were also 471,418 persons currently in Mexico who were 15 years old or over, habitual residents of Mexico, and who had worked or looked for work in the United States for at least one day since January 1974. The researchers also reported that about 750,000 persons had worked in the United States sometime during 1978, and that during 1978 the seasonal peak in the number of such workers was around 625,000 and the seasonal minimum approximately 500,000.[31]

However, it cannot be assumed that all of the habitual residents of Mexico who worked in the United States on a temporary basis were undocumented. A decision of the U.S. Supreme Court in 1929 established that persons who have been admitted to the United States as permanent legal residents do not lose that status even if they do not reside in the United States provided they have been absent from a U.S. job for no more than six months. The Supreme Court reiterated this opinion in another decision handed down in 1974.[32]

Arthur Corwin estimates the total number of permanent legal residents of the United States who are habitual residents of Mexico as around 100,000.[33] It is probable that close to half of these persons live in Mexican border cities and commute daily into the twin city on the U.S. side of the boundary. The remainder live in the interior of Mexico and commute seasonally to jobs in the United States. Two field studies, one conducted in a village in the state of Zacatecas and the other conducted in a rural community in Michoacán, each revealed the presence of legal seasonal commuters, although much more frequent in the Michoacán community.[34] Official data collected by the INS for the month of March 1975 revealed that 43,030 daily commuters entered the United States from Mexico that month and 8,892 seasonal commuters; the monthly figure for seasonal commuters is probably congruent with an annual figure of about 50,000, assuming all seasonal commuters entered the United States during the first six months of the year.[35]

If we accept the 750,000 workers enumerated by CENIET as having worked in the United States sometime during 1978, and then subtract the estimated 100,000 legal commuters, we end up with 650,000 as an upper limit on the number of undocumented seasonal Mexican workers in the United States.

The Warren and Passel estimate

Let us turn now to the estimate of the number of undocumented persons in the United States who were counted in the 1980 Census. The method used by Warren and Passel is simple but in its details complicated. Basically, it involves subtracting the adjusted number of legal aliens from each nation who were registered as living in the United States by the INS in January 1980 from the adjusted number of persons born in each foreign country and not naturalized citizens who were counted by the 1980 Census. Estimates of undocumented immigrants were developed for forty countries of birth, and for each of these nations separate calculations were done for thirteen age groups for each sex by four periods of entry. In a later analysis, separate estimates were made for each state, Standard Metropolitan Statistical Area, and county.

The methodology for making the adjustment for underregistration of legal aliens in January 1980 was very complicated and will not be described here. Suffice to say that for all countries of birth it was decided that the underregistration in this survey had been 11.1 percent and that for Mexico it had been 7.3 percent. The numbers registered were accordingly inflated to account for the estimated underregistration and were also adjusted to compensate for the fact that the date of the census was April 1.

Consider the adjustments made to the census population. The census questionnaire asked for place of birth of persons born outside the United States. For such persons it also asked a question on citizenship. What was desired was the true number of persons who were born outside the United States and were not naturalized citizens. Three types of adjustment were made to obtain this true number. First, approximately 6 percent of the foreign-born population had not reported a specific country of birth. Countries of birth were allocated to these persons *pro rata*. Second, a comparison of the census data on the number of naturalized citizens with data from the INS on naturalization events revealed that the census count was considerably overstated. The adjustment for overcount of naturalized citizens in the census increased the alien population for all nations by 12 percent and that for Mexico by 21 percent.

Finally, it was determined on the basis of an analysis of both the 1970 census and the 1980 Census that there appeared to be an overcount in 1980 of persons reported to be of Mexican origin but born in the United States. The excess persons thus reported were assumed to have been born in Mexico. This adjustment increased the Mexican-born population by an additional 8.8 percent. (The last adjustment was made by Warren and Passel at my suggestion after I had read an earlier version of the work.)

According to the Warren and Passel estimates, there were 2,057,000 undocumented persons in the United States counted in the 1980 Census; of these 1,131,000, 55 percent of the total were from Mexico. From only two other nations were there as many as 50,000 undocumented immigrants; 58,000 from Iran and 51,000 from El Salvador.

Table 3.1 compares the results obtained by Warren and Passel with the results of the previous studies.

The figure of 1,131,000 undocumented aliens from Mexico, estimated by Warren and Passel, was only negligibly less than the 1,195,000 legal aliens they estimated from that nation. Table 3.2 shows the estimated number of undocumented and legal aliens from Mexico by period of entry. Notice a strong association between whether the alien was undocumented or legal and the year of entry. For the most recent period, 1975 to 1980, the large majority of all immigrants were undocumented; for the period 1969 and earlier, the reverse was the case. These data are compatible with the hypothesis that legalization generally occurs somewhat later than entry.

Table 3.3 presents a breakdown of the estimated number of undocumented Mexican immigrants by age, sex, and year of entry. A surprising feature of the estimate is that there are almost as many females among the undocumented Mexican immigrants as males. Only 55 percent are male. In contrast, among Mexican immigrants apprehended by the INS and interviewed in 1977 by CENIET upon their return to Mexico, the proportion male was 88 percent.[36] Furthermore, the 1978–79 CENIET survey of habitual Mexican residents who were working in the United States (both undocumented and legal) showed that 84 percent were male.[37]

The difference in sex ratio between the undocumented Mexicans counted in the 1980 U.S. Census and that among the habitual residents of Mexico working in the United States illustrates a fundamental difference between the undocumented immigrants counted in the 1980 Census and the shuttle migrants counted in the 1978–79 CENIET survey. It is likely that the majority of adult undocumented immigrants counted in the 1980 Census were married with spouse present and that many of these had children with them born in the United States; the shuttle migrants may have been married or single but, if married, they kept their wives and children in Mexico while working in the United States. Evidence of the high proportion of married with spouse present among the undocumented immigrants counted in the 1980 Census in Los Angeles county is presented by Heer and Passel.[38]

Table 3.1. *Estimates (in millions) of the stock, net flow, and gross flow of undocumented Mexican immigrants in or to the United States*

Estimate	Stock	Net flow	Gross flow
Goldberg		.16	
		(1960–70)	
Lesko Associates	5.2	.95	.97
	(1975)	(1975)	(1975)
Lancaster and Scheuren	2.6		
(total whites 18 to 44 years old)	(1973)		
Heer		.082–.232	
(1970–75)			
Robinson	.4–2.5	.062–.357	
(white males in 5 southwestern	(1975)	(1970–75)	
states)			
Diez-Cañedo	.2–2.9		
	(1975)		
García y Griego	.481–1.22	.05–.158	.629–2.04
	(1977)	(1972–76)	(1972–76)
Bean et al.	1.5–4.0		
	(1980)		
CENIET	.891		
(maximum number who are habitual	(1978–79)		
residents of Mexico less estimated			
legal immigrants habitually residing			
in Mexico)			
Warren and Passel	1.131		
	(1980)		

Note: Years to which estimates refer shown in parentheses. If estimate is not for undocumented Mexicans, population to which estimate refers is defined in parentheses.

Evidence concerning the marital and family status of shuttle migrants is found in several studies focusing on particular Mexican communities. These include one by Mines in Las Animas in the state of Zacatecas, one by Stuart and Kearney in San Jeronimo in the state of Oaxaca, one by Reichert and Massey in Guadalupe in the state of Michoacán, and one by Cornelius in nine separate rural villages in the state of Jalisco.[39] For example, Reichert and Massey found that only 19 percent of 177 adult, current illegal migrants to the United States in Guadalupe were female. Moreover, among illegal migrants, the average size of the migrating family unit was only 1.3; 75 percent of the 124 such units consisted of only one person, and the wife was a migrant in only 17 percent of all the 121 such families with a wife.

Table 3.2. *Number (in thousands) of undocumented and legal resident aliens from Mexico in the United States, 1980, by period of entry*

Category	All periods	Entered 1975–80	Entered 1970–74	Entered before 1970
Undocumented aliens				
Number	1,131	559	343	228
Percentage of total	100.0	49.4	30.3	20.2
Legal resident aliens				
Number	1,195	293	282	620
Percentage of total	100.0	24.5	23.6	51.9

Source: Robert Warren and Jeffrey S. Passel, "A Count of the Uncountable: Estimates of Undocumented Aliens Counted in the 1980 Census," *Demography 24*, no. 3 (August 1987): 375–93, Table 1.

Cornelius found that 54 percent of the 230 men he interviewed who had been illegal migrants to the United States in the 1969–76 period were already married at the time of their first trip to the United States. Nevertheless, less than 1 percent had taken their wives and children with them to the United States.

Was the methodology of Warren and Passel sound? In my judgment, the adjustments made with respect to underregistration in the January 1980 survey of legal aliens were reasonable although made on a somewhat unsubstantiated basis. It would be difficult to argue that registration had been complete. Moreover, a degree of underregistration much greater than that assumed would be inconsistent with other data on the volume of emigration. Hence, even if the adjustment made by Warren and Passel was somewhat too high or somewhat too low, the resulting number of undocumented persons would not have been changed very much. The adjustments made by Warren and Passel to the Census counts of naturalized and native-born citizens also appear to me to be reasonable.

An earlier published article by myself and Passel compared the estimate of undocumented Mexican adults in Los Angeles County according to the Warren and Passel method with estimates developed from data of the Los Angeles County Parents Survey.[40] The relatively small differences between Warren and Passel's figures and figures based on the Los Angeles County Parents Survey enhance the credibility of the Warren and Passel estimate on the national level. Warren and Passel's methodology yielded a total of 317,800 undocumented Mexicans in Los Angeles County who were either males 18 to 44 or females 18 to 39 years of age. A method based on proportions undocumented from the Los Angeles County Parents Survey and on an unadjusted count of the Mexican-origin population of Los Angeles County by nativity from the 1980 Census yielded a smaller figure (228,729) equal to 72 percent of the Warren and Passel estimate. Finally, an estimate based on the proportions undocumented from the Los Angeles County Parents Survey and on Warren and Passel's adjusted count of the Mexican-origin population by nativity yielded an estimate of 264,821 such persons, equal to 83 percent of the Warren and Passel estimate.

Nevertheless, the article by Heer and Passel indicated one interesting difference. According to the methods based on the Los Angeles County Parents Survey, a higher proportion of the undocumented had arrived in 1975 or later than the estimate made according to the methods of Warren and Passel would indicate. This difference suggests there may be a bias in Warren and Passel's estimates of the number of undocumented persons subdivided by year of entry. How might this bias occur?

The data from the INS concerning legal aliens refer to the year in which the individual obtained permanent legal residence in the United States. However, many persons have come to the United States before succeeding in gaining legal entry. The question on the 1980 Census read, "When did this person come to the United States to stay?" The accompanying instruction read, "If the person has entered the U.S. more than once, fill the circle for the year he or she came to stay permanently."[41] In my opinion, individuals who by 1980 were permanent legal residents but who had first entered the United States illegally would have answered the census question according to the period in which they came to the United States to stay rather than with reference to the period in which they became a permanent legal resident. Thus it may not be correct to subtract from the census count of persons who came in a given period the INS count of persons who obtained legal entrance during the same period. By doing so, one underestimates the number of undocumented persons who entered the United States during the latest period and overestimates the number who entered during the earlier periods.

The total number of undocumented Mexicans in the United States in 1980

The total number of Mexicans in the United States at any one moment is the sum of the permanent residents of the United States, who are supposed to be included in the U.S. census, and the shuttle migrants, who, because their stay in the United States is only temporary, should not be included in the U.S. census. A likely estimate of the total number of undocumented Mexicans present in the United States at any time during 1980 can probably be obtained by adding the 1,131,000 undocumented

Table 3.3. *Estimates of illegal aliens born in Mexico counted in the 1980 census, by age, sex, and period of entry (populations in thousands; figures rounded independently)*

Age in 1980 and period of entry	Both sexes	Male	Female
Entered since 1960			
All ages	931	531	400
Under 5	47	24	23
5–14	161	83	77
15–24	323	193	129
25–34	274	162	112
35–44	90	53	37
45–64	28	13	14
65 +	10	2	7
Entered 1975–80			
All ages	476	278	198
Under 5	47	24	23
5–14	95	50	45
15–24	211	130	80
25–34	83	50	33
35–44	20	12	8
45–64	17	10	7
65 +	3	1	2
Entered 1970–74			
All ages	280	159	121
Under 5	—	—	—
5–14	53	27	26
15–24	74	42	32
25–34	113	67	46
35–44	28	15	12
45–64	11	7	4
65 +	1	0	1
Entered 1960–69			
All ages	138	77	61
Under 5	—	—	—
5–14	12	6	6
15–24	34	19	15
25–34	64	37	28
35–44	31	19	12
45–64	0	−2	2
65 +	−2	−1	−1

Table 3.3. *(cont.)*

Age in 1980 and period of entry	Both sexes	Male	Female
Entered before 1960			
All ages	36	17	19
Under 5	—	—	—
5–14	—	—	—
15–24	4	2	2
25–34	13	7	6
35–44	11	6	5
45–64	0	−2	1
65 +	8	3	6

Source: Robert Warren and Jeffrey S. Passel, "A Count of the Uncountable: Estimates of Undocumented Aliens Counted in the 1980 United States Census," *Demography 24,* no. 3 (August 1987): 375–93, Table 2.

Mexicans counted in the 1980 Census to the figure mentioned earlier: 650,000 undocumented Mexicans who were in the United States sometime during 1978 but were habitual residents of Mexico. This sum is 1,781,000.

I consider this likely, first, because I believe that such a sum provides a double count of many persons. For example, migrants who spent 6 to 11 months in the United States would probably stand a good chance of having been counted both in the 1980 Census and by CENIET. For reasons that I will state below, shuttle migrants with such a length of stay should constitute about one-half of all of the shuttle migrants. Moreover, it is likely as well that the CENIET survey also picked up some migrants, particularly those who were young and unmarried, who had been in the United States more than one year, all of whom should have been counted in the 1980 Census. In my opinion this double counting should approximately make up not only for (1) the undercount in the 1980 Census among persons who were truly permanent residents of the United States and should not have been enumerated by CENIET, but also for (2) the small undercount in the number of shuttle migrants because the CENIET survey excluded any shuttle migrants who were not workers, and (3) the fact that the CENIET survey preceded the 1980 Census by about two years.

Furthermore, I do not believe that the undercount in the 1980 Census was particularly large. Passel and Woodrow have stated,

The actual coverage of undocumented aliens in the 1980 Census, either for the entire nation or by state, remains unknown. A number of factors point toward reasonably complete coverage of this group. First, coverage of housing units in the 1980 census was virtually complete and undercount of all legal residents was on the order of 1 percent. Given these assertions and the marked increases in the number of foreign-born counted in 1980 relative to 1970, it seems unreasonable to claim that undercoverage of undocumented aliens was 3 or more times the undercoverage of the group with the highest recently measured undercount, black males in their 30s who were missed in 1980 at a rate of 1 in 6.[42]

My personal experiences in observing the interviewer–respondent interaction in my own study lead me to the belief that it would be difficult for undocumented Mexicans to avoid being counted. Furthermore, as pointed out by both Crewdson and Corwin, the Census Bureau went out of its way to convince undocumented immigrants that it was safe to be counted in the 1980 Census.[43] As Crewdson also emphasized, local officials in cities with large numbers of undocumented persons were fully aware that federal funding was dependent on the size of the census count and were motivated to take action to ensure that substantial undercount would not occur.[44] I might add that many Chicano-led organizations were also dependent on such federal funding and thus were also encouraged to make efforts to see that undocumented Mexicans were counted. Moreover, I believe that many undocumented Mexicans wanted to be counted in the 1980 Census as proof of residence in case an amnesty program were passed and U.S. residence in that year were required as a condition of receiving amnesty.

Some calculations of the estimated number of person-years spent in the United States in 1980 by undocumented Mexican immigrants may also be of interest. Let me present two estimates of this number. The first, 1,456,000, is perhaps on the low side; the second, 1,618,500, is perhaps on the high side. Each of these estimates assumes that the 1,131,000 persons counted in the 1980 Census spent one year in the United States, possibly an overestimate. Let's examine the basis of both low and high person-year estimates.

Let me first present a rationale for the low estimate. In Cornelius's sample in nine villages in the state of Jalisco, of 230 men with a history of illegal entry to the United States during the previous seven years, the median length of the last stay in the United States was only 5.5 months.[45] Furthermore, life tables were developed by Cervera from the migration histories of 9,992 undocumented Mexicans forcibly removed from the United States and interviewed by CENIET immediately thereafter. One life table refers only to migratory stays in the United States that did not include an apprehension by the INS. This life table gave a median length of stay of 5.65 months.[46] Assuming that the mean length for shuttle migrants may be slightly higher than the median, let us assume that the mean length of stay for shuttle migrants is 6 months. Then the number of person-years spent in the United States by undocumented shuttle migrants would be 325,000, which is one-half of the estimated 650,000 present at some point in the year. Adding this figure to 1,131,000 from the 1980 Census, we obtain a total of 1,456,000 person-years spent in the United States by undocumented Mexicans in 1980.

The higher estimate is obtained by assuming that the person years spent in the United States by shuttle migrants, both legal and undocumented, was the mean of the upper and lower seasonal numbers presented by CENIET. This mean is 562,500 (the sum of 625,000 and 500,000 divided by 2). If we then assume that 50,000 daily legal commuters worked all year in the United States and that 50,000 legal seasonal commuters worked one-half a year, we can conclude that the number of person-years spent in the United States by undocumented shuttle migrants was 487,500. Adding this figure to 1,131,000, we obtain 1,618,500 person-years spent in the United States in 1980 by undocumented Mexicans.

The geographic concentration of undocumented Mexican immigrants

Passel and Woodrow published additional findings concerning the number of undoc- umented and legal resident aliens by nationality for each state.[47] Passel also released estimates of the numbers of undocumented and legal resident aliens by nationality for the major metropolitan statistical areas.[48] A summary of these data, for persons of Mexican birth in each state and Standard Metropolitan Statistical Area (SMSA) with 15,000 or more persons of Mexican birth according to the 1980 Census, is shown in Table 3.4.

The data refer to the resident population only. In many SMSAs, such as those in the Central Valley of California, a large proportion of all the undocumented workers may have been seasonal agricultural laborers who may not have been counted in the 1980 Census. In other areas, particularly those adjacent to the Mex- ican border, a large proportion of all the undocumented workers may have been occasional or daily commuters from Mexico who should not have been counted in the 1980 Census. Also, the adjustments made concerning the naturalized Mex- ican population and the U.S.-born population of Mexican descent were made pro- portionally for each area. To the extent that the true adjustments should not have been proportional, the estimates for particular areas will be in error. In particular, one can expect greater error in the estimates for small areas than for large ones.

The most striking feature of Table 3.4 is the concentration of undocumented aliens in California and particularly in the Los Angeles–Long Beach SMSA (con- terminous with Los Angeles County). Sixty-seven percent of all undocumented Mexicans were calculated to be in California and 44 percent in Los Angeles County alone.[49] Another striking feature of the table is the fact that while Cal- ifornia had 67 percent of all of the undocumented Mexicans in the United States,

Table 3.4. *Geographic distribution of undocumented and legal aliens born in Mexico for each state and SMSA with 15,000 or more persons born in Mexico according to the 1980 Census (numbers in thousands)*

Area	Undocumented		Legal alien		Percentage undocumented
	Number	Percentage of total	Number	Percentage of total	
United States	1,131	100	1,195	100	49
Arizona	20	2	50	4	29
Phoenix SMSA	12	1	15	1	45
California	763	67	615	51	55
Anaheim–Santa Ana–Garden Grove SMSA	62	5	33	3	65
Bakersfield SMSA	9	1	13	1	40
Fresno SMSA	14	1	18	2	44
Los Angeles–Long Beach SMSA	500	44	261	22	66
Oxnard–Simi Valley-Ventura SMSA	12	1	25	2	32
Riverside–San Bernardino–Ontario SMSA	23	2	33	3	41
Sacramento SMSA	5	0	11	1	29
Salinas–Seaside–Monterey SMSA	15	1	14	1	51
San Diego SMSA	34	3	57	5	37
San Francisco–Oakland SMSA	25	2	32	3	44
San Jose SMSA	15	1	22	2	41
Visalia–Tulare–Porterville SMSA	9	1	10	1	48
Colorado	11	1	6	1	65
Illinois	101	9	83	7	55
Chicago SMSA	97	9	80	7	55
New Mexico	10	1	15	1	40
Texas	147	13	358	30	29
Brownsville–Harlingen–San Benito SMSA	3	0	33	3	9

Table 3.4. *(cont.)*

Area	Undocumented		Legal alien		Percentage undocumented
	Number	Percentage of total	Number	Percentage of total	
Dallas–Fort Worth SMSA	32	3	23	2	59
El Paso SMSA	15	1	66	6	18
Houston SMSA	41	4	63	5	39
Laredo SMSA	−1	N.A.	19	2	N.A.
McAllen–Pharr– Edinburg SMSA	2	0	49	4	3
San Antonio SMSA	12	1	34	3	25
Washington	11	1	6	0	65
Remaining states	68	6	68	6	50

Sources: Jeffrey S. Passel and Karen A. Woodrow, "Geographic Distribution of Undocumented Aliens: Estimates of Undocumented Aliens counted in the 1980 Census by State," *International Migration Review 18,* no. 3 (1984): 642–71; memorandum of August 16, 1985 from Jeffrey S. Passel to Roger Herriot; personal communication from Jeffrey S. Passel.

it had only 51 percent of the legal aliens born in Mexico. By way of contrast, Texas had only 13 percent of the undocumented Mexicans in the nation but fully 30 percent of the legal aliens born in Mexico.

Another surprising aspect of the data is the small proportion of the aliens who were undocumented in the SMSAs located on the Texas–Mexico border (Brownsville–Harlingen–San Benito, El Paso, Laredo, and McAllen–Pharr– Edinburg). In the Laredo SMSA, the number of undocumented Mexicans calculated was actually negative. An important reason for these small proportions may be that the undocumented workers in these SMSAs commute from the Mexican cities across the Rio Grande. The Mexican cities across the river from the four Texas SMSAs mentioned above are all sizable, and in two cases (El Paso and Laredo) the city on the Mexican side of the river is larger than its counterpart SMSA on the American side.

On the other hand, it is possible that the estimates of the number of legal and illegal aliens for these SMSAs are in error because some legal residents of the United States who actually commuted from across the river registered with the INS as having an address in the Texas SMSA where they worked. A person who allows the INS to mark his or her Form I-51 (green card) to indicate he or she is either

Table 3.5. *Geographic distribution of undocumented Mexican immigrants and of the total Mexican-origin population for each state with 50,000 or more persons of Mexican origin and at least 3 percent of total population of Mexican origin (numbers in thousands)*

Area	Undocumented Mexicans		Total Mexican-origin population		Percent undocumented in total Mexican-origin population
	Number	Percent	Number	Percent	
United States	1,131	100	8,740	100	13
Arizona	20	2	396	5	5
Phoenix SMSA	12	1	178	2	7
Tucson SMSA	4	0	100	1	4
California	763	67	3,637	42	21
Anaheim–Santa Ana– Garden Grove SMSA	62	5	232	3	27
Bakersfield SMSA	9	1	87	1	10
Fresno SMSA	14	1	141	2	10
Los Angeles–Long Beach SMSA	500	44	1,651	19	30
Oxnard–Simi Valley– Ventura SMSA	12	1	101	1	12
Riverside–San Bernardino– Ontario SMSA	23	2	253	3	9
Sacramento	5	0	79	1	6
Salinas–Seaside– Monterey SMSA	15	1	65	1	23
San Diego SMSA	34	3	228	3	15
San Francisco–Oakland SMSA	25	2	190	2	13
San Jose SMSA	15	1	227	3	7
Stockton SMSA	4	0	57	1	7
Visalia–Tulare– Porterville SMSA	9	1	69	1	13
Colorado	11	1	207	2	5
Denver–Boulder SMSA	7	1	109	1	6
Illinois	101	9	408	5	25
Chicago SMSA	97	9	369	4	26
New Mexico	10	1	234	3	4
Albuquerque SMSA	3	0	72	1	4

Table 3.5. *(cont.)*

Area	Undocumented Mexicans		Total Mexican-origin population		Percent undocumented in total Mexican-origin population
	Number	Percent	Number	Percent	
Texas	147	13	2,752	31	5
Austin SMSA	3	0	94	1	3
Brownsville–Harlingen– San Benito SMSA	3	0	139	2	2
Corpus Christi SMSA	2	0	158	2	1
Dallas–Fort Worth SMSA	32	3	233	3	14
El Paso SMSA	15	1	282	3	5
Houston SMSA	41	4	375	4	11
Laredo SMSA	−1	N.A.	87	1	N.A.
McAllen–Pharr– Edinburg SMSA	2	0	222	3	1
San Antonio SMSA	12	1	447	5	3

Sources: For undocumented Mexicans, same as for Table 3.4; for total Mexican-origin population, U.S. Bureau of the Census, *1980 Census of Population,* Vol. 1, Characteristics of the Population, PC80-1-B1 (Washington, D.C.: Government Printing Office, 1983), Tables 63 and 70.

a daily or seasonal commuter loses the right to remain a permanent legal resident if he or she remains without a job in the United States for more than six months.[50] Accordingly, the number of legal residents who actually commuted may be greater than the number whose green card marked them as such. Correspondingly, the number registered by the INS as living in the Texas border SMSAs may have been greater than the actual number who reside there. The negative estimate for the number of undocumented Mexicans in the Laredo SMSA would change into a positive number if the true number of legal aliens in the Laredo SMSA had been inflated by only 1,000 persons, or slightly more than 5 percent of the 19,000 estimated by Passel. Moreover, the survey conducted in March 1975 by the INS showed almost 2,400 daily commuters into Laredo from Mexico.[51] Assuming a survey would show the same number of registered commuters in 1980, the true number of commuters would have to be only about 40 percent higher than the registered number to obtain a positive number of undocumented Mexicans for the Laredo SMSA.

The data in Table 3.4 may also be contrasted with the data collected in the 1978–79 CENIET survey of the 519,301 habitual residents of Mexico, both legal and undocumented, who were currently working in the United States. According to that survey, the proportions of all such workers found in each of the states with the most such workers were as follows: California, 49.2 percent; Texas, 22.0 percent; Illinois, 8.6 percent; New Mexico, 2.0 percent; Colorado, 1.9 percent; and Arizona, 1.8 percent.[52] Thus California would seem to have a much higher proportion of the permanent undocumented Mexicans than of shuttle migrants, either legal or undocumented.

We have now completed our discussion of the geographic distribution of the absolute numbers of undocumented Mexicans. It is also important to consider their numbers relative to the total population of Mexican origin in separate areas within the United States. Table 3.5 presents data on the geographic concentration of the undocumented Mexican population in relationship to the total population of Mexican origin. It shows that the distribution by area of undocumented Mexicans differed substantially from the distribution of all persons of Mexican origin.

Data are presented for those states and SMSAs containing at least 50,000 persons of Mexican origin according to the 1980 Census in which the population of Mexican origin was at least 3 percent of the total population. I have restricted the areas to ones with at least 3 percent of total population of Mexican origin because the U.S. Bureau of the Census has determined that in areas with only a small percentage of Mexican population, the recorded Mexican-origin population was substantially overcounted due to respondent error.[53]

California had 67 percent of all undocumented Mexicans and only 42 percent of the population of Mexican origin; Texas, in contrast, had only 13 percent of the undocumented Mexican population but 31 percent of the population of Mexican origin. The Los Angeles–Long Beach SMSA (Los Angeles County) had 44 percent of all undocumented Mexicans and only 19 percent of the Mexican origin population; the San Antonio SMSA, on the other hand, had only 1 percent of all undocumented Mexicans but 5 percent of the Mexican-origin population. As a consequence of these differences in geographic concentration, Table 3.5 also shows considerable variation by area in the percentage of the Mexican-origin population that were undocumented. This proportion was high in two states (California and Illinois) and quite low in the remaining four states shown (Arizona, Colorado, New Mexico, and Texas). Three SMSAs had very high proportions undocumented among the Mexican-origin population. These were Los Angeles–Long Beach (30 percent), Anaheim, Santa Ana–Garden Grove (27 percent), and Chicago (26 percent). The SMSAs in southern Texas and along the Rio Grande River, by contrast, uniformly had percentages undocumented of 5 percent or less.

What factors determine the number of undocumented Mexicans in each locality? Our earlier discussion indicated that distance and the magnitude of prior migration chains were two important factors. We also emphasized the importance of economic opportunities. If we divide the number of undocumented Mexicans in each locality

Table 3.6. *Percentage undocumented among persons of Mexican origin, 1980, and correlates thereof, six selected states*

	AZ	CA	CO	IL	NM	TX	Value of r
Percentage undocumented among persons of Mexican origin, 1980	5.1	21.0	5.3	24.8	4.3	5.3	—
Median earnings in 1969 of the male experienced civilian labor force of Spanish language or surname[a]	6,103	6,993	6,032	6,839	5,247	4,599	.787
Percent of all persons in poverty, 1970	15.4	11.1	12.3	10.2	22.8	18.7	.724
Average monthly AFDC payments, 1970	128	192	168	232	122	119	.913
Median earnings in 1979 of the male experienced civilian labor force of Spanish origin	11,052	10,535	11,614	11,080	10,364	9,423	.138
Percentage of all persons in poverty, 1980	13.2	11.4	10.1	11.0	17.6	14.7	.527
Average monthly AFDC payment, 1980	174	399	239	277	185	109	.769

[a]For Illinois, of Spanish language.
Sources: For median earnings in 1969, Table 175 of U.S. Bureau of the Census, *1970 Census of Population,* PC(1)-D4, PC(1)-D6, PC(1)-D7, PC(1)-D15, PC(1)-D33, and PC(1)-D45 (Washington, D.C.: Government Printing Office, 1973); for percentage of all persons in poverty in 1970, Table 69 of *1970 Census of Population,* PC(1)-C4, PC(1)-C6, PC(1)-C7, PC(1)-C15, PC(1)-C33, and PC(1)-C45; for average monthly AFDC payments 1970 and 1980, U.S. Bureau of the Census *Statistical Abstract of the United States, 1982–83* (Washington, D.C.: Government Printing Office, 1983) p. 342; for median earnings in 1979, Table 175 of *1980 Census of Population,* PC80-1-D4, PC80-1-D6, PC80-1-D7, PC80-1-D15, PC80-1-D33, and PC80-1-D45; for percentage of all persons in poverty in 1980, Table 104 of *1980 Census of Population,* PC80-1-C4, PC80-1-C6, PC80-1-C7, PC80-1-C15, PC80-1-C33, and PC80-1-C45.

by the total population of Mexican origin in that locality, we obtain a variable (shown in the first row of Table 3.6) that, in large part, controls both for distance from Mexico and also for the strength of the prior migration chain. Let us now relate this variable, as a dependent variable, to six independent variables relating to economic opportunity (rows 2–7 of Table 3.6).

Table 3.6 shows the correlation of the six economic-opportunity variables with

Table 3.7. *Comparison of correlation coefficients and slopes for dependent variables of percentage undocumented among the Mexican-origin population and percentage legal aliens among the Mexican-origin population*

| | Dependent variables | | | |
| | Percentage undocumented | | Percentage legal aliens | |
Independent variables	r	b	r	b
Median earnings in 1969 of the male experienced civilian labor force of Spanish language or surname	.787	.008	.486	.003
Percentage of all persons in poverty, 1970	−.724	−1.38	−.468	−.617
Average monthly AFDC payments, 1970	.913	.187	.566	.080

the dependent variable (the proportion of undocumented immigrants in the total population of Mexican origin in 1980), for a universe of the six states shown in Table 3.5 (Arizona, California, Colorado, Illinois, New Mexico, and Texas). Three of the independent variables are measured from the 1970 Census: (1) the median earnings in 1969 of the male experienced civilian labor force of Spanish language or surname, (2) the percentage of all persons in poverty, and (3) the average monthly Aid to Families with Dependent Children (AFDC) payment. The remaining three are corresponding variables measured from the 1980 Census.

Each of the three correlations from the 1970 Census is stronger than its counterpart correlation with an independent variable from the 1980 Census. What emerges clearly from the table is that the three 1970 variables are all highly related to the dependent variable.

It can be inferred from these data that undocumented Mexicans responded strongly to differences in local economic opportunities. The fact that the highest of the correlations is for the average monthly AFDC payment in 1970 suggests the possibility that undocumented immigrants may have responded not only to the wages available to them but also to opportunities for support of their American-born children (who are eligible for AFDC payments provided other requirements of the AFDC program are met). Nevertheless, this suggestion need not be true. Because the average AFDC payment may affect the reservation wage of citizen and legal immigrant workers, the level of such payments may simply be a more accurate reflection of the earnings available to undocumented Mexicans than is either the median earnings of males of Spanish language or surname or the proportion of all persons in poverty.

The three 1970 variables are much more appropriate for a study of causality than are the three 1980 variables. The fact that in all cases the 1980 variables show a lower correlation than the 1970 variable can be considered to be a consequence of the flow of undocumented Mexicans to specific localities during the 1970–80 decade.

There is further evidence for the validity of the economic-opportunity hypothesis. Within the state of Texas the proportion of undocumented Mexicans in the Mexican-origin population also appears to have responded strongly to economic opportunity. In 1970 the proportion of all persons in poverty ranged from 10 percent to 14 percent in the Dallas–Fort Worth, and Houston SMSAs; from 15 to 25 percent in the Austin, Corpus Christi, El Paso, and San Antonio SMSAs; and from 45 to 50 percent in the Brownsville–Harlingen–San Benito, Laredo, and McAllen–Pharr–Edinburg SMSAs.[54] As shown in Table 3.5, the proportions of undocumented to total Mexican-origin population in these SMSA's are inverse to the proportions in poverty in 1970.

Did the proportion of legal Mexican aliens in the total Mexican-origin population respond as strongly to measures of economic opportunity as did the proportion of undocumented Mexican aliens? One would expect the relationship to be less strong because the chances of receiving a visa for legal immigration depend so heavily upon kinship factors. Table 3.7 presents the values of the correlation coefficients and slopes for the six states shown in Table 3.6 for the two dependent variables. The three independent variables are those measuring economic opportunity in 1970 as previously used in Table 3.6. It is readily seen that the slopes for the impact of each of the opportunity variables on the percentage of legal aliens are much smaller than on the percentage of undocumented aliens; the former slopes are invariably less than one-half the size of the latter.

We have now shown that economic opportunity strongly affects where undocumented Mexicans settle in the United States. We are now prepared to examine the impact of their presence in the communities to which they move.

⋋ Social consequences of undocumented immigration

Let us first consider the apparent impact of undocumented Mexican immigration on changes in the proportion of the Mexican-origin population living in poverty. This discussion will focus on the six states for which I presented data in the previous section. I shall then review studies made by other scholars concerning the apparent impact of undocumented Mexican immigration on Los Angeles County, the five counties constituting the Los Angeles–Long Beach–Anaheim Standard Consoli-

Table 3.8. *Percentage of Mexican-origin persons in poverty, 1970 and 1980, and percentage of Mexican-origin population that was undocumented in 1980 for six selected states*

State	Percentage in poverty			Percentage undocumented among Mexican-origin population
	1970	1980	Difference	
Arizona	27.0	21.4	−5.6	5.1
California	19.6	20.1	0.5	21.0
Colorado	27.6	20.8	−6.8	5.3
Illinois	12.5	18.0	5.5	24.8
New Mexico	37.7	24.9	−12.8	4.3
Texas	39.7	28.5	−11.2	5.3

Note: r between percent undocumented and poverty difference $= .926$. Slope of percent undocumented on poverty difference $= .692$.

dated Statistical Area, and the State of California as a whole. The scholars conclude that some persons benefit from the presence of the undocumented whereas others lose out.

Changes in the incidence of poverty

Table 3.8 presents data for six states – Arizona, California, Colorado, Illinois, New Mexico, and Texas – on the proportion of the Mexican-origin population that was in poverty according to the 1970 and 1980 censuses. (Poverty is defined by the U.S. Bureau of the Census for persons in families and for unrelated individuals. For persons in families, the poverty level depends on family income during the preceding year, the age of the householder, and the number of persons in the family. For unrelated individuals, it depends upon income in the preceding year and age.[55]

The data in Table 3.8 constitute impressive evidence that the influx of undocumented Mexicans during the 1970–80 decade was instrumental in producing either an increase in poverty, if the volume of undocumented immigration was large, or a decrease in poverty, if the volume was small. According to the 1970 Census, 13.7 percent of the U.S. population was in poverty; according to the 1980 Census 12.4 percent.[56] As can be seen from the table, the proportions of the Mexican-origin population in poverty in these states was considerably higher than the proportion of the total U.S. population for either 1970 or 1980. For 1970 there was considerable variation in the proportion of the Mexican-origin population in poverty from a high of almost 40 percent in Texas to a low of almost 12 percent in Illinois. By 1980 the differentials in poverty had been considerably muted. The incidence of poverty increased in Illinois and in California, the two states with the lowest incidence of poverty in 1970, and decreased in the remaining four states of Arizona, Colorado, New Mexico, and Texas. Table 3.8 also shows a strong correlation between the change from 1970 to 1980 in the proportion in poverty and the percentage of the Mexican-origin population in 1980 that was undocumented. The value of *r* is .926 and the slope measuring the impact of the proportion undocumented on the change in poverty is .692.

From the data shown above I have inferred that change in the proportion of the proportion of the Mexican-origin population living in poverty was affected by the magnitude of the flow of undocumented Mexicans into the area. One might object that such an inference is invalid because we do not actually measure the change from 1970 to 1980 in the proportion of the Mexican-origin population in each of these states that is undocumented. The objection has merit but is mitigated by the fact that there is very little variation among these six states in the proportions of the undocumented Mexican population in 1980 that came to the United States since 1970. This proportion varies only from a low of 75 percent in Arizona to 81.8 percent in Colorado.[57]

Impact on Los Angeles County, the Los Angeles SCSA, and California

This section reviews three major studies: (1) a study by the staff of the Southern California Association of Governments, (2) a major study performed by several scholars at the Urban Institute, and (3) another major study by the Rand Corporation.[58] None of the studies uses data concerning the characteristics of undocumented persons. What these studies do is to examine data from the 1970 and 1980 censuses and other official sources to look at changes in Los Angeles County, the Los Angeles–Long Beach–Anaheim SCSA, Southern California, and the state of California as a whole. I shall argue that these changes were the likely consequence of the high volume of undocumented Mexican immigration into the state, into southern California, and into Los Angeles County in particular.

Let me give a summary of the conclusions from these studies. First, they found a high volume of out-migration on the part of non-Hispanic whites from Los Angeles County in particular but also from Southern California as well. Second, they found that wage levels in low-wage manufacturing industries had been depressed. Third, they found that the school systems in Los Angeles County had been heavily affected by students who did not speak English. Fourth, they found little or no impact of Mexican immigration on rates of unemployment. Fifth, they

Table 3.9. *Number of undocumented Mexicans, percentage of total population which is undocumented Mexican, and percentage of total population black for the Los Angeles–Long Beach SMSA (by age and by sex) and for the other SMSAs in the Los Angeles–Long Beach–Anaheim SCSA*

Area, age, and sex	Undocumented Mexican population	Total population	Percentage undocumented Mexican in total population	Percentage black in total population
Los Angeles–Long Beach SMSA (Los Angeles County)	500,200	7,477,503	6.7	12.6
Male, total	266,500	3,648,361	7.3	12.2
Under 18 years	71,300	1,034,203	6.9	15.3
18 to 44 years	180,500	1,625,037	11.1	11.9
45 years and over	14,700	989,121	1.5	9.7
Female, total	233,700	3,829,142	6.1	13.0
Under 18 years	69,700	997,085	7.0	15.5
18 to 44 years	145,700	1,620,707	9.0	13.7
45 years and over	18,300	1,211,350	1.5	9.9
Anaheim–Santa Ana–Garden Grove SMSA (Orange County)	62,000	1,932,709	3.2	1.3
Oxnard–Simi Valley–Ventura SMSA (Ventura County)	12,000	529,174	2.3	2.1
Riverside–San Bernardino–Ontario SMSA (Riverside and San Bernardino Counties)	23,000	1,558,182	1.5	5.0
Los Angeles–Long Beach–Anaheim SCSA	597,000	11,497,568	5.2	9.2

Sources: For the undocumented Mexican population of Los Angeles County by age and by sex, David M. Heer and Jeffrey S. Passel, "Comparison of Two Methods for Estimating the Number of Undocumented Mexican Adults in Los Angeles County," *International Migration Review 21*, no. 4 (1987): 1446–73; for the undocumented Mexican population in the remaining SMSAs, Memorandum of August 16, 1985 from Jeffrey S. Passel to Roger Herriot, Chief,

Table 3.9. (*cont.*)
Population Division, U.S. Bureau of the Census; for the total and black population of each SMSA, U.S. Bureau of the Census *1980 Census of Population*, PC80-1-B6, (Washington, D.C.: Government Printing Office, 1980), p. 7.

found little or no impact of Mexican immigration on the incomes of black persons but some negative influence on the earnings of U.S.-born persons of Spanish origin. Finally, they found that the influx of Mexicans probably had a negative effect on the tax burden but served to reduce prices and to increase the size of the local economy.

However, before considering the findings in more detail, let us look at more of Passel's findings concerning the relationship between total population and the number of undocumented Mexican immigrants for Los Angeles County and for the Los Angeles–Long Beach–Anaheim SCSA in 1980. Table 3.9 presents the relevant data with somewhat more detail for Los Angeles County than for the entire SCSA.

We see that undocumented Mexicans constitute 6.7 percent of the population of Los Angeles County and 5.2 percent of the population of the entire Los Angeles–Long Beach–Anaheim SCSA. However, within Los Angeles County their proportion varies substantially by age. Among males 18 to 44, undocumented Mexicans constitute 11.1 percent of the population, but among either males or females 45 years of age or older only 1.5 percent. The table also allows a comparison of the number of undocumented Mexicans with the number of blacks. Although blacks constituted 12.6 percent of the Los Angeles County population and undocumented Mexicans only 6.7 percent, among males 18 to 44 there were almost as many undocumented Mexicans in the county as blacks. Another interesting fact is that, in two of the SMSAs shown in the table, the number of undocumented Mexicans was larger than the number of blacks. In the Anaheim–Santa Ana–Garden grove SMSA, the number of undocumented Mexicans was more than twice the number of blacks.

Additional data of interest relate to the numbers of undocumented Mexicans to the total population of Mexican origin in particular age-sex groups. Although there are no published data from the 1980 Census concerning the distribution of the Mexican-origin population in Los Angeles County by age and by sex, such data were available from a tape. Accordingly, I made tabulations from the 1980 Census Public Use Microdata Sample tape for the county to count the total number of Mexican-origin males 18 to 44 and Mexican-origin females 18 to 39. From these tabulations and from the estimates of undocumented Mexicans made by Passel, I calculated that, among Mexican-origin males 18 to 44 years of age, 47.7 percent were undocumented; among Mexican-origin females 18 to 39 years of age, 43 percent were undocumented.

Finally, although we do not have data on the increase between 1970 and 1980 in the size of the undocumented Mexican population in Los Angeles County, we do know that the vast majority of the current undocumented population arrived

Table 3.10. *Change in ethnic composition*[a] *for Los Angeles County and for the Los Angeles–Long Beach–Anaheim Standard Consolidated Statistical Area, 1970 to 1980 (numbers in thousands)*

| | | | Not of Hispanic origin | | |
Area	Total population	Hispanic origin	White	Black	Other race
Los Angeles County					
1970 population	7,042	1,046	5,020	746	225
1980 population	7,478	2,066	3,985	926	501
1970–80 change	436	1,020	−1,035	180	276
1970–80 percentage change	6	97	−21	24	123
Los Angeles–Long Beach–					
Anaheim SCSA					
1970 population	9,981	1,376	7,530	811	268
1980 population	11,498	2,754	7,033	1,038	673
1970–80 change	1,517	1,379	−497	227	405
1970–80 percentage change	15	100	−7	28	151

[a]Numbers for ethnic composition are based on sample data and do not add across to the figures on total population.
Sources: For data on total population, U.S. Bureau of the Census, *Statistical Abstract of the United States, 1985* (Washington, D.C.: Government Printing Office, 1985), p. 20; for data on ethnic composition, Southern California Association of Governments, *Southern California: A Region in Transition,* Vol. 3, (Los Angeles: SCAG, December 1984), p. 8.

in the United States since 1970.[59] Passel's calculation is that for Los Angeles County 79.6 percent came since 1970. As I stated earlier, I believe that Passel's method for determining the numbers by year of arrival is biased, and that the actual proportion coming since 1970 should be somewhat higher.

The 1980 Census showed that 949,000 persons born outside the United States who came to the United States in 1970 or later were living in Los Angeles County. Of these, 456,000, or 48 percent, were born in Mexico.[60] Passel's estimate is that there were 399,000 undocumented Mexicans in Los Angeles County who came to the United States during this decade.[61] These would then constitute 42 percent of all of the 949,000 persons in Los Angeles County in 1980 who came to the United States during the previous decade.

Let us now consider some results from the study performed by the Southern California Association of Governments (SCAG). This study presented data on the changes in the ethnic composition of Los Angeles County and the five-county SCSA. These data are shown in Table 3.10. For Los Angeles County the two most striking facts are the large increase in the Hispanic-origin population and the equally large decline in the non-Hispanic white population. For the entire SCSA it is also striking that the non-Hispanic white population was reduced by almost a half million persons during the decade coupled with an increase of almost 1.4 million persons of Hispanic origin.

The population decline for non-Hispanic white persons shown in Table 3.10 must imply an even greater out-migration. No figures on the net out-migration of this group for Los Angeles County are available. However, a tabulation performed as part of the Urban Institute study revealed that from 1970 to 1980 the net out-migration of native-born persons in Los Angeles County was 1.008 million. Moreover, for Southern California as a whole (defined as the Los Angeles SCSA, the Santa Barbara SMSA, the San Diego SMSA, and Imperial County), the net out-migration of the native-born was 223,000.[62]

Moreover, the Urban Institute study also discussed additional data, collected from the Current Population Survey, on net migration for the State of California from within the United States by ethnic status.[63] A 1980 Census publication, which appeared after the Urban Institute paper, provides more precise results than the CPS. Therefore, I shall not discuss the CPS results but only those from the 1980 Census. As shown in Table 3.11, total net in-migration into California from other states was 94,458. This included a net out-migration of 16,253 whites, a net in-migration of 75,746 blacks, and a net out-migration of 6,409 Hispanics.[64] The figure for the latter group's out-migration to other states is of particular interest because in the past California had experienced a substantial net in-migration of Hispanics, particularly from Texas.

The Urban Institute study also computed, from Current Population Survey data, net migration rates within the United States for the state of California for persons 18 years old or older by educational attainment.[65] Subsequently published and more precise data from the 1980 Census are also shown in Table 3.11. According to the Census, there was net out-migration for persons 25 and over in all educational attainment groups below the level of college graduate. For all such persons the net out-migration was 46,625; for whites it was much higher, 83,699. On the other hand, for all persons 25 and older who were college graduates or more, the net in-migration was 84,981; for whites it was 64,858.[66]

The authors of the Urban Institute study also detailed how the recent situation with respect to net migration to California from other states differed radically from that in the past. In prior decades the net migration to California from other states had always been strongly positive. However, since the 1955–60 period there has been both a decline in the rate of gross in-migration to California from other states and an increase in the rate of gross out-migration from California to other states.[67]

The authors of this Urban Institute study concluded, "The similarity in the socio-

Table 3.11. *Net interstate migration for various population subgroups, California, 1975–80*

Subgroup	Net interstate migration
Total	94,458
Whites	−16,253
Blacks	75,746
Other races	34,965
Hispanic origin	−6,409
Persons 25 and over, total	38,356
Less than college graduate	−46,625
College graduate or more	84,981
White persons 25 and over, total	−18,841
Less than college graduate	−93,699
College graduate or more	64,858
Black persons 25 and over, total	33,376
Less than college graduate	26,625
College graduate or more	6,751

Source: U.S. Bureau of the Census, *1980 Census of Population*, Vol. 2, Subject Reports, PC80-2-2A (Washington, D.C.: Government Printing Office, 1985), Tables 22 and 28.

economic characteristics of net out-migrants from California and those of Mexican immigrants suggests that the flow from Mexico substituted for internal migration."[68]

Oregonians are fond of bumper stickers that proclaim, "Don't Californicate Oregon." However, it would appear that the Mexican immigration into California helped to produce precisely that phenomenon. According to the 1980 Census, during the 1975–80 period the net out-migration from California to Oregon was 105,818. Moreover, the net out-migration from California to Washington was of almost equal magnitude. Furthermore, there was net out-migration from California to every other state within the Pacific division except Hawaii, to every single state within the Mountain division, and to every state within the West South Central division with only the single exception of Louisiana.[69] In an interesting recent paper, Philip Martin, a labor economist, describes in detail how he believes job displacement of non-Hispanic whites by undocumented Mexican immigrants occurs.[70] He emphasizes that in most small firms the hiring is done by the foreman from among friends and acquaintances. Once a foreman of Mexican origin is hired, he, with the approval of his boss, hires many undocumented Mexicans and no longer hires non-Hispanic whites. The persons hired are generally persons to whom the foreman has kinship ties or whose origin is the same local community in Mexico. In such an atmosphere, workers who do not speak Spanish soon find themselves culturally out of place and decide that they would be better off with a job elsewhere.

The study conducted by SCAG discussed the impact of Mexican immigration on the public school system. The Los Angeles Unified School District (including the city of Los Angeles and a few other communities) enrolls certain of its students in its Limited English Program. In 1981–82, 22 percent of all of the system's 536,000 students were enrolled in this program. Of the 117,000 enrolled students, there were 102,000 whose native language was Spanish. The authors of the SCAG study believe that the later achievement of these numerous Spanish-speaking students will be adversely affected by their lack of English-speaking ability and that as a consequence many will drop out of school before high-school graduation.[71]

The Urban Institute study considered the impact of Mexican immigration on wages in Los Angeles County. They showed that Mexican immigrants constituted 47 percent of all workers in low-wage manufacturing industries (e.g., apparel, leather goods, and furniture), 19.5 percent of all workers in high-wage manufacturing (e.g., metals, machinery, and transportation equipment) and 9.9 percent of all workers. There was a very high correlation between the proportion of all workers who were Mexican immigrants and the increase in the wage from 1972 to 1980 in Los Angeles relative to that in the United States. For low-wage manufacturing the relative increase in the Los Angeles County wage was only 77 percent of that in the United States, for high-wage manufacturing it was only 91 percent, but for all workers it was 109 percent.[72] The authors concluded, "there is some evidence of wage depression attributable to immigrants."[73]

The Urban Institute study also considered trends in unemployment in the Los Angeles SCSA relative to that in the United States. They found that in 1970, for persons of all races and also for black persons, the unemployment rate had been higher in the Los Angeles SCSA than in the United States. Nevertheless, by 1980 it was lower. Thus they concluded that the influx of Mexican immigrants had had no effect on unemployment.[74]

The Urban Institute study also included regression analyses relating average black family income in SMSAs across the nation and in the southwest to the proportion of the total labor force of Hispanic origin.[75] They concluded, "the presence of Hispanic immigrants in local labor markets has little effect, positively or negatively, on black family income."[76] The Urban Institute study did not attempt to examine how the income of families headed by persons born in the United States of Mexican origin was affected by competition from Mexican immigrants.

The third study, conducted by the Rand Corporation, does shed some light on how the influx of undocumented Mexicans affected the income of U.S.-born Mexicans, the group ignored in the Urban Institute study. For California as a whole and also for Los Angeles County, the Rand Corporation study reported the increase in earnings for U.S.-born, full-time year-round workers of Hispanic origin relative to that in the nation as a whole. The relative increase in such earnings in Los Angeles County was only 59 percent of that in the nation, and the relative increase for California as a whole only 71 percent that of the nation. For Los Angeles County, the average earnings of U.S.-born Hispanic-origin year-round full-time workers had been 25 percent higher than the national average, whereas by 1980 they were only 99 percent of the U.S. average.[77]

Additionally, the Urban Institute scholars calculated the difference between taxes paid to California or local taxing agencies and financial benefits received from these governmental bodies for those households in Los Angeles County in which the householder was a Mexican immigrant. They showed a net deficit (financial benefits minus taxes) of $1,779 with respect to the State of California and of $466 with respect to local taxing agencies, for a total net deficit of $2,245. Expenditures on behalf of Mexican immigrant households were higher than for all households in the county mainly because of the greater expenses for school enrollment of the Mexican-origin children.[78]

The Urban Institute scholars also showed that the consumer price index had increased somewhat more slowly in the Los Angeles area than in the nation as a whole, particularly for personal care, apparel, and entertainment.[79] Thus consumers in Los Angeles County would appear to have benefited from the presence of undocumented Mexican immigrants.

The Urban Institute scholars estimated that 52,000 low-wage jobs in highly competitive manufacturing industries would not exist if Mexican immigrants were not present.[80] According to Thomas Muller of the Urban Institute, "The net result was to preserve the area's competitive advantage in manufacturing and to modestly increase profit margins."[81]

In his summary of the impact of Mexican immigration on the Los Angeles economy, Muller concluded, "There is little question that when all factors are considered Mexican immigrants are a definite plus to the local economy. This is not to say, however, that everybody benefits from the immigrants' presence. Some residents pay higher state and local taxes but enjoy few if any direct benefits. Other residents who hold semiskilled jobs may earn less than people with similar skills in localities where few immigrants are present."[82]

But in this summary statement Muller ignored the undocumented as a constituent of the total population. Table 3.12 presents data on the percentage of persons in poverty and on per capita income in Los Angeles County and the nation according to the censuses of 1970 and 1980.

In 1970 Los Angeles County, as compared to the nation, had both a higher per

Table 3.12. *Percentage in poverty and per capita income, Los Angeles County and United States, 1970 and 1980*

	Los Angeles County	United States
Percentage in poverty		
1970	10.9	13.7
1980	13.4	12.4
Absolute change	+2.5	−1.3
Per capita income		
1970	3,884	3,139
1980	8,303	7,298
Percentage change	113.8	132.5

Sources: For 1970 data, U.S. Bureau of the Census, *1970 Census of Population*, PC70(1)-C1 (Washington, D.C.: Government Printing Office, 1973), p. 398 and p. 400, and PC70(1)-C6, p. 558 and p. 574; for 1980 data, U.S. Bureau of the Census, *1980 Census of Population*, PC80-1-C1 (Washington, D.C.: Government Printing Office, 1983), p. 78 and p. 79 and PC80-1-C6, p. 303 and p. 318.

capita income and a lower percentage in poverty. By 1980, although the per capita income was still considerably above the U.S. average, the proportion in poverty was higher than for the nation as a whole. Moreover, while the proportion in poverty declined over the decade for the nation, it rose substantially in Los Angeles County from 10.9 to 13.4 percent. Thus in Los Angeles County the gap between rich and poor, many of the latter undocumented immigrants, would appear to have increased during the decade. That there is a growing gap between rich and poor in Los Angeles County is of course fully congruent with Muller's own findings concerning relative increase in wages by type of industry.

Finally, we may ask what was the conclusion of the Urban Institute scholars concerning the impact of the Mexican immigration on the economy of California as a whole? Muller summarized: "Public-sector impacts are primarily redistributional with the state's economy only marginally affected by the combination of higher taxes and higher expenditures induced by Mexican immigrants. There are, however, substantial transfers from people living outside Los Angeles to those living inside the county. Although the state as a whole benefits from added manufacturing employment in Los Angeles, these benefits are concentrated in the county with only limited spillover to other areas. Thus, while it appears that the economic effects of Mexican immigration are positive to Los Angeles County, the effects on the rest of California are decidedly mixed."[83]

4. Alternative ways of surveying the undocumented and some results

Because undocumented Mexican immigrants in the United States are here illegally, it is difficult for investigators to survey them according to methods commonly used in other surveys. This chapter describes various methods of survey and presents two types of results from actual surveys. The first type concerns variables for which the distribution varies considerably between studies, a variation resulting because of the way in which the respondents were located. These variables include sex, marital status, and intention to reside permanently in the United States. The second concerns the results of variables that were not covered in my own survey. These include geographic origin in Mexico, use of coyotes (guides), apprehension history, remittances to Mexico, size of place of employment, labor union membership, and level of psychological stress. (See Chapters 7 and 8 for discussion of most of the variables that were covered in my own survey.)

Alternative methods for surveying the undocumented

The Census

For a rather obvious reason the U.S. Census has never asked persons in the United States whether they had a legal right to be here. Undocumented persons would certainly be reluctant to inform U.S. Census enumerators of their status. Because the prime aim of the census is to produce a complete population count, a question on legal status would be undesirable as it would limit the number of persons responding.

Conceivably, the census of Mexico might provide an opportunity for some relevant questions. It would probably be technically feasible for the Mexican census to have a question on whether persons who were habitual residents of Mexico were in the United States for an intended stay of less than one year. For such persons, a second question could be asked as to whether they had legal authorization for their stay. However, it is not likely that the Mexican government would wish to include the latter question. Even without this last question, the results of the first question would nevertheless prove useful because the number of legal immigrants to the United States who are habitual residents of Mexico is presumably so small. Consequently, the characteristics of the uncounted number of the undocumented

72

who migrate to the United States but are habitual residents of Mexico would differ little from the characteristics of the counted number of all persons who migrate to the United States but habitually reside in Mexico.

Thus it is useful to find a group who are believed to be for the most part undocumented and then use the characteristics of this group to represent those of the undocumented. Such a technique may be applied to the U.S. Census. Two recent studies make use of it.[1] One by James Pearce and Jeffrey Gunther made use of the 1980 Census Public Use Microdata Sample to isolate persons in Texas who were born in Mexico and spoke no English. The researchers then assumed that this group could be used as a proxy for undocumented Mexican immigrants and proceeded to examine the occupations, educational attainment, and earnings of adults in this group. In my opinion, the results of that study seem suspect. According to the results of my survey in Los Angeles County, among respondents who were undocumented fathers only a little more than one-quarter spoke no English. Moreover, the educational attainment, occupational status, and earnings of Mexican immigrants who speak no English may be heavily affected by their inability to speak the language of the United States.

The second study, by Bean et al., assumed that an appropriate proxy for undocumented Mexican immigrants in the 1980 Census Public Use Microdata Sample would be noncitizens born in Mexico who came to the United States since 1975. Almost two-thirds of this group was undocumented. Characteristics of persons in this group were hence likely to be close to those of all undocumented Mexicans who came to the United States since 1975.

Thus, a judicious use of this proxy-group method may be warranted. What is important is to try to judge what will be the biases in using it.

The area-probability survey

Other than census data, the major source of information concerning demographic characteristics of a population is an area-probability survey. In the United States the Current Population Survey, an area-probability survey conducted monthly by the U.S. Bureau of the Census, is the major source of annual information concerning the basic characteristics of the U.S. population. The major disadvantage of the Current Population Survey, compared to the census, is that it cannot provide data for small areas, nor can it be used to provide descriptive data for subgroups that form only a small part of the total U.S. population.

A question on the legal status of immigrants cannot be asked in the Current Population Survey for the same reason it cannot be asked in the decennial census of the United States. Nevertheless, it is conceivable that other area-probability surveys might include a question on the legal status of immigrants. One problem with conducting such a survey is that undocumented Mexicans constitute such a small proportion of the total U.S. population. Hence any survey attempting to obtain characteristics of undocumented Mexicans would have to oversample those areas where undocumented Mexicans are known to live. Three sources of data provide an excellent basis for a sampling scheme that would heavily oversample areas with a high concentration of undocumented Mexicans. These are (1) Jeffrey Passel's tabulations on the estimated count of undocumented Mexicans for each county in the United States in 1980, (2) data on the proportion of persons born in Mexico in each census tract, and (3) forthcoming data on legalizations of status by country of birth and place of residence under the 1986 Immigration Reform and Control Act. Hence it would appear technically feasible to conduct such a study if the funds were made available.

In fact the Immigration and Naturalization Service did commission a survey in 1978 to determine the size and characteristics of the deportable population in the United States. Reyes and Associates was given a contract to survey 10,000 households in twelve states thought to have large numbers of undocumented immigrants. For reasons that have never fully been explained, the INS canceled the survey on August 15, 1978 after 9,600 of the 10,000 planned household interviews had been made and $890,000 of government funds spent.[2] It is possible that the actual reason for the cancellation was a high rate of nonresponse among contacted households.

In Chapter 3 I mentioned the area-probability survey (conducted in Mexico in late 1978 and early 1979 by Centro Nacional de Información y Estadísticas del Trabajo, CENIET) of habitual residents of Mexico that counted the number who were either working in the United States temporarily or had done so within the preceding five years. This survey of 62,500 households did not ask the legal status of those persons who were or had been workers in the United States. However, its results are valuable because we do know that the vast majority of such workers must have been undocumented. In the second section of this chapter we shall describe results from this survey as if it pertained only to undocumented Mexicans.

Specialized samples of persons known to be undocumented

A very large number of studies have been conducted to determine the characteristics of specialized groups of persons, all of whom are known to be undocumented. With three exceptions, these studies have involved apprehended individuals. The exceptions are the major study by Van Arsdol et al. of the clients of the One Stop Immigration Center in Los Angeles, a smaller study done by Jones in San Antonio among 181 clients seeking advice to legalize their status, and another small study done in Houston among 105 parents attending special private schools for the undocumented.[3]

Ideally, all such surveys of persons known to be undocumented should be conducted either as a census (a complete count) or as a survey from a probability sample. Unfortunately, not all of the studies have been able to follow this ideal; some of the surveys of this class have been quota samples. However, even if we had a representative sample or complete count of such a special population, it would not necessarily be representative of the complete population of undocumented persons.

Let us first discuss the studies of apprehended individuals. Many of these studies have been conducted within the United States. Many others have been conducted in Mexico among deportees immediately upon their being turned back to Mexican authorities on their side of the border.[4]

Do such studies give an accurate picture of the characteristics of all apprehended persons in the United States? I think we can be assured that they do not, at least with respect to certain characteristics, because certain types of undocumented individual have a much higher probability of being apprehended than others.

North and Houstoun, authors of one of the most important of the studies of apprehended aliens, have been well aware of these biases. In particular, according to these researchers, the INS is much more concerned with apprehending men than women. Furthermore, as they point out, there are logistical problems associated with the apprehension of women; the INS does not have overnight detention facilities for women, and there are special problems when the woman is the mother of small children.[5]

Moreover, as I pointed out in Chapter 2, the INS has been much more active in pursuing illegal aliens who work in agriculture than those who work elsewhere. Until 1986 arrests could be made in the fields without a warrant. Arrests have never been possible in factories or other business establishments without either a warrant or the consent of the employer. Hence samples of apprehended individuals have been biased in favor of including agricultural workers. North and Houstoun point out that this bias also results in lower levels of educational attainment and ability to speak English. Finally, shuttle migrants will be very much overrepresented in samples of apprehended aliens. Unlike permanent immigrants, they are apt to cross the border frequently; furthermore, the chance of apprehension is very much greater at the border than elsewhere. Shuttle migrants in turn can be expected to have characteristics that differ from those of undocumented immigrants intending a more permanent stay.

Finally, samples of apprehended aliens may differ depending upon the areas in which interviews take place. Some of the major studies of apprehended aliens have been conducted in a single place; others have been conducted in a multitude of places. The survey by CENIET of apprehended persons, conducted in 1977, is noteworthy for having been conducted at twelve Mexican ports of entry and having a larger sample size (1,992) than any other such survey conducted in recent years.[6]

The survey conducted in 1975 by North and Houstoun is important because it was restricted to persons who had worked in the United States at least two weeks

before apprehension. Thus it allowed for greater attention to labor force characteristics than the usual sample of apprehendees, many of whom have been apprehended
prior to any U.S. employment. North and Houstoun's planned quota sample consisted of 800 persons, 600 of whom had been apprehended by the staff of INS district offices and only 200 of whom had been apprehended by the INS border patrol.
Interviews were actually obtained from 793 apprehendees from all nations of the
world, of whom 481 were born in Mexico.[7]

Let us now examine details of the large-scale survey of undocumented persons seeking to legalize their status conducted by Van Arsdol et al. in Los Angeles.[8] The respondents for the study consisted of all of the undocumented clients of the One Stop
Immigration Center who were from Spanish-speaking Latin American nations and who
first came there for legal counseling beginning January 1, 1972, and continuing through
part of 1975. One Stop Immigration Service Center was originally funded with federal
Model Cities funds to provide legal services connected with immigration. In addition
to providing legal assistance concerning adjustment of status, it also assisted with applications for naturalization. The total number of respondents included in the study was
2,845 of which 2,634 were from Mexico. One may surmise that this sample was biased
toward the inclusion of undocumented persons who had good reason to believe that they
could legalize their status.

Snowball samples

Several researchers have used snowball samples to gather data on undocumented
Mexicans. With a snowball sample, the researcher first interviews one or more persons whom he already knows to be undocumented. Each person interviewed then
provides the researcher with additional names of undocumented persons. These
additional undocumented persons are then interviewed. Obviously, the snowball
samples are not probability samples. It is never certain how much bias snowball
samples have. Wayne Cornelius has discussed the relative value of snowball samples
in comparison to probability samples with a high nonresponse rate (such as my
own sample of Los Angeles County parents). He has concluded that such probability
samples do not seem "to be an adequate substitute . . . ."[9] I will not dispute with
him concerning the desirability of a low rate of nonresponse; instead I would like
to emphasize that snowball samples are not adequate substitutes for probability samples, even those with high nonresponse rates. For populations for which probability
samples will produce a high nonresponse rate, I think it is valuable to have both
snowball samples and probability samples.

Reynaldo Baca and Dexter Bryan made use of a snowball sample to interview
1,400 undocumented Mexican workers in Los Angeles County.[10] Their sample was
built upon initial contacts within the restaurant industry.

Gilbert Cárdenas describes the details of his snowball sample of undocumented Mexicans in San Antonio.[11] He succeeded in interviewing 99 undocumented Mexicans. He also interviewed, for purposes of comparison, 126 Mexican-Americans, 35 blacks, and 104 white Anglos, all of whom lived in poor neighborhoods in the city. As a further comparison, he obtained data from the San Antonio district office of the INS concerning the characteristics of 747 Mexicans they had apprehended during the first months of 1975. With respect to length of residence in the United States, Cárdenas's sample differed significantly from the INS San Antonio district office data; in his sample 36 percent had lived in the United States for four years or more, whereas in the INS sample the percentage was only 4 percent. With respect to Mexican state of origin, however, the two samples gave very similar results.

Snowball samples have also been used that built from a base of field investigation in Mexico. Wayne Cornelius conducted a field investigation in nine rural communities in the northeastern part of the state of Jalisco. From names received by respondents in these communities, he initiated a snowball sample of 185 immigrants from these communities living in 1978 in six cities in California and four cities in Illinois.[12] About one-half of those interviewed were undocumented. Richard Mines conducted a similar survey of 66 individuals living in California, all of whom had come from the same town in a rural community in the state of Zacatecas.[13] If one wants to generalize to all undocumented Mexicans in the United States, an obvious type of bias in each of the two preceding studies is that all of the interviewees come from rural communities. However, the studies done by Cornelius and Mines are not only illustrations of snowball samples but also of sampling from a specialized population, the topic we shall next pursue.

Surveys from specialized populations with a known high proportion of undocumented persons

Surveys of specialized populations known to have a high proportion of undocumented persons are advantageous in that they are relatively inexpensive. They also allow comparison of the undocumented persons in a population with others who are not undocumented. Nevertheless, such surveys do not in general represent the entire undocumented population whether the survey is done on a complete-count basis or as a probability sample.

A large number of surveys have been done of rural communities in Mexico known to have large numbers of individuals who are shuttle migrants to the United States. Joshua Reichert and Douglas Massey surveyed 919 shuttle migrants to the United States after first conducting a census of the entire population of a rural community in the state of Michoacan.[14] Surprisingly, only 21 percent of these stated that they were undocumented. Cornelius conducted 994 usable interviews from a random sample among adult male respondents in nine rural communities in the state of Jalisco; of these 487 involved men who had worked in the United States, and 317 were of men who had last worked in the United States illegally.[15] Mines conducted interviews with a random sample of 67 adult males in a village in the state of Zacatecas.[16] Past shuttle migrants to the United States were asked their legal status; 10 were legal and 53 undocumented. Mines also questioned each of the 67 village men interviewed, and an additional 75 men from the village then living in either California or Tijuana, concerning their close relatives. In this larger sample of 1,454 persons, 174 out of 193 shuttle migrants were illegal.

Sheldon Maram conducted two important surveys in Los Angeles County in 1979.[17] The first involved workers in the garment industry and the second workers in the restaurant industry. It was known in advance that a high proportion of workers in each of these industries were undocumented. Interviewing for these two studies was conducted by employees of the State of California (staff of the Concentrated Enforcement Program of the Division of Labor Standards Enforcement of the Department of Industrial Relations). The study design called for quota sampling in each industry of Hispanic workers. A variety of workplaces in each industry were selected, and for each workplace a minimum of two interviews and a maximum number of interviews equal to 10 percent of the workforce was stipulated. In all 499 garment workers and 327 restaurant workers were interviewed. Among the garment workers interviewed 81 percent were undocumented; among workers in the restaurant industry, 75 percent were undocumented.

The study by Lisa Kubiske mentioned in Chapter 2 is also an example of a survey of a specialized population with a very high proportion of undocumented persons. Between September and November of 1984, Kubiske interviewed 1,225 persons applying at the U.S. Embassy in Mexico City for permanent legal residence in the United States. Applicants in Mexico City comprise about 40 percent of all applicants from Mexico but generally exclude persons originally from the northern states of Mexico because these persons go to consulates closer to the U.S. border. For the 979 applicants who were illegal residents of the United States, Kubiske obtained data on ability to speak English, number of years in the United States and, for those in the labor force, data on occupation, industry, union membership, and earnings. In March 1985, from an additional sample of 348 applicants who had worked in the United States, she obtained data on remittances back to Mexico.[18]

My own study also exemplifies a survey from a specialized population with a known high probability of undocumented respondents. My survey attempted to obtain two probability samples of the parents of babies born in Los Angeles County. In the first, either the mother or the father of the baby was reported on the birth certificate to be of Mexican origin and the mother was born outside the United States. In the second, either the mother or the father or the baby was reported on the birth certificate to be of Mexican origin and the mother was born in the United States. To the extent that parents of babies differ in their characteristics from other undocumented persons, my results will differ from those of a survey of the entire undocumented Mexican population.

Surveys from specialized populations in which the proportion of undocumented persons is highly relevant to policy

I shall cite only one set of surveys of this type. Periodically, the California State Department of Social Services conducts a random survey of its AFDC case load throughout the state. The object of the survey is to determine characteristics of the persons receiving AFDC that are relevant to policy with respect to the receipt of AFDC benefits. Current policy is to provide AFDC assistance to the American-born children of undocumented immigrants but not to provide assistance to undocumented persons in the same family who would otherwise be eligible for assistance. However, to evaluate the consequences of any change in that policy, it is important to know the number of cases in which not all members of the household are being assisted. Accordingly, three of the recent surveys conducted by the California State Department of Social Services have made inquiries into the number of illegal aliens residing in the same household as assisted persons.[19]

Some important results from the existing surveys

In this section we look first at some variables the distribution of which differs markedly by type of population surveyed: sex, marital and family status, and intention to settle in the United States permanently. We then examine some variables that are important but do not appear in the questionnaire of my own study; these are geographic origin in Mexico, use of coyotes, apprehension history, remittances to Mexico, size of place of employment, and labor union membership. I shall defer discussion of studies with respect to variables appearing in my own questionnaire. These will be considered together with my own results in Chapters 6–11.

Variables that differ markedly by population studied

Sex. Let us first consider the sex of undocumented immigrants. In their study of undocumented Mexicans counted by the 1980 Census, Robert Warren and Jeffrey Passel estimated that only 55 percent of all such persons were males; even among persons 15 and over the proportion male was only 56 percent.[20] These proportions differ markedly from those obtained in most but not all of the studies mentioned so far in this chapter. Among apprehended Mexicans, the proportion male has been very high. In the 1977 survey conducted by CENIET, the proportion male was 88 percent;[21] in that of North and Houstoun, 91 percent;[22] in that of Samora, 88 percent.[23] The Mexican-based studies with the requisite data have also shown a very high proportion male. For example, Reichert and Massey's study of shuttle migrants from a rural community in Michoacan showed 81 percent male among current undocumented migrants.[24] On the other hand, the study by Van Arsdol et al. of Los Angeles clients of the One Stop Immigration Service Center showed only 65 percent to be male.[25] Moreover, Baca and Bryan's snowball sample in Los Angeles County was 60 percent male.[26] The only study to report a lower proportion male than that reported by Warren and Passel was Maram's study of workers in the garment industry.[27] Maram reported that only 27 percent of the interviewed Mexican undocumented workers were male. On the other hand, in his study of Mexican undocumented workers in the restaurant industry, he found the proportion male to be 82 percent.[28]

Marital and family status. Existing studies show strong differences with respect to the proportion of male undocumented immigrants in the survey who are married and, among surveyed males who are married, the proportion who bring their wives and children with them to the United States. In their important study of apprehended aliens, North and Houstoun reported that "roughly half" of the Mexicans were married. They further reported that among the married apprehendees from Mexico, only 11 percent had their spouses in the United States, and only 10 percent had children in this country.[29] North and Houstoun's proportions refer to both sexes but can hardly be different for males because 91 percent of all apprehended persons in the study were men. In his study of males from nine rural communities in the state of Jalisco, Cornelius reported that, among the 230 men residing in Mexico at the time of the interview who had been undocumented when they last worked in the United States during 1969–76, 53.5 percent were married at the time of their first trip to the United States, but that fewer than 1 percent had taken their wives and children with them.[30]

Some other studies have markedly contrasting results. In the study of Los Angeles clients of the One Stop Immigration Center, Van Arsdol et al. reported 85 percent of all of the male clients to be currently married. (Not all of these were Mexicans, but in the total male sample, Mexicans formed 94 percent.) Van Arsdol et al. also reported that 64 percent of all One Stop clients had at least one child who was a legal resident of the United States (and presumably born here).[31] In Baca and Bryan's survey in Los Angeles County, 48 percent of the males were married, and of these 45 percent were living with their wives.[32] In his study of garment industry workers in Los Angeles, Maram showed that 40 percent of all of the undocumented Mexican male workers were married; of those who were married, 63 percent had their wives living with them in the United States.[33] In his study of workers in the restaurant industry, Maram showed that 52 percent of all of the male Mexican undocumented workers were married; among those married, 57 percent had their wives living with them in the United States.[34]

Settlement intention.   Related to whether an immigrant man brings wife and children to the United States is the question of whether an undocumented person considers himself or herself to be a permanent settler in the United States or a shuttle migrant. From his survey of nine communities in the state of Jalisco, Cornelius reported that, among 230 men who had been undocumented when they last worked in the United States during 1969–76, only 19 percent wanted to live permanently in the United States, even assuming they could get legal authorization to do so.[35] On the other hand, Maram, in his studies of Mexican undocumented workers in the Los Angeles garment and restaurant industries, showed an apparently different picture. Among garment-industry workers, Maram reported that 69 percent of the undocumented Mexican males and 70 percent of the undocumented Mexican females had never returned to Mexico since coming to the United States.[36] Among restaurant workers, the proportions were similar: 61 percent among males and 73 percent among females.[37]

Summary.   In summary, the various studies of undocumented Mexicans differ markedly with respect to certain variables because they vary in the extent to which they are tapping the permanent immigrants versus the shuttle migrants. Shuttle migrants tend mostly to be males who leave their wives and children in Mexico. Males who intend permanent residence soon have wives and children with them in the United States. Whether married or unmarried, undocumented females tend to be permanent settlers in the United States. Obviously, not all undocumented persons can be clearly categorized as either shuttle migrants or permanent settlers. As has been pointed out by Mines, first-time visitors to the United States must decide whether to become shuttle migrants or permanent settlers; they may take some time to make this decision.[38]

Results for variables not included in my own study

Geographic origin in Mexico.   Let us begin with results describing the state of birth in Mexico or the state of last current residence in Mexico. Many studies, particularly those of apprehended persons, include one or both of these two variables.[39] Manuel García y Griego has provided a summary of results that would apply either to state of birth or state of last residence. According to him, a line drawn from the state of Veracruz to the state of Guerrero divides Mexico into two regions (northwest and southeast) whose participation in migration to the United States is very different. Historically, half of Mexico's population has lived in the northwestern states (Baja California, Sonora, Chihuahua, Coahuila, Nuevo León, Tamaulipas, Baja California del Sur, Sinaloa, Durango, Zacatecas, San Luis Potosí, Nayarit, Jalisco, Guanajuato, Querétaro, Colima, and Michoacán) and half in the southeastern states (Veracruz, Hidalgo, Puebla, Tlaxcala, Morelos, Distrito Federal, México, Guerrero, Oaxaca, Chiapas, Tabasco, Campeche, Yucatán, and Quintana Roo). Nevertheless, the southeastern states have contributed only about 5 to 10 percent of the immigrants to the United States while the northwestern states have contributed all the rest.[40]

Undocumented Mexicans living in Texas tend to have somewhat different origins from those living in California.[41] This difference would be expected because certain of the northwestern Mexican states are nearer to California and others are nearer to Texas. Thus, in the Van Arsdol et al. study of 2,634 One Stop clients in Los Angeles born in Mexico, the five states of birth in order of the largest number of respondents were Jalisco, Michoacán, Chihuahua, Zacatecas, and Durango.[42] In contrast are the results of Bustamante's study of 401 Mexicans interviewed in Matamoras after expulsion from the United States near Brownsville, Texas, in the lower Rio Grande Valley.[43] He found the following order of place of birth by number of respondents: Guanajuato, San Luis Potosí, Jalisco, Michoacán, and Zacatecas.

Moreover, geographic origins may differ even within the state of Texas. Cárdenas provided results for 100 undocumented Mexicans living in San Antonio. Cárdenas reported the following order of states with respect to place of original residence in Mexico: Coahuila, Guanajuato, Nuevo León, Zacatecas, and Tamaulipas tied with Jalisco.[44] The difference between his results and Bustamante's with respect to this variable may reflect in part the fact that San Antonio is northwest of Matamoras (and its American twin city of Brownsville, Texas) and is considerably closer to the state of Coahuila.

Bustamante's study (and two additional studies of apprehended Mexicans) shows some tendency for the Mexican border states to have higher numbers of respondents with respect to state of last residence than with respect to state of birth; the reverse was true of the states not on the U.S. border.[45] However, in his Matamoras survey the ranking of the top five states with respect to state of last residence was identical to that of the ranking by state of birth except for a reversal in rank for Michoacan and Zacatecas.

Existing studies also concur that the majority of undocumented Mexicans come from rural areas in Mexico and that around one-half have a background in farm occupations. In Bustamante's study of 401 Mexicans interviewed in Matamoras,

61 percent came from localities with fewer than 2,500 persons.[46] In North and Houstoun's study of apprehended persons who had worked at least two weeks in the United States, among 407 respondents from Mexico, 49.3 percent had last worked in farm occupations in Mexico.[47]

Use of coyotes. Wayne Cornelius provides data on the guides known as coyotes from his study of shuttle migrants in nine rural communities in the state of Jalisco. Among the 230 undocumented male immigrants whose last trip to the United States was in the period from 1969 to 1976, 41 percent had used a coyote during their last trip to the United States; only 30 percent of these men had used a coyote for their first trip. The average amount paid the coyote for the first trip was $126 and for the last trip $200. Among the 87 undocumented men whose last trip to the United States was before 1969, only 24 percent had used a coyote during their first trip and 14 percent during their last.[48]

The data reported by Cornelius for the pre-1969 entrants are consistent with those of Zazueta and Zazueta. From data gathered in the 1977 CENIET survey of expelees from the United States, they found that male respondents report the use of a coyote more frequently during their first trips than their later ones.[49] The data for Cornelius's respondents who last entered the United States in 1969–76 are not consistent with this; instead they imply that over time it has become harder to cross the U.S. border without assistance. However, Cornelius's data on the amount paid to the coyote are consistent with the range of $150 to $250 reported by Zazueta and Zazueta.[50] Cornelius's data are also consistent with those of Villalpando, who interviewed 217 detainees at the Chula Vista detention center in San Diego County, California. He found that 34 percent had paid a coyote with an average payment of $172.[51]

Very much in contrast to the aforementioned results are those reported by Cárdenas from his snowball sample of 100 undocumented persons in San Antonio. His figures are that only 6 percent of those in his sample had used a coyote to get to San Antonio. According to Cárdenas most of the respondents in his sample declared they could not afford to pay anyone. Among those who did pay for a coyote the average payment was only $25 to $50.[52]

Perhaps the use of coyotes is more common among persons planning a destination in a high-wage area such as California as compared to a destination in a low-wage area such as South Texas. This would imply that it is easier to get across the border in Texas than in California.

Apprehension history. Data on apprehension are quite scarce. The study conducted by Van Arsdol et al. among clients of the One Stop Immigration Service Center in Los Angeles reported that only 36 percent of the 1,714 Mexican male clients and 14 percent of the 920 Mexican female clients had ever been apprehended by the INS.[53]

In sharp contrast to those mentioned results are the results from Cornelius's survey of shuttle migrants from Jalisco. Among 230 undocumented men whose last trip to the United States was from 1969 to 1976, 69 percent had been detained by the INS at least once.[54]

One reason for the difference in results between these two studies may be that the shuttle migrants interviewed by Cornelius crossed the border many more times than the permanent settlers interviewed in the One Stop study.

Remittances.   Several studies have data on monetary remittances to family in Mexico. They provide different results depending on the degree to which shuttle migrants versus permanent settlers are tapped.

In Cornelius's survey of undocumented shuttle migrants in Jalisco, 79 percent of the 230 men who had last been in the United States during 1969–76 reported sending remittances during their last trip.[55] Among male undocumented shuttle migrants whose last trip to the United States was in 1976, the median monthly remittance was $150 per month, which constituted 31 percent of the median monthly earnings while in the United States. In addition, the median amount brought home at the end of the trip was $255.[56]

In North and Houstoun's 1975 survey of apprehended aliens who had worked at least two weeks in the United States, 77 percent of the 481 Mexican apprehendees had made remittance payments. Among persons making payments the average amount paid monthly was $169, which constituted 37 percent of the average monthly wage.[57]

In Villalpando's sample of Mexican apprehendees detained at the Chula Vista detention center in Southern California in 1976, among the 160 men who had been employed prior to apprehension, 71 percent had sent remittances. Among those sending remittances the average amount was $138 monthly, representing 37 percent of the average monthly wage.[58]

In Kubiske's March 1985 sample of 348 currently undocumented visa applicants who had worked in the United States, applicants were asked concerning remittances back to Mexico. In this sample, nearly 70 percent sent home money to Mexico. The average amount remitted annually was $1,100, or about 6 percent of the income earned by the applicant and his family.[59]

At the other end of the pole are the results reported by Maram. Among 346 undocumented Mexicans working in the garment industry in Los Angeles County in 1979, 37 percent never sent remittances to Mexico and only 38 percent sent remittances home monthly. Among those sending remittances at least once every three months, the median monthly remittance was $60 and the mean $91.[60] Similarly among 225 undocumented Mexicans working in the restaurant industry in Los Angeles County in 1979, 40 percent never sent remittances to Mexico and only 46 percent sent remittances at least once a month. Among those sending remittances at least once every three months the median remittance was $100 and the mean $132.[61]

Size of place of employment. Given the recent enactment of employer-sanction legislation, the size of place of employment is relevant to the effectiveness of enforcement. Presumably, enforcement of such sanctions will be easier the larger the average size of place of employment. Indeed, the existing studies are quite consistent in showing that the size of place of employment for undocumented Mexicans is quite small.

The survey conducted in Mexico by CENIET in 1978–79 of returned workers from the United States (not all of whom were undocumented) showed that about 50 percent had worked in enterprises with fewer than 20 employees.[62] Cornelius's survey of undocumented shuttle migrants in Jalisco showed that among those who last worked in the United States in 1969–76, 59 percent had worked in an enterprise with fewer than 25 employees.[63]

Cornelius's snowball survey of Mexicans in ten U.S. cities (all respondents originally from the state of Jalisco) showed that for undocumented workers the average workplace had twenty employees.[64] Maram's survey of undocumented Mexican garment workers in Los Angeles County showed that 53 percent of the respondents worked in an establishment with less than twenty employees.[65] His survey of undocumented restaurant workers showed 57 percent working in a place of that size.[66]

Labor union membership. Surveys conducted to date show a relatively small proportion of undocumented Mexicans reported membership in a labor union. North and Houstoun's study showed 11 percent of the 481 undocumented Mexicans surveyed to have union membership. They also reported that, for the total sample, union membership varied substantially by city of employment; it was highest in New York, followed in order by Chicago and Los Angeles, and lowest in San Antonio, where there were no union members.[67]

Cárdenas reported for his San Antonio sample that undocumented Mexicans "rarely belong to labor unions."[68] In his survey of Mexicans from Jalisco living in California and Illinois, Cornelius found that only 3 percent of the undocumented workers were members of labor unions, whereas 56 percent of the legal-immigrant workers in his sample were members.[69] Kubiske reported that among the undocumented visa applicants in her survey who had worked in the United States, 11 percent were labor union members.[70] Maram found that less than 1 percent of the undocumented Mexican garment workers in his Los Angeles County survey belonged to a labor union.[71] Among undocumented Mexicans working in the restaurant industry in Los Angeles County, only 4 percent belonged to a union.[72]

How does the labor-union membership of undocumented Mexicans compare to that of the entire U.S. work force? According to data published in the *Statistical Abstract of the United States,* in 1982, 21.9 percent of nonagricultural workers in the United States belonged to a labor union. Thus labor-union membership among undocumented Mexicans would appear to be much lower than the national average.[73]

Level of psychological stress.   In two interesting articles, Ramón Salcido examined the level of psychological stress among undocumented Mexican immigrants. In his first study, Salcido compared the level of stress among 25 undocumented mothers with that among 25 mothers who were legal immigrants. All 50 mothers were selected from a file of cases at an agency in Los Angeles that assisted aliens with free legal counseling. All 50 mothers had been in the United States at least two years and had intact families, including a husband with the same legal status. The index of stress employed in this study was the Health Opinion Survey developed by Alexander Leighton. This index was based on the answers to 20 separate questions. Salcido showed that the level of stress was higher (with statistical significance at the .05 level) among the 25 undocumented mothers than among the twenty-five mothers who were legal immigrants.[74]

In a second article, Salcido examined the level of stress among 34 undocumented Mexican mothers who were either clients of a community service center in Los Angeles serving immigrants or who were acquaintances of such clients. Again, all of the mothers had been in the United States at least two years and had intact families, including a husband with the same legal status. The Health Opinion Survey was again used to measure stress. Salcido found that the level of stress was substantially higher for those undocumented mothers who had been in the United States for more than five years as compared to those who had been in the United States for from two to five years.[75] Salcido did not provide a test of statistical significance. However, according to my own computation, the difference was not statistically significant.

Moreover, the data gathered by Salcido do not answer the further question of whether the undocumented mothers from the first study had higher stress only because they had been in the United States for a longer period than the mothers who were legal immigrants. In my opinion, Salcido's pioneering work deserves to be replicated on much larger samples allowing more detailed analysis.

Summary.   The vast majority of undocumented immigrants come from the northwestern part of Mexico. Their use of coyotes is variable and may be related to whether they intend to cross the border into California or into Texas. There is considerable variation in whether undocumented immigrants have ever been apprehended, apparently related to whether they are shuttle migrants or permanent settlers. The volume of their remittances to Mexico is also apparently related to whether they are shuttle migrants or permanent settlers. The size of their place of employment tends to be small and few of them join labor unions. They appear to suffer a higher level of psychological stress than do legal immigrants.

5. How the Los Angeles County Parents data were obtained

The proposed research design and its genesis

The Los Angeles County Parents Survey was conducted in response to a Request for Applications issued on May 11, 1979 by the National Institute of Child Health and Human Development for research on Implications of International Migration for the United States. My grant application requested costs for a project to begin July 1, 1980. It stipulated the following research design. I would use the file of Los Angeles County birth certificates as the universe. From this file I would draw two systematic samples each with random starts. The first sample would be from the frame of babies for whom either the mother or the father was reported to be of Mexican ethnicity and for whom the mother was reported to be born outside the United States. The second sample would be the frame of babies for whom either the mother or the father was reported to be of Mexican ethnicity and for whom the mother was reported to be born in the United States. I would attempt to obtain 700 interviews from the first frame and 300 interviews from the second. The sampling fractions for each of the frames could be adjusted over time to ensure the desired number of interviews from each.

In my grant application I stressed the cost effectiveness of this design compared to that of an alternative design that would call for area-probability sampling of all households in Los Angeles County. As I pointed out, the cost of such an alternative design would be greatly inflated by the necessity to screen each contacted household for the presence of persons of Mexican origin. In my proposed design no such screening would be necessary.

I proposed that interviews would take place approximately two months following the birth of the child. Information would be collected from a respondent who could be either the mother or the father of the child (the latter possibility only if the father was married and living with the mother). The respondent would provide information concerning self and spouse (if any). If the respondent was of Mexican origin, she (or he) would provide information about a brother 18 to 44 who was not married, wife present, but was living in Los Angeles County (if any such brother existed) and about a childless sister 18 to 39 years old living in Los Angeles County (if

88

any). If the respondent had more than one eligible brother or more than one eligible sister, either the oldest or the youngest would be selected for the desired information on a random basis. One-half of the questionnaires that were to be printed were to stipulate that the oldest brother and sister were to be the subject of response and the other one-half were to stipulate the youngest brother and sister.

For each person who was to be the subject of inquiry a question on legal status was to be asked that would separate out those who were U.S. citizens by birth, naturalized U.S. citizens, legal resident aliens, and undocumented persons. In addition, respondents claiming to be legal alien residents were to be asked to show the interviewer their alien registration cards. Moreover, it was proposed that at the end of the interview all respondents be questioned again concerning their own legal status by means of the randomized-response technique. (In the randomized-response technique, respondents are asked to play a game in which they turn away from the interviewer and draw either a white marble or a black marble from a bag. The respondent is then showed a card in which two questions appear. The first question is irrelevant but it is known how many persons will answer positively. A typical first question is "Were you born in April?" The second question is the relevant one. If the respondent picked the white marble out of the bag, he or she is told to answer the first question; if the respondent picked the black marble, he or she is told to answer the second question. Because the proportion of persons who will answer the first question positively is known and because one-half of the marbles in the bag are white and one-half are black, one can ascertain the proportion of all respondents who answered the relevant question positively. However, the interviewer will not know which question the respondent has answered. Research indicates that use of the randomized-response technique results in higher proportions of persons reporting deviant behavior than does a simple question on that behavior.[1]) I proposed that at the very end of the interview all respondents be asked three questions by means of the randomized-response technique that they had already answered at the beginning of the interview. The first concerned whether they were born in the United States, the second whether they were a citizen of the United States, and the third whether they were either a citizen or had currently valid legal documents permitting their residence in the United States.

Most of the questions proposed for the questionnaire, other than those concerning legal status, were identical to those that had appeared in the 1980 Census of Population. However, several items on the proposed questionnaire were not items from the 1980 Census. Many of these items concerned the use of health and welfare services.

It was proposed that questionnaires be prepared both in Spanish and in English and in separate versions for male and female respondents. It was proposed that respondents sign a consent form and that they be paid $10 if the interview were completed. It was further proposed that the interviewing be conducted by the Chicano Pinto Research Project following a pretest of each version of the questionnaire by that organization. All interviewers on the staff of the Chicano Pinto Research Project spoke both Spanish and English with full fluency.

The Chicano Pinto Research Project had been originally established to interview former convicted drug addicts of Mexican descent in the Los Angeles area. These interviews were the substance of the book, *Homeboys: Gangs, Drugs and Prison in the Barrios of Los Angeles,* written by Joan W. Moore (with contributing authors), which won the 1979 Spivack Award.[2] Following the completion of this work, Robert S. García, the president of the CPRP, had decided that he wanted to convert the organization into a generalized social survey organization specializing in the interviewing of Mexican Americans. It was proposed that Moore, *Homeboys* principal author and a professor at the University of Wisconsin, Milwaukee, be a paid consultant to advise on the content of the questionnaire and on interviewing procedures.

The proposal recognized that access to the California birth certificates would not be possible without the approval of the state of California Vital Statistics Advisory Committee. Moreover, the research could not be conducted unless it was approved by the Human Subjects Committee of the University of Southern California. The regulations of the National Institutes of Health allowed for a grant proposal to be submitted without these approvals as long as they were obtained before the meeting of the National Institute of Child Health and Human Development Council. Accordingly, my proposal was submitted without either of these necessary approvals.

Modifications made to meet human subjects' constraints

The California Vital Statistics Advisory Committee has the function of advising the California State Department of Health Services whether researchers will be allowed access to the confidential sections of vital statistics certificates. In the case of the birth certificate, information concerning the address of the mother and information concerning the mother and father's ethnicity were considered confidential. Nine of the eleven members of this committee were appointed by the governor of California, who at the time was Jerry Brown. One member was designated by the chairperson of the California Senate Health and Welfare Committee and another by the chairperson of the California Assembly Health Committee. The members of this Committee were supposed to represent all segments of the community in California as well as health professionals.

I decided it would be best if I first obtained the approval of the University of Southern California Human Subjects Committee. In reviewing the introduction to my questionnaire, the USC Human Subjects Committee came to the conclusion that it was not sufficiently explicit concerning the fact that questions on legal status would be included. Thus it did not allow potential respondents to reach informed consent. The USC committee also concurred that I must promise to destroy any records identifying the name and address of respondents as soon as possible after they had been interviewed. The Committee decided that I ought to revise the introduction and appear in person at their next meeting on December 13. At that meeting the USC Human Subjects Committee did approve the project.

I flew to San Francisco on December 11 to attend the meeting of the California Vital Statistics Advisory Committee. I soon found out that the committee had two serious objections to my proposal. First, although I had now promised to destroy identifying records as soon as possible, I could not guarantee that my records would not be subpoenaed by the INS before I had had time to destroy them, and thus there was a possibility that my research might lead to the deportation of some of my respondents. Second, I had not shown the Committee that my project had the support of the Mexican-American community. Because of these two objections, the Committee voted, 4 to 2, to disapprove my project in its current form. I was urged: (1) to find a way to guarantee that no one could ever find evidence of the name and address of an undocumented resident from my study and (2) to obtain a large number of letters of endorsement for my project from the Mexican-American community. I was told I could then come back to meet with the committee at its next meeting, on March 25 in Los Angeles. I was also informed that should the committee approve my project, I must refrain from interviewing mothers under age 18, or who had experienced a complication of pregnancy or birth, or whose baby was disabled, had died, or been adopted.

To avoid any possibility that my records might be subject to subpoena, I devised the following procedure. The only record of a potential respondent's name and address would be placed on a glued paper tape that would be fastened to the interviewer's work-progress form. Immediately after the interview, the interviewer would peel off this tape and give it to the respondent. Accordingly, the permanent records would not contain the name and address for any respondent whose interview had been completed.

Robert S. García (president of the CPRP) very kindly agreed to solicit letters from leaders of the Mexican-American community in support of the project. In a short time, twenty-two Mexican-American community leaders had written letters to the California State Department of Health Services endorsing the project. Both Mr. García and I attended the March 25, 1980, meeting of the California Vital Statistics Advisory Committee. At this meeting the proposal was unanimously approved provided I would furnish a written statement on how I would screen out from my sampling frame the addresses of recent mothers: (1) who were under 18, (2) for whom there had been a complication of pregnancy or birth, (3) whose child had already died, (4) whose child had been adopted, or (5) whose child had a severe defect. After consultation with Martin Donabedian of the Los Angeles County Health Department, I prepared such a statement; on April 8, 1980, I received permission to have access to the Los Angeles County birth records for the purpose of selecting my study population.

These several modifications in my research design made necessary by the demands of the California Vital Statistics Advisory Committee and the University of Southern California Human Subjects Committee had consequences for my research which, in my opinion, were both positive and negative. In my opinion, the fact that Robert S. García took the time to solicit twenty-two letters of recommendation from Mexican-American community leaders had the very beneficial consequence of increasing community acceptance for the study. Thus, I am sure that the rate of response was better than it would have been otherwise. On the other hand, I see two detrimental consequences. Because I was required to leave with the interviewee all records of name and address, the supervisors of the interviewers could not go back and check, on a random basis, the quality of the interviewers' performance. Such a check is a standard procedure for most interviewing organizations and facilitates the process of separating out good interviewers from bad ones. Second, I was now restrained from interviewing a fairly sizable proportion of all of my original universe. I did not know exactly what proportion this was. However, it seemed obvious to me that there were probably many persons in the originally proposed universe who were either under age 18 or who had suffered complications of pregnancy or birth (such as a cesarean delivery). Chapter 7 will provide evidence that the proportion of all births omitted from the study population for human-subjects consideration was about 20 percent for mothers born outside the United States and about 31 percent for mothers born in the United States.

Details of the data collection

The name-selection process

Dee Falasco, my chief research assistant throughout the course of the project, was in charge of selecting candidates for interview. Names were selected at the office of the Los Angeles County Department of Health Services. The birth certificate files were arranged in chronological order by week of registration and within that chronological order by hospital. Falasco confined her search to files where the birth had taken place at least two months previously. For her first sampling frame she had to find those births where either the mother or the father of the baby was reported to be of Mexican ethnicity and the mother was born in the United States; for her second sampling frame she had to confine herself to births where either mother or father was of Mexican ethnicity and the mother was born outside the United States. For either sampling frame she was obliged to omit those births where the mother's age was under 18, the baby's birthweight was less than 2,000 grams, the baby had died, had a birth injury or congenital malformation, or had been adopted, or where the mother had suffered complications of pregnancy or concurrent illness or complications of labor or delivery (including a cesarean section). All of these facts could be ascertained from the birth certificate except for whether the baby had died. Accordingly, at each of her visits to the County Department of Health Services, Falasco made a list of the first and last birth certificate numbers of all births to be sampled that day. Then, each time using a different random start, she drew two systematic samples, one for each of the two frames. The sampling fractions would differ on each occasion of name selection but were always higher for births where the mother was born outside the United States than for the births where the mother was born in the United States.

Having selected a name, she would determine its eligibility, and, if it was eligible, she would write down the names of the baby and of its mother and father, the address of the mother, whether the mother was born in the United States, and the sampling weight to be assigned the name (the inverse of the sampling fraction). Each selected name would then be checked with the file of infant deaths for the month of birth and the following months. If the baby was found to have died, the name was eliminated from the list of eligible names.

However, before giving over any names to the CPRP, Falasco performed an additional screening operation. She checked the reported address of each mother with the 1980 census tract edition of the Thomas Brothers Street Atlas for Los Angeles County. If the address did not show up within the range of addresses shown for that street in the street atlas, the name was not given to the CPRP. If the address was within the listed range of addresses, the census tract of the mother's residence was also determined.

Finally, the following items were placed on an Interviewer Work Form made out separately for each eligible birth and delivered to the CPRP: the date the name was submitted, the census tract number, the page and quadrant of the Thomas Brothers Street Atlas in which the address was located, the sampling weight, the birthplace of the mother (outside or inside the United States), the ID number, and the names and address of the baby, the mother, and the father (only on the glued paper tape).

The pretest and the resulting modifications of the questionnaire

Work on the pretest began July 28, 1980. The survey's consultant, Joan Moore, was in Los Angeles throughout the pretest and played an active role in assessing the pretest results.

Two major issues emerged from the pretest. The first had to do with the three questions at the end of the interview on the respondent's legal status making use of the randomized-response technique. The interviewers were unanimous in stating that they were uncomfortable in asking these questions; moreover, the permanent staff members of the CPRP concurred that the questions should not be asked in order to preserve the morale of the interviewers. As a result, I reluctantly decided that the questions must be dropped. In their stead, I substituted questions on legal status very similar to those asked at the beginning of the interview.

A second major question arose as to exactly what classes of fathers should be subjects for the interview questions. I had originally proposed that fathers be subjects if they were married and living with the mother of the child. However, I had not defined whether the state of being married was to be confined to legal marriages or to include consensual marriages. From pretest interviews it soon emerged that there were some mothers who were not legally married, were living with the baby's father, but were adamant that they would give no information concerning characteristics of the baby's father. Presumably this reluctance occurred because they were receiving AFDC payments and did not want anyone to know the father's income. I myself observed one interview with a respondent of this type. As a result, we decided to reverse the order of the question concerning the household roster relative to the question on marital status. We now asked the household roster question first and found out if the mother of the baby considered the baby's father to be her husband. If she did, we would then ask her questions about her husband even though she stated she was not married in answer to the question on marital status. On the other hand, if we had listed the baby's father as a partner but not as a husband, we asked no further questions concerning him.

We also created a concept called partnership status that allowed for four classes of response: (1) legally married and living with spouse, (2) not legally married but living with a person considered to be a "spouse," (3) not legally married and living with a partner not considered to be a "spouse," and (4) not living with a partner. We later consulted with Arthur Norton, in charge of Family Statistics at the U.S. Bureau of the Census, and found out that the categories we planned allowed for consistency with U.S. Census Bureau procedure. The Bureau's procedure stipulated that if on the relationship item both a householder and spouse were reported, these two would be considered to be married on the marital status item.

Altogether, 54 interviews were completed during the pretest period, that ended on August 21, 1980. Because the question wording for these 54 interviews differed from that decided on for the regular interviews, these pretest interviews were not used for any later data analyses.

The course of the interviewing

Interviewers were paid an hourly rate of $4.50. It was stipulated that interviewers would make three attempts to contact each respondent. Respondents were each paid $10 at the end of the interview. Unfortunately, the progress of the interviewing was slower than anticipated, largely due to a higher than anticipated personnel turnover among the interviewers.

The original goal had been to obtain approximately 1,000 interviews, of which 300 were to be from mothers born in the United States and the remainder from mothers born outside the United States. However, the CPRP budget was fixed; late in the interviewing it became evident that the original goal could not be reached within the budget. Accordingly, I made a decision to cease interviewing mothers born in the United States and henceforth interview only mothers born outside the United States.

As a result of this decision, of 903 interviews obtained before interviewing ceased on March 30, 1981, 724 concerned mothers who, according to the birth certificate, were born outside the United States, and 179 concerned mothers reported to have been born in the United States. The average sampling weight for interviews with mothers selected from the frame of mothers born outside the United States was 7.276 and of those selected from the frame of those born in the United States 11.229. Although the respondent for the interview could be either the mother or the father of the baby, in 777 of 903 cases the mother was the respondent. Moreover, in 689 of the 903 interviews the language of the interview was Spanish.

Data were collected concerning the mother in all 903 interviews. Data were collected concerning the father in 759 interviews.

The nonresponse rate

Table 5.1 presents a detailed statement concerning the nonresponse rate separately for mothers reported to have been born in the United States or outside the United States. The table shows that the weighted nonresponse rate for respondents gathered from the frame of mothers born outside the United States was 48.5 percent and that for respondents from the frame of mothers born in the United States 52.9 percent. These rather high nonresponse rates are not directly comparable to nonresponse rates for household surveys because they included such categories as nonexistent addresses; the move of a mother to a new, unknown address; names never assigned to the interviewing organization; names never used by the interviewing organization; and names that were found not to be qualified. These categories were in addition to the categories of nonresponse found for household surveys:

Table 5.1. *Percentage distribution of weighted results of interview attempts for sample drawn from births in Los Angeles County to women stating that they or the father of the baby were of Mexican descent (and whose births met qualifying specifications), by whether birth record indicated the mother was born inside or outside the United States*

	Mother's birthplace	
	Outside United States	Inside United States
Total	100.0	100.0
Prospective respondent contacted		
Interview completed	51.5	47.1
Not qualified, neither parent Mexican	1.4	2.9
Refused to be interviewed	8.9	10.9
Prospective respondent not contacted		
Moved to known location	1.6	1.8
Moved, location not given	11.5	11.7
Address not located by interviewer	2.3	3.2
Unknown at address given on birth record	1.6	1.0
No contact before last day of interviewing	2.4	2.6
No contact after third attempt	6.4	7.2
No interview attempt made		
Names given to interviewing agency:		
Never assigned to interviewer	5.0	4.6
Assigned to interviewer, no interview attempt	1.7	0.6
No record of further processing	1.6	4.1
Names never given to interviewing agency because address not found in Thomas Brothers Street Atlas	4.1	2.4
Weighted number of cases	10,236	4,265

refusals, names in which three unsuccessful attempts at contact had been made, and names for which no contact had been achieved by the end of the interviewing.

One may note in particular that the weighted refusal rate for mothers with a birthplace outside the United States was only 8.9 percent and that for mothers with birthplace in the United States only 10.9 percent. On the other hand, there is a high proportion of cases where no interview attempt was made (12.4 percent if the mother was born outside the United States and 11.7 percent if the mother was born in the United States). This high proportion results from a fixed interview budget as well as from more names being drawn than were actually necessary. The category

"Names given to interviewing agency: no record of further processing" deserves special mention. This category was created to count the number of cases where a name was given to the CPRP on an Interviewer Work Form, but this form was not returned to the University of Southern California. It is most likely that all of these names should belong in the category of names given to the interviewing agency and never assigned to interviewer.

It is also possible that some of the many cases in which the respondent was reported to have moved actually consist of polite refusals. On the other hand, geographic mobility following a birth is a common event.

A very important question is the extent to which the observed nonresponse rate biases the proportion of the sample that reported it was undocumented. Does Table 5.1 shed any light on this? I think that it does. What is significant to me is that the nonresponse rates are so similar for the two subgroups subdivided by mother's birthplace. Mothers born in the United States do not have to fear that they will be reported as undocumented. Yet the total nonresponse rate and the refusal rate are very similar for the two subgroups. If the nonresponse rate for the women born outside the United States were much higher than for those born in the United States, then one would have had good reason to suspect that the nonresponse rate for undocumented women was especially high.

Was there any difference in the response rate within geographic segments of Los Angeles County? Using a classification developed elsewhere, the county was subdivided into ten segments. Outcomes were tabulated separately for women reported on the birth certificates to be born inside or outside the United States. There were no large differences in the percentage of names resulting in an interview with the exception of the north county segment. Lancaster, the chief city in this part of the county, is located about 80 miles from the CPRP headquarters. For this region, 66 percent of the weighted number of names were never assigned to an interviewer.

6. The validity of data on legal status

The crux of the Los Angeles County Parents Survey was to distinguish the characteristics of undocumented parents from those who had a legal right to be in the United States. Obviously, therefore, it is essential to know to what extent undocumented persons told the whole truth concerning their legal status. It would appear that not all undocumented persons did tell the whole truth. However, for persons claiming to be permanent legal residents, we did devise a means of separating out those who had a very high probability of telling the whole truth from those with a lower probability.

Categorizing legal status of the immigrants

We distinguished five categories of legal status for mothers and fathers: (1) undocumented, (2) permanent legal resident who showed an alien registration card, (3) permanent legal resident who did not show the interviewer such a card, (4) naturalized U.S. citizen, and (5) native-born citizen. On the questionnaire, the first question was whether the person was born in the United States. If the person answered negatively, the next question was whether the person was a naturalized citizen of the United States. If again the answer was negative, the next question was whether the person had an alien registration card (a green or a brown card) that permits residence in the United States. If the answer was positive, the interviewer asked to see the card.

Regarding the legal status of unmarried brothers and childless sisters, it was not possible to ask to see the alien registration card. Hence for them we distinguished only four categories of legal status. The weights for the data for unmarried brothers and childless sisters need to be explained. Of the 903 respondents, only 194 had an eligible unmarried brother and only 131 had an eligible childless sister. On the other hand, many respondents had more than one eligible unmarried brother or childless sister. Since information was gathered for only one brother, the weight for each unmarried brother was determined by multiplying the weight assigned to the respondent by the number of eligible brothers the respondent had. Unfortunately,

Table 6.1. *Percentage distribution by legal status for mothers, fathers, unmarried brothers, and childless sisters of Mexican origin*

Legal status	Mothers	Fathers	Brothers	Sisters
Total	100.0	100.0	100.0	100.0
Undocumented	48.2	48.1	39.7	32.9
Legal immigrants, total	25.0	28.9	18.2	22.9
Permanent legal resident	23.3	26.2	18.2	20.2
Showed card	11.6	8.0	N.A.	N.A.
Did not show card	11.7	18.2	N.A.	N.A.
Naturalized citizen	1.7	2.7	0.0	2.7
Native-born citizen	26.8	23.0	42.1	44.2
Weighted number of cases	6,840	5,727	2,504	1,531
Unweighted number of cases	857	724	194	131

the questionnaire inquired only whether the respondent had one eligible childless sister or more than one. As a result, if a respondent had more than one eligible sister, it was assumed that she had 2.50 such sisters. (The value 2.50 was taken from the average number of eligible unmarried brothers among respondents with at least two such brothers.) Thus the weighted number of eligible unmarried brothers and childless sisters approximates the total number of such persons among the respondents of the survey. Respondents born in the United States had more eligible brothers and sisters than respondents born outside the United States. Hence the reported distributions by legal status of unmarried brothers or childless sisters will not approximate the actual distributions by legal status of unmarried adult males or childless adult females.

Table 6.1 presents a detailed categorization of the legal status of mothers and fathers of Mexican origin and a more abbreviated categorization for unmarried brothers and childless sisters. The most striking feature of the table is the high proportion of mothers and of fathers who were undocumented, in each case almost one-half of the total. For mothers and fathers, only about one-quarter were native-born citizens of the United States and an additional one-quarter legal immigrants. Of the legal immigrants, very few were naturalized citizens. For brothers and sisters, the proportion who were U.S. citizens by birth was much higher (over 40 percent) than for mothers or fathers. This proportion is expectable given the weighting system used.

Table 6.2. *Weighted number of mothers who were questionnaire respondents by legal status (initial questions) and by respondent's legal status (final questions)*

Legal status (initial questions)	Respondent's legal status (final questions)				
	Undocu-mented	Permanent legal resident	Natural-ized citizen	Native-born citizen	Total
Total	2,937	1,463	111	1,802	6,313
Undocumented	2,885	28	0	0	2,913
Permanent legal resident					
Showed card	12	720	0	0	732
Did not show card	30	701	0	0	731
Naturalized citizen	10	0	111	0	121
Native-born citizen	0	14	0	1,802	1,816

Assessing the validity of the responses

How valid are the answers to the questions concerning legal status? In Chapter 3, I discussed the substantial downward adjustment that Warren and Passel had made to the number of individuals who reported in the 1980 Census that they were naturalized citizens of Mexican origin and the smaller downward adjustment made to the number who reported themselves to have been born in the United States and of Mexican origin. Ought similar downward adjustments be made in my own data to obtain a valid distribution by legal status?

I do think some downward adjustment might be desirable. However, it is not certain how much. Some light on this matter can be obtained if we cross-tabulate the data on legal status, as shown in Table 6.1, with data on another variable that I call respondent's legal status. The variable I here call legal status was obtained in answer to initial questions concerning the legal status of self and questions in the middle of the interview concerning the legal status of spouse. The variable I here call respondent's legal status was taken from the questions on the respondent's own legal status asked at the very end of the questionnaire. Thus the data on respondent's legal status are available for only 777 of the 903 mothers in the study and for 126 of the 759 fathers.

Table 6.2 shows the cross-tabulation of legal status (initial questions) with respondent's legal status (final questions) for mothers. It is evident from Table 6.2 that

Table 6.3. *Percentage distribution by legal status for mothers subdivided by their birthplace as reported on the birth certificate*

| | Place of birth from birth certificate | | |
Legal status	Total	Outside United States	Inside United States
Total	100.0	100.0	100.0
Undocumented	46.6	63.9	1.3
Permanent legal resident			
Showed card	11.4	15.8	0.0
Did not show card	11.7	15.8	1.1
Naturalized citizen	2.0	2.2	1.1
Native-born citizen	28.3	2.4	96.3
Weighted number of cases	7,278	5,268	2,010

the variable of respondent's legal status shows a slightly higher proportion to be undocumented than does the question on legal status. With respect to the variable of legal status, 46.1 percent are reported as undocumented; with respect to the variable of respondent's legal status, 46.5 percent report as undocumented. However, some women who reported themselves as undocumented with respect to the variable of legal status report themselves as legal residents on the variable of respondent's legal status.

Additional data relevant to the validity of the data on legal status can be obtained by separate tabulations on this variable for women reported to have been born in or outside the United States according to the birth certificate. These data are reported in Table 6.3. In general this cross-tabulation shows that the two sources of data with respect to whether the respondent was born in the United States are highly reliable. Among mothers reported on the birth certificate to have been born in the United States, 96.3 percent stated in the survey that they were born in the United States. Among mothers reported on the birth certificate to have been born outside the United States, 97.6 percent said they were born outside the United States. Thus, there is a very slight tendency to overreport birth in the United States in the survey as compared to the birth certificate. The survey finds that 28.3 percent are born in the United States, whereas according to the birth certificates only 27.6 percent are born in the United States.

The validity of the reported data on the number of naturalized citizens can also be examined. In Chapter 3, I pointed out that the 1980 Census was subject to con-

Table 6.4. *Percentages of naturalized citizens among persons born outside the United States by sex and family status from the Los Angeles County Parents Survey and percentages of naturalized citizens in comparable populations from the 1980 Census and from the 1980 Census as adjusted by Passel for the misreporting of naturalized citizens*

	Percentage naturalized citizens
Los Angeles County Parents Survey	
Mothers	2.3
Fathers	3.5
Unmarried brothers	0.0
Childless sisters	4.8
1980 Census (Los Angeles County, persons of Mexican origin born outside the United States)	
Females, parity 1[+], ages 18–39	14.8
Males, married and not separated, ages 18–44	15.0
Males, other marital status, ages 18–44	12.4
Females, parity 0, ages 18–39	14.2
1980 Census as adjusted by Passel for misreporting of naturalized citizens (Los Angeles County, persons born in Mexico with proportionate adjustment for unknown country of birth)	
Males, ages 18–44	3.5
Females, ages 18–39	3.3

Sources: For 1980 Census data, David M. Heer and Jeffrey S. Passel, "Comparison of Two Methods for Estimating the Number of Undocumented Mexican Adults in Los Angeles County, *International Migration Review 21*, no. 4 (Winter 1987).

siderable overreporting in the category of naturalized citizen.[1] Accordingly, when Warren and Passel made their estimates of the number of undocumented persons in the United States, they first had to add to the total alien population a large proportion of all of those persons who had reported themselves as naturalized citizens.

Table 6.4 shows the percentages of naturalized citizens among persons born outside the United States from the Los Angeles County Parents Survey together with the percentages who were naturalized citizens in comparable populations both in the unadjusted data from the 1980 Census and in the 1980 Census data as adjusted by Passel for the misreporting of the number of naturalized citizens. Table 6.4 reveals that the percentages of naturalized citizens from the Los Angeles County

Table 6.5. *Percentage distribution by whether a card was shown for mothers and fathers of Mexican origin reported to be legal residents of the United States subdivided by whether or not they were respondents and for mothers of Mexican origin reported to be legal residents subdivided by number of children under age 3*

Subgroups	Total	Showed card	Did not show card	Weighted number of cases
Mothers, total	100.0	49.9	50.1	1,594
Respondent	100.0	50.6	49.4	1,380
Not respondent	100.0	45.8	54.2	214
Fathers, total	100.0	30.5	69.5	1,503
Respondent	100.0	45.2	54.8	208
Not respondent	100.0	28.1	71.9	1,295
Mothers				
Only one child less than 3 years old	100.0	52.8	47.2	1,174
Two or more children less than 3 years old	100.0	41.9	58.1	420

Parents Survey were very close to the 1980 Census percentages *after* adjustment for the misreporting of the number of naturalized citizens and were very much lower than the actually reported percentages from the 1980 Census.

Finally, we can examine differences in the characteristics of those persons reported as legal residents of the United States and who showed the interviewer a card as compared to those who stated they were legal residents but did not show the interviewer a card. One may surmise that if no card was shown, the person is more likely not to have been in fact a legal resident. However, before one concludes that perhaps all the persons who did not show a card were not telling the truth, one must recognize that there are many reasons why a card might not be shown. In particular, it should be remembered that the respondent reported legal status both for self and for spouse.

As shown in Table 6.5, whether the person was his own respondent does make a difference, particularly for fathers. Among fathers who were their own respondents, 45 percent showed a card; among fathers who were not respondents, only 28 percent showed a card. It is true that whether a mother was a respondent made little difference. However, this finding can be explained by the fact that when the father was the respondent, usually the mother was also present. Moreover, all of

Table 6.6. *Differences in characteristics between legal residents who showed a card and those who did not for mothers and fathers of Mexican origin*

	Percentage with characteristic	
Characteristics	Showed card	Did not show card
Mothers		
Aged 25 years old or over	79.7	63.7
With 7 or more years of completed schooling	53.9	40.6
In United States 11 years or longer	49.3	33.6
Speak no English	24.1	32.6
Weighted number of respondents	796	798
Fathers		
Aged 25 years old or over	93.4	83.7
With 7 or more years of completed schooling	56.7	56.0
In United States 11 years or longer	60.5	49.1
Speak no English	7.0	9.2
Weighted number of respondents	458	1,045

the female respondents had just had a baby; it may have been inconvenient for them to have gotten up to bring back the evidence of their legal status. For example, I remember observing one interview where the mother was holding her sleeping baby throughout the interview and told the interviewer she could not get up to fetch her green card because it would disturb the baby. Additional complications in showing a card occurred for women with small children other than the baby. Data on this point are also shown in Table 6.5. Among legal-resident women who had only one child less than three years old, 53 percent showed a card, whereas among those with two or more such children only 42 percent showed a card.

Table 6.6 summarizes some additional differences between mothers and fathers for whom a card was shown and for whom a card was not shown. As can be seen, for both mothers and fathers those who did not show a card were younger, had fewer years of schooling, had been in the United States a shorter period, and were less likely to speak any English. Data to be presented in the next chapter will demonstrate that, with respect to all of these characteristics, mothers and fathers who did not show a card were intermediate in characteristics between the legal residents who showed a card and those who were reported as undocumented. This tendency gives ground for the suspicion that some of those who did not show a card were in fact undocumented.

Were persons who said they were legal residents but had no card conscious liars, or were they simply stretching the truth? I think there is evidence that many were simply stretching the truth. For example, I observed one interview where the father said he was a legal resident, did not show a card, but did show a Silva letter. As I mentioned in Chapter 2, the U.S. government sent out 250,000 Silva letters and eventually granted legal status to 145,000 of those receiving letters. The Silva letter gave hope of legalization but did not guarantee it. Moreover, it is highly likely that many of the other reported legal residents who did not show a card had applied for visas under one of the preference categories but were still on the waiting list. These waiting lists can be very long. For example, in February 1979, persons admitted from Mexico under the second preference (spouses and unmarried sons and daughters of permanent legal aliens) had waited more than nine years to receive their visa, and persons admitted under either the fourth (married sons and daughters of U.S. citizens) or fifth (brothers and sisters of U.S. citizens 21 years of age and over) preference had waited between one and two years.[2]

In summary, I believe there is evidence that the great majority of those persons who were reported as legal residents but for whom no card was shown either had such a card or, if not, had applied for a visa and had good reason to believe that they would eventually receive it. As a result, except in special instances, I do not separate out among those reported to be legal residents those who showed a card from those who did not. Moreover, because so few persons were reported to be naturalized citizens, I decided not to separate out this group. Accordingly, in most of the tabulations to be presented in the later chapters of this book, type of legal status is subdivided into only three categories: (1) undocumented, (2) legal immigrant (legal resident or naturalized citizen), and (3) native-born citizen.

7. A comparison of the social characteristics of undocumented immigrants, legal immigrants, and U.S. natives of Mexican origin

This chapter explores the extent to which the undocumented, who form a legal underclass, also possess social characteristics commonly associated with a lower societal status. Data from the Los Angeles County Parents Survey are compared with data from other studies if such a comparison is warranted, for each of seven social characteristics: (1) age, (2) marital and family status, (3) immigration history, (4) educational attainment and ability to speak English, (5) geographic location, (6) fertility, and (7) children's school enrollment.

Methodological notes

All of the interviews were conducted in Los Angeles County, the place of residence of 44 percent of all undocumented Mexicans enumerated in the 1980 Census. It is obvious that the characteristics of the undocumented in Los Angeles County are not necessarily the same as for the United States as a whole. Most important, there were relatively few opportunities for agricultural work in this county, which was the nation's largest in population size and one of the most urbanized. Second, the proportion of undocumented Mexicans counted in the 1980 Census who were female was somewhat higher in Los Angeles County (46.7 percent) than for the nation (45.1 percent).[1]

In the sections of this chapter dealing with births, household size and composition, and geographic location, I shall present data concerning all mothers and fathers in the study. In the remaining sections, I shall present data concerning only persons of Mexican origin. In these sections of the chapter, a small proportion of all persons in the study will be excluded from the analysis because the base for inclusion in the study was that either the mother or the father of the baby had to be of Mexican origin. Further details are provided in Table 7.1, which presents the percentage distribution by Mexican origin for mothers and fathers of the study sample subdivided by legal status.

For many, but not all characteristics I will also include data concerning the unmarried brothers and childless sisters of respondents of Mexican origin. It will be remembered that the unmarried brothers were defined as those brothers 18 to

106

Table 7.1. *Percentage distribution by whether of Mexican origin for mothers and fathers subdivided by legal status*

	Mother's legal status			Father's legal status		
	Undocumented	Legal immigrant	Native-born citizen	Undocumented	Legal immigrant	Native-born citizen
Total	100.0	100.0	100.0	100.0	100.0	100.0
Mexican origin	97.3	93.8	88.8	98.1	95.1	88.0
Not of Mexican origin	2.7	6.2	11.2	1.9	4.9	12.0
Weighted number of cases	3,391	1,825	2,062	2,806	1,740	1,500

Table 7.2. *Average weights assigned to mothers, fathers, unmarried brothers, and childless sisters by Mexican origin and by legal status*

	Mother's legal status			Father's legal status		
	Undocumented	Legal immigrant	Native-born citizen	Undocumented	Legal immigrant	Native-born citizen
All persons	7.29	7.30	10.97	7.44	7.57	9.87
Persons of Mexican origin	7.30	7.22	10.90	7.42	7.59	9.78

	Brother's legal status			Sister's legal status		
	Undocumented	Legal immigrant	Native-born citizen	Undocumented	Legal immigrant	Native-born citizen
	10.93	12.67	15.72	9.33	10.94	15.05

Table 7.3. *Estimated number and percentage distribution of all births in Los Angeles County to the study population during the name-selection periods by legal status of the mother*

	Births to study pop- ulation during the name- selection periods	Legal status of mother		
		Undocu- mented	Legal immi- grant	Native- born citizen
Numbers of births	13,986	6,419	3,458	4,109
Percentage distribution of births in study population	100.0	45.9	24.7	29.4

44 living in Los Angeles County who were not married with wife present, and that the childless sisters were defined as those sisters 18 to 39 years of age living in Los Angeles County who had never born a child.

With one exception, all tables in this chapter describing characteristics of the surveyed persons are based on weighted data, and the weighted number of cases is set forth. For the reader to calculate the actual number of unweighted cases upon which the findings of the table are based, Table 7.2 provides the average weights for all mothers and fathers subdivided by legal status, for mothers and fathers of Mexican origin subdivided by legal status, and for unmarried brothers and childless sisters (all of whom are of Mexican origin) by legal status. I might add that the results for weighted and unweighted data are quite similar as long as one looks at a percentage distribution composed only of persons born outside the United States or only of persons born in the United States. However, when a percentage distribution includes both persons born in and outside of the United States, the unweighted results can differ more substantially from the weighted results.

Births

Perhaps the most important finding of the Los Angeles County Parents study relates to the proportion of all births in the county that took place to undocumented women with either the mother or the father of Mexican origin. To make a long story short, I estimate that at least 18.6 percent of all births in Los Angeles County in 1980–81 took place to parents with at least one parent of Mexican origin and with the mother undocumented. Let me now present the data for that conclusion.

Table 7.3 presents data on the estimated distribution of births by the legal status of the mothers falling within the frame of the study during the periods in which names were selected for the study. (The estimated numbers of births in the study

Table 7.4. *Number and percentage distribution of births in Los Angeles County,*
August 1, 1980, through March 31, 1981, by birthplace of mother by whether at
least one parent of Mexican origin

	Total	Mother's birthplace		
		Outside United States	Inside United States	Un-known
Total births				
Number	93,356	40,685	52,613	58
Percent	100.0	43.6	56.4	0.1
One or both parents of Mexican origin				
Number	39,111	26,515	12,587	9
Percent	100.0	67.8	32.2	0.0
Neither parent of Mexican origin				
Number	54,245	14,170	40,026	49
Percent	100.0	26.1	73.8	0.1

population by legal status of the mother were obtained after inflating the weighted number of respondents for whom the birth certificate reported birth of the child's mother to be in the United States by the reciprocal of the response rate for such mothers, and by inflating the weighted number of respondents for whom the birth certificate reported birth of the child's mother to be outside the United States by the reciprocal of the response rate for those respondents.)

Among the 13,986 estimated number of births to the study population during the intervals in which names were drawn, 45.9 percent are estimated to have occurred to mothers who were undocumented, 24.7 percent to women who were legal immigrants, and 29.4 percent to women who were born in the United States. However, the frame of the study excluded many births for human-subjects considerations, specifically, all births where the mother was under 18, or where the baby was disabled, had died or been adopted, or was of low birth weight or where the mother had suffered complications of pregnancy, labor, or delivery.

To calculate how many births took place to undocumented Mexican women who were excluded from the study because of human-subjects considerations, I made tabulations from the tapes concerning the annual number of California births in 1980 and 1981 (which were made available to me by the State of California Department of Health Services). Tabulations were made of all births that took place to residents of Los Angeles County in the period from August 1, 1980, through March 31, 1981. This period corresponded to the period during which names had been drawn for the study.

Table 7.5. *Number and percentage distribution by whether met human subjects specifications of all births in Los Angeles County, August 1, 1980, through March 31, 1981, with at least one parent of Mexican origin*

	Total	Met human-subjects specifications	
		Yes	No
Total births with at least one parent of Mexican origin			
Number	39,111	29,795	9,316
Percent	100.0	76.2	23.8
Mother born outside United States			
Number	26,515	21,134	5,381
Percent	100.0	79.7	20.3
Mother born inside United States			
Number	12,587	8,656	3,931
Percent	100.0	68.8	31.2
Mother's birthplace unknown			
Number	9	5	4
Percent	100.0	55.6	44.4

Table 7.4 presents the data from the birth tapes concerning the total number of births to women residents in Los Angeles County during this period subdivided by whether one or both parents were of Mexican origin and by whether the mother was born in the United States.

Table 7.5 presents further data on the 39,111 births occurring in Los Angeles County from August 1, 1980, through March 31, 1981, in which either the mother or the father of the baby was of Mexican origin. The table provides a cross-classification of these births by whether they met the human-subjects specifications demanded for the study population and by whether the mother was born in the United States.

The table shows that only 76 percent of these 39,111 births met the human-subjects specifications. Moreover, the proportion meeting the human-subjects specifications was substantially higher among women born outside the United States (80 percent) than among women born in the United States (69 percent). (The two major reasons for this discrepancy were the much greater prevalence of cesarean deliveries and of women under age 18 among women born in the United States.)

Table 7.6 addresses the question of whether there was bias in the extent to which

Table 7.6. *Comparison of data from birth tape and study population concerning place of birth of mother for all births where either parent was of Mexican origin and which met the human subjects specifications*

	Total	Birthplace		
		Inside United States	Outside United States	Unknown
Los Angeles County Births, August 1, 1980, through March 31, 1981				
Number	29,795	21,134	8,656	5
Percent	100.0	70.9	29.1	0.0
Births to study population				
Number	13,986	9,877	4,109	—
Percent	100.0	70.6	29.4	—

the weighted number of births in the study sample differed by place of residence from the distribution by place of residence of all eligible births that took place from August 1, 1980, through March 31, 1981. The answer is negative. Just 71 percent of the births in the study population were to women born outside the United States, while, according to the data from the birth tapes, 71 percent of all eligible births from August 1, 1980, through March 31, 1981, were to women born outside the United States.

I shall now present the rationale for my estimate that at least 18.6 percent of all births in Los Angeles County in the period from August 1, 1980, through March 31, 1981, occurred to undocumented mothers in which either the mother or the father of the baby was of Mexican origin. The crucial assumption is that one can merge: (1) the data from my study concerning the proportion of all births to women born outside the United States taking place to undocumented mothers with (2) data from the birth tapes concerning the distribution of all births by origin of mother and father and by mother's birthplace. From Table 7.3 we see that, in the study population, 64.99 percent of all births to women born outside the United States reportedly took place to undocumented women (6,419 of 9,877). As was discussed in Chapter 6, this percentage is probably an underestimate. From Table 7.4 we see that from August 1, 1980, through March 31, 1981, there were 26,515 births in which one or both parents were of Mexican origin and the mother was born outside the United States. Accordingly, it can be estimated that there were at least 17,344 births in which either the mother or the father was of Mexican origin and the mother was undocumented. This number represents 18.58 percent of all births in Los

Table 7.7. *Estimated number and percentage distribution of births in Los Angeles County, August 1, 1980, through March 31, 1981, by whether at least one parent is of Mexican origin and, if so, by birthplace and legal status of mother*

	Number	Percent
All births	93,356	100.0
Neither parent of Mexican origin	54,245	58.1
One or both parents of Mexican origin, total	39,111	41.9
Mother born outside United States	26,515	28.4
Legal immigrant	9,171	9.8
Undocumented	17,344	18.6
Mother born inside United States	12,587	13.5
Mother's birthplace unknown	9	0.0

Angeles County during the period. Table 7.7 presents the complete breakdown of births in Los Angeles County during the specified period by Mexican origin, mother's birthplace, and mother's legal status.

Age

Table 7.8 presents data on the age distribution of mothers, fathers, unmarried brothers, and childless sisters of Mexican origin by legal status. An important finding is the much younger age of the undocumented mothers and fathers as compared to the mothers and fathers who were legal immigrants. On the other hand, parents of Mexican origin born in the United States tended to be even younger than those who were undocumented immigrants.

Among unmarried brothers and childless sisters, it is also evident that those who were undocumented were younger than those who were legal immigrants. On the other hand, unlike the case with fathers, undocumented unmarried brothers tended to be even younger than native-born unmarried brothers.

The younger age of the undocumented as compared to the legal immigrants is congruent with Passel's data for Los Angeles County.[2]

Marital and family status

As was mentioned in Chapter 5, we discovered during the pretest interviews that a substantial proportion of respondents were in consensual marriages. Accordingly, we developed a variable called partnership status. This variable merges information

Table 7.8. *Percentage distribution by age group of mothers, fathers, unmarried brothers, and childless sisters of Mexican origin subdivided by legal status*

Age group	Mother's legal status			Father's legal status			Brother's legal status			Sister's legal status		
	Un-docu-men-ted	Legal immi-grant	Native-born citizen	Un-docu-men-ted	Legal immi-grant	Native-born citizen	Un-docu-men-ted	Legal immi-grant	Native-born citizen	Un-docu-men-ted	Legal immi-grant	Native-born citizen
Total	100.0	100.0	100.0	100.0	100.0	100.0	100.0	100.0	100.0	100.0	100.0	100.0
18 and 19	7.0	6.0	11.5	1.4	1.6	4.3	28.2	9.4	17.1	25.0	19.4	25.7
20 to 24	42.2	24.7	36.6	22.7	12.0	25.2	37.0	45.3	33.1	38.5	26.3	43.3
25 to 29	29.1	32.3	34.4	33.0	28.6	35.6	26.8	28.3	37.3	22.8	27.7	9.3
30 to 34	13.9	21.6	12.0	25.1	33.4	18.0	3.9	13.0	9.4	9.3	16.3	15.7
35 and over	7.9	15.4	5.4	17.7	24.3	16.9	4.3	4.0	3.1	4.4	10.3	6.0
Mean age	25.8	27.8	25.3	29.0	30.6	28.6	23.1	25.0	24.0	23.4	25.4	23.8
Weighted number of cases	3,298	1,711	1,807	2,746	1,613	1,305	987	446	1,053	504	350	677

Table 7.9. *Percentage distribution by partnership status for mothers and fathers of Mexican origin subdivided by legal status and percentage distribution by marital status for unmarried brothers, and childless sisters of Mexican origin subdivided by legal status*

Partnership status	Mother's legal status			Father's legal status		
	Undocu-mented	Legal immigrant	Native-born citizen	Undocu-mented	Legal immigrant	Native-born citizen
Total	100.0	100.0	100.0	100.0	100.0	100.0
Legally married, spouse present	72.1	86.9	65.1	86.6	94.8	93.0
Consensually married, spouse present	12.4	2.3	4.0	13.2	4.2	5.9
Partner (not a spouse) present	0.2	0.6	0.8	0.0	1.0	0.0
Legally married, spouse not present	0.0	0.4	0.8	0.2	0.0	0.0
No partner present	15.3	9.9	29.3	0.0	0.0	1.1
Weighted number of cases	3,298	1,711	1,931	2,752	1,655	1,320

Marital status	Brother's legal status			Sister's legal status		
	Undocu-mented	Legal immigrant	Native-born citizen	Undocu-mented	Legal immigrant	Native-born citizen
Total	100.0	100.0	100.0	100.0	100.0	100.0
Never married	92.4	84.7	86.4	70.4	59.4	73.8
Married, spouse present	—	—	—	24.6	40.6	22.7
Married, spouse absent						
Separated	2.8	1.8	5.1	5.0	0.0	0.9
Not separated						
In Mexico	4.2	0.0	0.0	0.0	0.0	0.0
Not in Mexico	0.6	0.0	0.0	0.0	0.0	1.3
Divorced	0.0	13.6	8.5	0.0	0.0	1.3
Weighted number of cases	456	1,053	504	350	677	995

from the relationship item concerning whether the mother of the baby considers herself to have a husband with data from the question on marital status. Table 7.9 presents the data for this variable for all mothers and fathers of Mexican origin subdivided by legal status.

It can be seen that (1) legal immigrant mothers or fathers had higher proportions legally married than the other two subgroups, (2) the undocumented mothers or fathers had the highest proportion with a consensual marriage (not legally married but living with a person they consider to be their spouse), and (3) mothers born in the United States had the highest proportion with no partner present.

The high proportion legally married among legal immigrants may possibly be explained by the provisions of the immigration law that grant legal immigrant status without quota to anyone who marries an American citizen. As was shown earlier, in Table 2.3, in 1981 more than 36 percent of all persons from Mexico admitted as permanent legal residents (other than Silva cases or refugees) were admitted as spouses of U.S. citizens. One may also speculate that the relatively high proportion of native mothers living without a partner and the relatively high proportion of undocumented mothers living in a consensual marriage are both related to provisions of the law relating to Aid to Families with Dependent Children. I shall present further details concerning this matter in Chapter 8.

Table 7.9 also presents data on the marital status of unmarried brothers and childless sisters of Mexican origin. For the unmarried brothers, a striking feature is the low proportion (4.2 percent) who were married with a wife living in Mexico. This percentage contrasts markedly with the data obtained by Cornelius in his study of returned U.S. migrants in nine rural communities in the state of Jalisco. Cornelius found that on their first trip to the United States, about an equal number had been never-married as had been married but had left their wives behind.[3] The data from this survey also contrast with Maram's data for undocumented Mexican male workers in the garment and restaurant industries. For such workers who were not married with wife present, 20 percent of those in the garment industry and 31 percent of those in the restaurant industry were married, wife absent.[4] It is possible that the unmarried brothers in the current sample had an unusual distribution by marital status because they all had a sibling in the United States. One may speculate that, in the presence of a sibling already here, married males had no hesitation in bringing their wives up from Mexico.

What difference does legal status make with respect to the total number of persons and of own children (including stepchildren) living in the household? Table 7.10 presents the mean, median, modal, and maximum numbers of persons and of own children living in the household for mothers subdivided by their legal status. The mean number of persons in the household was highest when the mother was undocumented, intermediate when the mother was a legal immigrant, and lowest

Table 7.10. *Summary measures of the number of persons and of the number of own children in the household for all mothers subdivided by legal status*

		Legal status of mother:	
	Undocumented	Legal immigrant	Native-born citizen
Number of persons			
Mean	5.49	5.27	4.76
Median	5	5	4
Mode	4	5	4
Maximum	18	12	12
Number of own children			
Mean	2.50	2.85	2.08
Median	2	3	2
Mode	2	3	2
Maximum	11	9	8
Weighted number of cases	3,391	1,825	2,062

when the mother was a native-born citizen. The maximum number of persons in the household, eighteen, was found in the household of an undocumented mother. The ranking by legal status of the average number of own children was not identical to the ranking of the average number of all persons. The mean number of children living in the home was largest for legal immigrants and least for the native-born. The maximum number of children, eleven, was found in the home of an undocumented mother.

Do undocumented Mexican immigrants live in nuclear or in extended households? Table 7.11 presents data on this topic for all mothers subdivided both by their legal status and by whether they were living with the father of the reference baby. If the mother lived only with the father of the reference baby and/or her children, she was defined as living in a nuclear household. If she lived with any other person, relative or nonrelative, she was defined as being in an extended household. Mothers whose husband was temporarily absent were included in the group of mothers not living with the baby's father.

The proportion of all mothers living in an extended household was greatest for the undocumented, intermediate for the native-born, and least for the legal immigrants. For each type of legal status, the proportion living in an extended household was much larger for mothers not living with the father than for mothers living with the father.

7.11. *Percentage distribution by whether in a nuclear or extended household and, if in an extended household, the mean number of persons in the household outside the nuclear family for all mothers subdivided by whether living with the father and by legal status*

	Legal status of mother		
	Undocumented	Legal immigrant	Native-born citizen
All mothers			
Total	100.0	100.0	100.0
In nuclear household	64.1	78.4	69.7
In extended household	35.9	21.6	30.3
Weighted number of cases	3,391	1,825	2,047
Mean number of other persons in extended households	3.17	2.41	3.09
Mothers living with the father			
Total	100.0	100.0	100.0
In nuclear household	70.2	81.8	82.3
In extended household	29.8	18.2	17.7
Weighted number of cases	2,886	1,650	1,510
Mean number of other persons in extended households	2.94	2.07	2.10
Mothers not living with the father			
Total	100.0	100.0	100.0
In nuclear household	28.9	46.3	34.5
In extended household	71.1	53.7	65.5
Weighted number of cases	505	175	537
Mean number of other persons in extended households	3.72	3.47	3.85

Immigration history

Three questions were asked concerning immigration history for mothers, fathers, unmarried brothers, and childless sisters. The first question asked the year in which the person first came to the United States to live. The second question asked whether the person had ever left the United States for six months or more since first coming there. The third question asked for the number of years the person had lived here counting only those years in which the person had lived here for six months or more.

Table 7.12. *Percentage distribution by year of first arrival in the United States for mothers, fathers, unmarried brothers, and childless sisters of Mexican origin born outside the United States subdivided by legal status*

Year of first arrival	Mother's legal status		Father's legal status		Brother's legal status		Sister's legal status	
	Undocu-mented	Legal immigrant	Undocu-mented	Legal immigrant	Undocu-mented	Legal immigrant	Undocu-mented	Legal immigrant
Total	100.0	100.0	100.0	100.0	100.0	100.0	100.0	100.0
Before 1965	1.7	18.1	2.4	20.2	0.0	32.0	1.2	19.8
1965–1969	7.6	24.6	12.9	33.5	9.7	28.4	11.3	23.6
1970–1971	5.9	17.2	12.2	15.6	5.6	14.2	5.6	23.9
1972–73	13.3	15.6	23.4	15.6	17.1	12.9	10.7	8.7
1974–1975	21.1	11.5	18.5	9.9	19.2	9.3	13.7	4.4
1976–1977	22.1	8.1	19.2	1.1	21.0	3.1	22.8	15.1
1978	11.9	3.0	5.7	2.9	16.1	0.0	11.9	1.7
1979 or later	16.3	2.1	5.7	1.2	11.4	0.0	22.8	2.9
Mean year of first arrival	'74.9	'69.6	'73.2	'68.2	'74.9	'67.5	'75.3	'69.6
Weighted number of cases	3,298	1,711	2,728	1,633	971	450	504	344

Table 7.13. *Percentage distribution by whether absent from the United States for a period of six months or longer since first arrival in the United States for mothers, fathers, unmarried brothers, and childless sisters of Mexican origin born outside the United States subdivided by legal status*

Whether absent	Mother's legal status		Father's legal status		Brother's legal status		Sister's legal status	
	Undocu-mented	Legal immigrant	Undocu-mented	Legal immigrant	Undocu-mented	Legal immigrant	Undocu-mented	Legal immigrant
Total	100.00	100.00	100.00	100.00	100.00	100.00	100.00	100.00
No	92.97	95.32	90.47	91.42	90.64	90.22	92.66	96.51
Yes	7.03	4.68	9.53	8.58	9.36	9.78	7.34	3.49
Weighted number of cases	3,298	1,711	2,740	1,655	983	450	504	344

The answers to these questions reveal some striking differences between legal and undocumented immigrants and between the four relationship categories.

Table 7.12 presents the percentage distribution by year of first arrival in the United States for mothers, fathers, unmarried brothers, and childless sisters of Mexican origin born outside the United States subdivided by their legal status.

It can be seen that the year of first arrival for undocumented persons (whether mothers, fathers, unmarried brothers, or childless sisters) was considerably later than the year of first arrival for legal immigrants. Looking only at undocumented persons, a higher proportion of mothers had arrived more recently compared to the fathers. Particularly striking is the distribution by year of first arrival of unmarried brothers who were legal immigrants. Fully 32 percent arrived before 1965 and none after 1977. Many of these persons apparently became legal immigrants by virtue of being minor children of parents who gained legal status many years ago. Few of them had entered in recent years, most probably because since 1977 it has been so difficult to achieve the status of legal immigrant without marrying an American citizen.

Table 7.13 presents the percentage distribution by whether absent from the United States for a period of six months or longer since first arrival for mothers, fathers, unmarried brothers, and childless sisters born outside the United States. The very small percentages ever absent for this period of time among mothers and fathers give striking proof that these persons who had decided to have a baby in the United States were very definitely permanent settlers. Even more striking are the small proportions ever absent for six months or more among the unmarried brothers and childless sisters. One might have expected a higher proportion of these persons to have been shuttle migrants.

In view of the small proportions of persons ever absent from the United States for six months or more, the tabulations on total years of continuous stay in the United States are not presented.

Educational attainment

In this section I shall present data concerning number of school years completed and whether the person was in the United States at the time schooling was completed. I shall show that with respect to educational attainment, native-born respondents average out to a high level, undocumented immigrants to a very low level, and legal immigrants to an intermediate one.

Table 7.14 presents the percentage distribution by number of school years completed by legal status for mothers, fathers, unmarried brothers, and childless sisters of Mexican origin. Vast differences are shown to exist in favor of those born in

Table 7.14. *Percentage distribution by years of school completed for mothers, fathers, unmarried brothers, and childless sisters of Mexican origin subdivided by legal status*

Years of school completed	Mother's legal status			Father's legal status			Brother's legal status			Sister's legal status		
	Un-documented	Legal immigrant	Native-born citizen	Un-documented	Legal immigrant	Native-born citizen	Un-documented	Legal immigrant	Native-born citizen	Un-documented	Legal immigrant	Native-born citizen
Total	100.0	100.0	100.0	100.0	100.0	100.0	100.0	100.0	100.0	100.0	100.0	100.0
Less than 4	21.9	12.0	0.0	21.6	7.8	0.5	11.1	2.6	0.0	19.4	0.0	0.0
4 or 5	19.1	12.1	0.0	14.8	11.7	1.2	16.8	10.5	0.0	16.5	0.0	0.0
6	33.5	25.7	1.3	37.3	21.0	1.7	40.3	8.8	0.0	40.5	18.0	0.0
7 or 8	9.6	8.7	3.2	9.1	9.8	3.7	11.0	25.4	0.0	2.0	10.0	0.0
9–11	13.0	19.6	36.4	14.6	24.2	31.8	12.8	10.5	38.4	16.1	18.6	33.2
12	2.4	16.8	41.4	1.9	18.6	35.1	8.0	22.4	49.5	4.4	40.0	51.7
13 or more	0.5	5.2	17.7	0.8	6.9	26.1	0.0	19.7	12.1	1.2	13.4	15.1
Mean years completed	5.60	7.61	11.57	5.72	8.29	11.71	6.44	9.70	11.57	5.77	10.30	12.04
Weighted number of cases	3,298	1,705	1,831	2,714	1,627	1,312	953	456	1,022	504	350	677

the United States compared to the undocumented immigrants. Legal immigrants have a distribution intermediate between the undocumented and the native-born.

Some additional light on these findings is shed by comparing these data with tabulations made by the Rand study for persons 25 to 34 in California according to the 1980 Census. That study showed that U.S.-born citizens of Mexican descent had slightly lower educational attainment than all persons, but that there was a very wide gulf between the educational attainment of Mexican immigrants and native-born U.S. citizens of Mexican origin.[5]

The data from the Los Angeles County Parents Survey can also be compared to the nationwide data for the Mexican-origin population in the 1980 Census reported by Bean et al. The educational attainment of the undocumented immigrants in the Los Angeles County Parents Survey was similar to that for all immigrants from Mexico who came to the United States in 1975–80. However, a substantially higher proportion of the native-born population of Mexican origin in the United States reported eight years or less of completed schooling than was the case among the native-born persons of the Los Angeles County Parents Survey.[6]

We have shown that legal immigrants had come to the United States earlier than the undocumented immigrants. Did this fact allow more of the legal immigrants to complete school in the United States? If so, how did the latter affect the educational attainment of the legal immigrants relative to that of the undocumented? Data from the questions on age, number of years in the United States for six months or more, and on years of completed schooling were used to estimate whether school had been completed in the United States for mothers and fathers born outside the United States. Specifically, school was presumed to have been completed in the United States if the difference between the person's age and the person's length of stay in the United States was less than six years plus the number of school years completed.

Table 7.15 shows that for both mothers and fathers, legal immigrants had a substantially higher proportion who completed school in the United States than did the undocumented. Table 7.15 also shows that for mothers and fathers among both the undocumented and the legal immigrants, the level of educational attainment was substantially higher among those who completed their education in the United States than for those who did not. Moreover, Table 7.15 also shows another very important fact. Among those persons who did not complete their schooling in the United States, there was a smaller difference in educational attainment between the legal and the undocumented immigrants than the difference in educational attainment between undocumented and legal immigrants in the whole sample. Finally, a comparison of the findings in Table 7.15 with those in Table 7.14 reveals very little difference in the educational attainment of legal immigrants who completed school in the United States and the native-born citizens.

Table 7.15. *Percentage distribution by whether school was completed in the United States for mothers and fathers of Mexican origin born outside the United States subdivided by legal status and percentage distribution by years of school completed for mothers and fathers of Mexican origin born outside the United States subdivided by whether school was completed in the United States and by legal status*

	Mother's legal status		Father's legal status	
	Undocu-mented	Legal immi-grant	Undocu-mented	Legal immi-grant
School completed in United States				
Total	100.0	100.0	100.0	100.0
No	94.7	72.0	97.0	73.7
Yes	5.3	28.0	3.0	26.3
Weighted number of cases	3,298	1,711	2,724	1,643
Years of school completed *School not completed in United States*				
Total	100.0	100.0	100.0	100.0
Less than 4	23.1	16.6	21.7	10.6
4 or 5	20.0	16.8	15.2	15.8
6	35.4	35.2	37.6	28.3
7 or 8	9.0	10.1	9.3	13.3
9–11	10.3	14.5	13.3	21.0
12	1.9	5.4	2.0	10.7
13 or more	0.4	1.3	0.8	0.3
Mean years completed	5.36	6.17	5.65	6.96
Weighted number of cases	3,122	1,226	2,619	1,193
School completed in United States				
Total	100.0	100.0	100.0	100.0
Less than 4	0.0	0.0	19.7	0.0
4 or 5	3.4	0.0	0.0	0.0
6	0.0	1.3	19.7	1.0
7 or 8	20.5	5.0	0.0	0.0
9–11	62.5	32.6	60.7	31.2
12	11.4	46.1	0.0	42.0
13 or more	2.3	15.0	0.0	25.9
Mean years completed	9.71	11.30	7.90	12.06
Weighted number of cases	176	479	61	417

Table 7.16. *Percentage distributions by mother tongue and ability to speak English for mothers, fathers, unmarried brothers, and childless sisters of Mexican origin subdivided by legal status*

	Mother's legal status			Father's legal status			Brother's legal status			Sister's legal status		
	Un-docu-men-ted	Legal immi-grant	Native-born citizen	Un-docu-men-ted	Legal immi-grant	Native-born citizen	Un-docu-men-ted	Legal immi-grant	Native-born citizen	Un-docu-men-ted	Legal immi-grant	Native-born citizen
Mother tongue, total	100.0	100.0	100.0	100.0	100.0	100.0	100.0	100.0	100.0	100.0	100.0	100.0
English	0.2	0.2	47.3	0.0	0.7	38.8	0.0	0.0	45.1	0.0	0.0	43.7
Spanish	99.6	98.0	32.9	99.6	98.4	42.7	100.0	97.4	34.1	100.0	100.0	32.9
Other language	0.0	0.0	0.0	0.4	0.9	0.0	0.0	0.0	0.0	0.0	0.0	0.0
Both English and Spanish	0.2	1.8	19.8	0.0	0.0	18.5	0.0	2.6	20.8	0.0	0.0	23.5
Ability to speak English, total	100.0	100.0	100.0	100.0	100.0	100.0	100.0	100.0	100.0	100.0	100.0	100.0
Fluent	1.3	18.7	94.4	3.4	22.1	91.8	9.9	49.1	92.3	3.6	49.7	99.1
Moderate	9.6	16.2	4.3	18.1	36.8	4.4	16.5	31.1	7.7	7.9	18.3	0.9
With difficulty	23.4	38.1	0.8	51.4	33.4	3.8	42.0	11.4	0.0	45.2	20.9	0.0
None	66.0	27.0	0.5	27.0	7.7	0.0	31.7	8.3	0.0	43.3	11.1	0.0
Weighted number of cases	3,298	1,711	1,831	2,752	1,655	1,320	995	456	1,053	504	350	677

Table 7.16 presents data on mother tongue and ability to speak English for mothers, fathers, unmarried brothers, and childless sisters by type of legal status. Almost all native-born persons spoke English fluently despite the fact that for a substantial proportion Spanish was the mother tongue. On the other hand, a high proportion of undocumented immigrants spoke no English. Legal immigrants were intermediate between the undocumented and the native-born in their ability to speak English. There was also a substantial difference between undocumented mothers and undocumented fathers in English-speaking ability. This fact is probably related to the longer stay in the United States of the fathers as compared to the mothers. It is also probably related to the greater exposure to English-speaking persons because more of the fathers than the mothers were working outside the home.

The data shown in Table 7.16 can be compared to the data on English proficiency for all persons of Mexican origin in the United States in 1980 as reported by Bean et al. For undocumented persons, the distributions by ability to speak English are not dissimilar to the distributions reported by Bean et al. for all Mexican immigrants who came to the United States in 1975 or later. For native-born persons in the Los Angeles County Parents Survey, the ability to speak English seems to be slightly superior to that for all native-born persons in the Mexican-origin population of the United States.[7]

Geographic distribution of residence

In Chapter 5, I mentioned a geographic breakdown of interview results in which Los Angeles County had been subdivided into ten segments. This typology, borrowed from elsewhere, concentrated too many of the interviews into too few of the segments. Accordingly, I decided to subdivide the two segments that had contained the largest number of interviews. I now subdivided the Central Los Angeles segment into two areas I named (1) Lincoln Heights and Boyle Heights and (2) Other Central Los Angeles. The first area is east of downtown; the second, and much larger, area is either downtown or to the west, northwest, or northeast. Then I subdivided the Southeast segment into four parts that I labeled (1) East Los Angeles, (2) South Gate and Huntington Park, (3) Pico Rivera and Whittier, and (4) Norwalk and Downey. (The use of city names to denote these areas does not imply that they are the only cities in the area.)

Figure 7.1 is a map of Los Angeles County that shows the location of each of the resulting fourteen areas.

Table 7.17 presents the percentage distribution by legal status for all mothers subdivided by the geographic area of their residence. Before discussing the results, it would perhaps be best to say something about each of the fourteen delineated areas as of the time of the 1980 census.

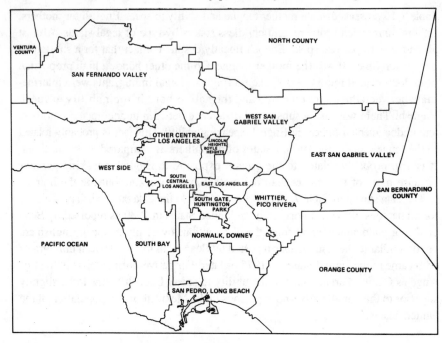

Figure 7.1: Districts within Los Angeles County

The San Fernando Valley is very large both in population and in area. In its southern and western portions, the population is very affluent; in its northern and eastern portions, the population tends to have substantial proportions of Hispanics and some blacks and be rather poor.

Lincoln Heights and Boyle Heights is part of the city of Los Angeles located northeast of downtown. It is relatively poor and has been a traditional center of Mexican settlement.

Other Central Los Angeles is rather heterogeneous in its ethnic composition but currently has a large Hispanic population, some portions of which are in traditional areas of Mexican settlement. It contains many poor persons.

South Central Los Angeles is predominantly black and one of the poorest areas of the county. Parts of the area experienced a massive shift from black to Mexican population during the 1970–80 decade.

The West Side is the most affluent portion of the county and a bastion of non-Hispanic White population.

San Pedro and Long Beach make up a mixed area with emerging Hispanic and black populations; some parts are quite affluent, others very poor.

The East San Gabriel Valley is the most eastern portion of the county and an area of new settlement. It is rather heterogeneous in income and has emerging black and Hispanic populations.

Table 7.17. *Percentage distribution by legal status for all mothers subdivided by geographic area of residence*

Area	Weighted Number of cases	Percentage distribution			
		Total	Undocu- mented	Legal immigrant	Native- born citizen
Total	7,278	100.0	46.6	25.1	28.3
San Fernando Valley	848	100.0	59.4	20.6	19.9
Lincoln Heights and Boyle Heights	439	100.0	46.9	36.0	17.1
Other Central Los Angeles	621	100.0	58.1	30.3	11.6
South Central Los Angeles	519	100.0	81.7	16.6	1.7
West Side	165	100.0	50.9	24.2	24.9
San Pedro and Long Beach	345	100.0	44.1	32.5	23.5
East San Gabriel Valley	620	100.0	25.7	18.6	55.8
West San Gabriel Valley	868	100.0	27.2	30.3	42.5
Whittier and Pico Rivera	471	100.0	17.8	14.4	67.7
East Los Angeles	705	100.0	51.9	28.4	19.7
South Gate and Huntington Park	598	100.0	59.7	25.8	14.6
Norwalk and Downey	746	100.0	42.1	28.7	29.2
South Bay	327	100.0	44.0	14.1	41.9
North County	6	100.0	0.0	100.0	0.0

Definitions of Areas: San Fernando Valley (census tracts 1000–1499 and 3000–3299); Lincoln Heights and Boyle Heights (census tracts 1991–2051); Other Central Los Angeles (census tracts 1800–1990 and 2052–2199); South Central Los Angeles (census tracts 2200–2499); West Side (census tracts 2600–2799 and 7000–8999); San Pedro and Long Beach (census tracts 2900–2999 and 5700–5799); East San Gabriel Valley (census tracts 4000–4099); West San Gabriel Valley (census tracts 4300–4899); Whittier and Pico Rivera (census tracts 5000–5299); East Los Angeles (census tracts 5300–5329); South Gate and Huntington Park (census tracts 5330–5399); Norwalk and Downey (census tracts 5400–5599); South Bay (census tracts 6000–6799); North County (census tracts 9000–9399).

The West San Gabriel Valley is similar in income and ethnicity to the East San Gabriel Valley area but is an area of older settlement.

Pico Rivera and Whittier are an area of emerging Hispanic settlement with relatively few poor people.

East Los Angeles is generally considered to be the heartland of the Mexican-origin population of Los Angeles. It is one of the poorer areas of the county but not the poorest.

South Gate and Huntington Park are an area in which Hispanics have recently become predominant. It is one of the poorer areas of the county.

Norwalk and Downey constitute another area of emerging Hispanic settlement,

Table 7.18. *Percentage distribution by area of residence for total population of Los Angeles County and for all surveyed mothers subdivided by legal status*

| Area | Los Angeles County population | Mother's legal status | | | |
		Total	Undocu- mented	Legal immigrant	Native- born citizen
Total	100.0	100.0	100.0	100.0	100.0
San Fernando Valley	17.1	11.7	14.9	9.6	8.2
Lincoln Heights and Boyle Heights	2.1	6.0	6.1	8.7	3.6
Other Central Los Angeles	10.5	8.5	10.7	10.3	3.5
South Central Los Angeles	6.6	7.1	12.5	4.7	0.4
West Side	8.5	2.3	2.5	2.2	2.0
San Pedro and Long Beach	7.7	4.7	4.5	6.1	3.9
East San Gabriel Valley	9.2	8.5	4.7	6.3	16.8
West San Gabriel Valley	8.5	11.9	7.0	14.4	17.9
Whittier and Pico Rivera	3.5	6.5	2.5	3.7	15.5
East Los Angeles	3.0	9.7	10.8	11.0	6.7
South Gate and Huntington Park	3.6	8.2	10.5	8.4	4.2
Norwalk and Downey	8.5	10.3	9.3	11.7	10.6
South Bay	8.6	4.5	4.3	2.5	6.6
North County	2.5	0.1	0.0	0.3	0.0
Weighted number of cases		7,278	3,391	1,825	2,062

but the area also contains the city of Compton, which is mostly black; it is generally an area of middle and lower-middle income.

The South Bay is generally affluent and mostly populated by non-Hispanic whites with the exception of Inglewood, which has recently become mostly black.

The North County area contains more than one-half of the area of Los Angeles County but very little of its population. It is generally a middle-income non-Hispanic white area.

If we ignore the North County (where there was only one interview), we see from Table 7.17 that the proportion of all of the surveyed mothers who were undocumented ranges from almost 82 percent in South Central Los Angeles to a low of 18 percent in Pico Rivera and Whittier.

In Table 7.18 we run the percentages a different way to show the percentage distribution by geographic area for the surveyed mothers subdivided by legal status and also for the total population of Los Angeles County.

We may also look at the joint distribution of mothers by legal status and by census tract of resident subdivided according to more analytical classifications. Table 7.19 presents the percentage distribution by legal status of the surveyed mothers depend-

Table 7.19. *Percentage distribution by legal status for all mothers subdivided by median 1979 family income in census tract of residence and percentage distribution by median 1979 family income in census tract of residence for all mothers subdivided by legal status*

Median 1979 family income in census tract	Weighted number of cases	Percentage distribution by legal status				Percentage distribution by census tract income			
		Total	Undocumented	Legal immigrant	Native-born citizen	Total	Undocumented	Legal immigrant	Native-born citizen
Total	7,268	100.0	46.5	25.1	28.4	100.0	100.0	100.0	100.0
Under $10,000	470	100.0	74.5	12.8	12.8	6.5	10.4	3.3	2.9
$10,000 to $14,000	2,547	100.0	58.5	27.8	13.7	35.0	44.0	38.9	16.9
$15,000 to $19,999	2,754	100.0	43.6	24.7	31.8	37.9	35.5	37.2	42.4
$20,000 and over	1,497	100.0	22.9	25.2	52.0	20.6	10.1	20.7	37.7
Weighted number of cases						7,268	3,381	1,825	2,062

Table 7.20. Percentage distribution by legal status for all mothers subdivided by percentage of the 1980 population in the census tract of residence which was Black and percentage distribution by 1980 percentage black in the census tract of residence for all mothers subdivided by legal status

Percentage black in census tract of residence	Weighted number of cases	Percentage distribution by legal status				Percentage distribution by census tract percent black			
		Total	Undocu-mented	Legal immi-grant	Native-born citizen	Total	Undocu-mented	Legal immi-grant	Native-born citizen
Total	7,278	100.0	46.6	25.1	28.3	100.0	100.0	100.0	100.0
Under 20	6,040	100.0	42.8	25.4	31.8	83.0	76.2	84.2	93.1
20 to 39	464	100.0	54.3	30.8	14.9	6.4	7.4	7.8	3.4
40 to 59	293	100.0	74.4	16.4	9.2	4.0	6.4	2.6	1.3
60 to 79	311	100.0	68.2	22.5	9.3	4.3	6.3	3.8	1.4
80 and over	170	100.0	72.9	16.5	10.6	2.3	3.7	1.5	0.9
Weighted number of cases		7,278					3,391	1,825	2,062

Table 7.21. Percentage distribution by legal status for all mothers subdivided by percentage of the 1980 population which was of Hispanic origin in the census tract of residence and percentage distribution by percentage of Hispanic origin in the census tract of residence for all mothers subdivided by legal status

Percentage of Hispanic origin in census tract of residence	Weighted number of cases	Percentage distribution by legal status				Percentage distribution by census tract percentage of Spanish origin			
		Total	Undocu-mented	Legal immi-grant	Native-born citizen	Total	Undocu-mented	Legal immi-grant	Native-born citizen
Total	7,278	100.0	46.6	25.1	28.3	100.0	100.0	100.0	100.0
Under 20	866	100.0	41.3	24.9	33.7	11.9	10.6	11.8	14.2
20 to 39	1,428	100.0	39.8	24.7	35.6	19.6	16.8	19.3	24.6
40 to 59	1,629	100.0	44.6	24.1	31.3	22.4	21.4	21.5	24.7
60 to 79	2,026	100.0	51.1	24.4	24.5	27.8	30.5	27.1	24.1
80 and over	1,329	100.0	53.0	27.8	19.2	18.3	20.8	20.3	12.4
Weighted number of cases		7,278				7,278	3,391	1,825	2,062

ing on the median family income in the census tract of residence. It also presents the percentage distribution by median family income in the census tract of residence depending on categories of legal status. We see a strong association between being undocumented and living in a census tract with a low median income, and being native-born and living in a tract of high income.

Table 7.20 presents the percentage distribution by legal status of the surveyed mothers depending on the proportion of the total population of the census tract in 1980 that was black and also the percentage distribution by percent black in the census tract of residence for mothers subdivided by legal status. There was a strong association between the mother's type of legal status and the proportion black in her census tract of residence. A possible interpretation of these findings is that all persons of Mexican origin would rather live apart from blacks but many undocumented Mexicans, because of their lower incomes, had no choice.

Table 7.21 presents data similar to the data of Table 7.20 except that we now look at the association between mother's legal status and the proportion of the population in her census tract of Hispanic origin. There was some tendency for the undocumented to be more predominant in the areas with the highest proportion of total population of Spanish origin. However, the association was only moderate. The reason why the association between these two variables is only moderate is that the undocumented were more likely to be living in tracts with a high proportion of blacks while the native-born were more likely to be living in tracts with a high proportion of the population either non-Hispanic white or Asian. Also less than half of all of the surveyed mothers lived in areas with 60 percent or more of the population of Hispanic origin. This proportion was slightly higher among undocumented mothers than among native-born mothers.

We may also say a word about the process of residential succession that took place in Los Angeles County during the 1970–80 decade. As was mentioned in Chapter 3, the total population of the county increased by only 436,000, while the Hispanic population increased by more than one million with a decline of approximately equal magnitude in the white population not of Hispanic origin. The major cause for the large increase in the population of Hispanic origin was that the reported number of persons born in Mexico increased from 206,831 to 697,771[8] and many of the newly arrived immigrants from Mexico bore children soon after arrival.

During the decade, undocumented Mexican immigrants displaced the black population in much of the northern and eastern fringe of South Central Los Angeles and also in parts of the South Gate and Huntington Park area. In turn blacks displaced white Anglos in areas (such as the city of Inglewood) to the south and west of the black ghetto as defined in 1970. Native-born Mexicans moved out of the traditional Mexican areas (such as East Los Angeles and Lincoln Heights and Boyle

Table 7.22. *Percentage distribution by number of children ever born standardized for age by the direct method*[a] *for mothers of Mexican origin subdivided by legal status*

	Legal status of mother		
Children ever born	Undocu-mented	Legal immigrant	Native-born citizen
Total	100.0	100.0	100.0
1 child	27.0	29.6	32.7
2 children	31.2	21.5	34.7
3 children	22.4	27.2	18.0
4 children	7.6	10.0	8.1
5 children or more	11.8	11.8	6.5
Median number of children ever born	2.24	2.45	2.00
Weighted number of cases	3,298	1,707	1,816

[a]Standard is the distribution by age of all Mexican-origin mothers.

Heights) and moved eastward (to such areas as West San Gabriel Valley and East San Gabriel Valley) and southeastward to such areas as Whittier and Pico Rivera, where in each case they displaced non-Hispanic whites.

Fertility

The first two types of data to be presented in this section – the age-adjusted number of children ever born to the surveyed mothers by legal status, and recent fertility of the surveyed mothers by legal status – come directly from the survey but are not the best measures of fertility for all women (as distinct from mothers). The last, the total fertility rate for women of Mexican origin 18 to 39 years old by legal status, is the best measure of fertility for all women but cannot be measured unequivocally.

Children ever born

Table 7.22 presents the age-standardized number of children ever born to mothers of Mexican origin subdivided by legal status. The method used was direct standardization with five-year age groups. It can be seen from the table that the median number of children ever born (when age-standardized) was lowest for those born in the United States (2.00), intermediate for those who were undocumented (2.24), and highest for those who were legal immigrants (2.45). However, the difference between the undocumented and the legal immigrants must be qualified because it is possible that a large number of the children born to women who were legal

Table 7.23. *Percentage distribution by number of children under age 2 in the home other than the reference baby for mothers of Mexican origin born outside the United States and residing in the United States for at least three years*

| | Legal status of mother | |
	Undocumented	Legal immigrant
Total	100.0	100.0
0	81.7	89.0
1	17.6	11.0
2	0.7	0.0
Age-standardized median number of children under age 2 besides the reference birth	0.13	0.05
Unweighted number of cases	289	216

Source: Dee Falasco, "Economic and Fertility Differences between Legal and Illegal Migrant Mexican Families: The Potential Effects of Immigration Policy Changes," unpublished Ph.D. dissertation, University of Southern California, April 1982, p. 80.

immigrants at the time of the survey had been born while their mothers were still undocumented.

Recent fertility

It seemed appropriate to look at differences in recent fertility as between the undocumented and the legal immigrant mothers of Mexican origin. Dee Falasco did this as part of her Ph.D. dissertation, findings from which have been previously published.[9] Current fertility was defined only for women currently with a husband who had been in the United States at least three years. Among these women, current fertility was defined as the number of children under age 2, other than the reference baby, who were living with the mother. The results of this analysis, shown in Table 7.23, reveal a somewhat higher proportion of the undocumented than of the legal immigrant women had born one or more children during the two-year period before the birth of the reference baby. However, these results do not control for age. Accordingly, the age-standardized median number of children under age 2 was computed and is also shown in Table 7.23. This median was 0.13 for the undocumented and 0.05 for the legal immigrants.

In a multivariate analysis of the determinants of recent fertility among mothers born in Mexico, Falasco examined whether type of legal status had an independent effect. Her analysis showed that the coefficient for being a legal immigrant was negative but not statistically significant. Three variables had a statistically significant effect on recent fertility. Years of completed schooling and duration of stay in the United States were negatively related; a categorical predictor concerning whether school had been completed in the United States was positively related.

Estimates of the total fertility rate

The results discussed so far pertain only to mothers. It is also desirable to look at the level of fertility for all women, including those who never become mothers. A commonly used measure of fertility for all women consists of a set of age-specific fertility rates, which can then be summarized into a total fertility rate. Conventionally, the total fertility rate is obtained by summing the age-specific fertility rates from 10 years to 49 years of age. Because of my research design, my data allow for the calculation only of age-specific fertility rates and of a total fertility rate for women 18 to 39 years old. However, the total fertility rate for females 18 to 39 is not substantially less than that for women 10 to 49 years of age. For example, for the United States in 1980 the total fertility rate for women 10 to 49 years of age was 1,836 per thousand, and for women 18 to 39 years of age 1,713 per thousand.[10]

I have computed three sets of estimates both of the age-specific fertility rates and of the total fertility rates for the females of Mexican origin 18 to 39 years old subdivided by their type of legal status. These three sets of estimates differ in their assumptions concerning the size of the respective base populations. Three assumptions are necessary because we cannot be certain what these sizes should be. However, even if we were certain concerning the correct population bases, these estimates can only be approximate for several reasons: we were not able to interview many mothers for human-subjects considerations, we had a high rate of nonresponse, and it is not certain that all of our respondents told the truth concerning their legal status. To compute these three sets of total fertility rates, it was necessary to estimate (1) as numerator for each rate, the number of births that occurred to women of Mexican origin subdivided by age and by legal status during calendar year 1980, and (2) as possible denominator for each rate, three sets of estimates of the number of women of Mexican origin on July 1, 1980 subdivided by age and by legal status. Complete details of the methodology are complicated and will not be presented here. (They may be obtained from the author upon request.)

To estimate the numbers of relevant births I made use of unpublished tabulations prepared by the National Center for Health Statistics; my tabulations of births in Los Angeles County during the period from August 1, 1980, through March 31, 1981, and data from my survey.

The three sets of estimates of the base populations were derived as follows: A previously mentioned publication by me and Passel describes in detail how three separate estimates of the total number of females of Mexican origin subdivided by age and by legal status were derived for the time of the 1980 Census.[11] For my first set of estimates of the total fertility rates, I made use of the "best" estimates as described in that article. For my second set of estimates I made use of the "composite" estimates. For my third set of estimates I made use of the "residual" estimates.

In the best estimates it was assumed that the 1980 Census's 5 percent sample count of the population of Mexican origin in Los Angeles County born outside the United States was correct. These estimates made use of my survey data to estimate the distribution of Mexican-origin women born outside the United States by legal status. It was assumed that for subgroups homogeneous in various relevant characteristics the proportion undocumented in the census population of Mexican origin born outside the United States was identical to that in my sample.

The composite estimates assumed the validity of the adjustments made by Passel to the count of the population born in Mexico and then made use of my survey data to estimate the distribution of Mexican-origin women born outside the United States by legal status in a manner identical to that employed for the best estimates. The Passel adjustments were previously briefly described in Chapter 3. To reiterate, Passel assumed that a substantial proportion of the population of Mexican origin who stated they were born in the United States were actually born in Mexico. Moreover, he also allocated as having been born in Mexico a substantial proportion of all persons enumerated in the 1980 Census as being of foreign birth but with nation of birth unknown.

The residual estimates used Passel's own estimate of the number of females of Mexican birth for Los Angeles County subdivided by age and by legal status. The residual estimates also used the same estimates of the native-born population of Mexican origin as was used for the composite best estimates. The methodology for Passel's estimates of the undocumented and legal immigrant populations has also been briefly described in Chapter 3. To reiterate, the essence of the residual method was to subtract from the adjusted population born in Mexico as counted in the 1980 Census the adjusted number of persons registered in January 1980 as legal aliens.

Table 7.24 presents the population bases according to the best, composite, and residual estimates. As of July 1, 1980, the number of undocumented females of Mexican origin 18 to 39 years old in Los Angeles County was smallest according to the best estimate and largest according to the residual estimates. The number of legal immigrants was smallest according to the residual estimates and largest according to the composite estimates. Finally, the number of native-born women was identical according to either the composite or residual estimates and in either case smaller than according to the best estimates.

Table 7.24. *Estimates of the total fertility rate per 1,000 women of Mexican origin in Los Angeles County by legal status for "best" estimate of the base population by legal status, for "composite" estimate of the base population by legal status, and for "residual" estimate of the base population by legal status*

	July 1, 1980, population			Birth rate per 1,000		
Age group	Undocu- mented	Legal immigrant	Native- born citizen	Undocu- mented	Legal immigrant	Native- born citizen
"Best" estimate						
Total, 18–39 years	93,185	87,799	142,623	238.3	127.7	83.6
18–19	6,945	8,264	19,813	373.4	148.2	99.1
20–24	32,234	17,026	45,272	293.1	168.4	109.2
25–29	25,737	23,321	34,613	238.5	151.8	92.7
30–34	17,258	22,582	24,852	171.9	106.1	56.2
35–39	11,010	16,606	18,073	96.4	71.1	23.0
Total fertility rate for women 18–39				4,746	2,783	1,604
Approximation of TFR for women 10–49				5,226	3,065	1,766
"Composite" estimate						
Total, 18–39 years	109,577	102,465	111,564	202.7	109.4	106.9
18–19	8,094	9,859	17,070	320.4	124.3	115.0
20–24	38,644	19,975	35,913	244.5	143.6	137.6
25–29	30,043	26,746	26,882	204.3	132.3	119.4
30–34	20,064	26,345	18,283	147.9	91.0	76.4
35–39	12,733	19,540	13,416	83.3	60.4	31.0
Total fertility rate for women 18–39				4,041	2,385	2,052
Approximation of TFR for women 10–49				4,449	2,626	2,259
"Residual" estimate						
Total, 18–39 years	138,380	67,374	111,564	160.5	166.4	106.9
18–19	13,515	4,236	17,070	191.9	289.2	115.0
20–24	45,084	12,406	35,913	209.5	231.2	137.6
25–29	38,327	16,743	26,882	160.1	211.4	119.4
30–34	26,224	18,457	18,283	113.1	129.9	76.4
35–39	15,129	15,432	13,416	70.1	76.5	31.0
Total fertility rate for women 18–39				3,148	3,823	2,052
Approximation of TFR for women 10–49				3,466	4,210	2,259

Arguments might be made for the greater accuracy of the age-specific and total fertility rates based on the best population, on the composite population, or on the residual population. I believe that the residual population is probably closer to the true numbers than the composite population, which in turn is probably closer to the true numbers than the best population. Nevertheless, I believe it is often inappropriate to adjust the denominator of a rate without adjusting the numerator. A likely reason why the residual estimate gives a higher number of undocumented females than the composite estimate is that some of the surveyed females who were actually undocumented claimed to be here legally. Accordingly, the number of births to undocumented women would also have been underestimated. Moreover, if persons who were born outside the United States falsely claimed to the Census that they were born in the United States, they might possibly make the same claim on the birth certificate. If so, use of the composite estimate would bias the age-specific fertility rates of the native-born population upward and those of the foreign-born population downward. On the other hand, if the nativity reporting on the birth certificate were correct, the most accurate estimate of the total fertility rate for the native-born population of Mexican origin could not be that based on the residual population.

I have the feeling that the reporting of nativity on the birth certificate is in fact subject to little error. I believe it would be difficult for an immigrant mother falsely to claim birth in the United States to the nurse or physician attending her. Accordingly, I believe that the most accurate total fertility rates will be those in which the composite population is taken as the base. However, the total fertility rates for undocumented and legal immigrants given the composite population as base refer to subgroups of immigrants who have claimed a certain legal status but not always truthfully.

The results with respect to age-specific and total fertility rates are also shown in Table 7.24. The table shows the total fertility rates for women 18 to 39 years old subdivided by type of legal status and also approximations of the total fertility rates for women 10 to 49 years of age. These last are based on the product of the respective total fertility rates for women 18 to 39 years of age times the ratio (1.101) of the total fertility rate at ages 10 to 49 to that at ages 18 to 39 for all women of Mexican origin in Los Angeles County in 1980.

Let us first consider the results with the composite population as base. Given this population base, undocumented women had the highest total fertility rate at ages 18 to 39 (4,041 per thousand); the total fertility rate of the legal immigrant women 18 to 39 years old was much lower (2,385 per thousand), and the native-born women had the lowest total fertility rate (2,052). However, I believe the substantial difference in total fertility rate between the undocumented and legal immigrants must not be treated as reflecting equally large differences in lifetime cumulative fertility between the two subgroups.

I believe that women who during their reproductive ages were first undocumented and then became legal immigrants were more motivated to have babies during the period of their illegal stay than during their period of legal stay. Remember that, prior to 1977, only if an undocumented woman gave birth to a baby in the United States were she and her husband allowed to apply for a permanent visa without the necessity of obtaining labor certification. Even with the current immigration law, an undocumented woman can always legalize her status after her first American-born child reaches age 21. Furthermore, as Harwood has shown, INS officials are reluctant to require the departure of undocumented mothers with small children because of the complications such a departure would cause.[12] This interpretation of the findings is also the only one consistent with the findings reported in Tables 7.22 and 7.23. Table 7.22 showed a small difference in age-standardized median number of children ever born to mothers in favor of the legal immigrants as compared to the undocumented. Nevertheless, Table 7.23 showed that recent fertility was considerably higher among the undocumented mothers than among the legal immigrant mothers.

With the "best" population as base, the total fertility rates for the two immigrant populations are inflated proportionately and the total fertility rate for the native-born population deflated. The total fertility rate of the legal immigrants 18 to 39 years of age becomes much higher (2,783) than that of the native-born women (1,604). The result for the latter group appears improbably low.

On the other hand, with the "residual" population as base, the total fertility rate of the undocumented women falls and that of the legal immigrant women rises. The total fertility rate of the native-born remains the same as in the estimate with the "composite"population as base. According to the results with the residual population as base, the total fertility rate of the undocumented (3,148) is substantially lower than that for the legal immigrants (3,823). This result contradicts the results with respect to recent fertility of mothers shown in Table 7.23. Accordingly, I believe that the results with the residual population as base are incorrect.

Let me now try to conclude what has been a long discussion. The results have been found to depend heavily upon the assumptions made. Nevertheless, four matters are quite clear.

First, regardless of the choice of population base, each of the subgroups of Mexican-born women had a higher total fertility rate for the ages from 18 to 39 than the total fertility rate for all women of those ages in the United States. In 1980 the total fertility rate for all women in the United States from 18 to 39 years of age was only 1,713 per thousand as opposed to possible rates for the two subclasses of Mexican-born women ranging from 2,385 to 4,746.

Second, the total fertility rate of the combined total of the three subgroups of Mexican-origin women 10 to 49 years of age in Los Angeles County (3,113) is not inconsistent with the total fertility rate of 2,901 per thousand estimated by the U.S. National Center for Health Statistics for all Mexican-origin women 10 to 49 years of age in the United States in 1980.[13]

Third, the positive difference found here, regardless of the population base chosen, between the total fertility rate of all immigrant women and of native-born women is consistent with previous results of Bean et al., and Bean and Swicegood.[14] Bean et al. in an analysis of 1970 Census data for ever-married women of Mexican origin in the United States showed that at each age recent fertility was higher for women of Mexican origin born outside the United States than for those born in the United States. Bean and Swicegood had earlier established the same fact for all ever-married women of Mexican origin in the United States 20 to 34 years of age enumerated in the 1976 Survey of Income and Education.

Fourth and finally, the total fertility rate for native-born women of Mexican origin 18 to 39 years old (ranging from 1,604 with the best population as base to 2,052 with the composite population as base) was very close to the total fertility rate of all women 18 to 39 in the United States (1,713). Accordingly, it would appear that with respect to fertility behavior the native-born women of Mexican origin in Los Angeles County have been quite completely assimilated to the mainstream.

School enrollment and relative progress in school

A very important question is the extent to which the children of undocumented Mexican parents will be hampered in their own quest for success in adult life. A prime determinant of such success is educational attainment. Accordingly, we examine, for children subdivided by the legal status of their mother, the proportions who were enrolled in school and, among those enrolled, the relative progress in school.

For all children in the household other than the American-born reference baby, a tabulation was made of nation of birth cross-classified by legal status of the mother. According to this tabulation, the following proportions of nonreference children were born outside the United States: 49.1 percent when the mother was undocumented, 20.3 percent when the mother was a legal immigrant, and 3.0 percent when the mother was born in the United States. This tabulation provides a close approximation to the proportion of school-age children who were born outside the United States subdivided by their mother's legal status. It also gives some indication of the language handicap faced by the children of the three respective subgroups.

School enrollment

Table 7.25 shows the school enrollment of the children of mothers in the study population who were 3 through 18 years of age by their own age and by their mother's

Table 7.25. *Percentage distribution by school enrollment status for children of mothers in the study population by age and by mother's legal status*

	Legal status of mother		
Age by enrollment status	Undocumented	Legal immigrant	Native-born citizen
Ages 3–5			
Total	100.0	100.0	100.0
Enrolled in school	29.4	39.1	41.8
Not enrolled	70.6	60.9	58.2
Weighted number of cases	1,658	934	710
Ages 6–13			
Total	100.0	100.0	100.0
Enrolled in school	98.0	99.0	100.0
Not enrolled	2.0	1.0	0.0
Weighted number of cases	1,435	1,620	839
Ages 14–18			
Total	100.0	100.0	100.0
Enrolled in school	76.4	100.0	100.0
Not enrolled	23.6	0.0	0.0
Weighted number of cases	220	200	81

legal status. School enrollment was defined to include nursery school and kindergarten as well as higher grades.

At ages 3 through 5, children of undocumented mothers had the lowest enrollment rates and children of mothers born in the United States the highest. At ages 6 through 13 the same pattern held, but almost all children were enrolled in school. At ages 14 through 18, almost 24 percent of the children of undocumented mothers were not enrolled in school whereas there were no children of this age not enrolled if their mother was native-born or a legal immigrant.

Relative progress in school

What about grade retardation or advance? I first defined a variable meant to measure relative progress in school. (If the current grade in which the child was enrolled less the child's own age plus 5 was greater than or equal to 1, the child's progress was defined to be advanced. If the current grade minus the child's age

Table 7.26. *Age-standardized percentage distribution by relative progress in school for children 5 to 17 years old of mothers in the study population subdivided by legal status of the mother*

Number of grades retarded or advanced	Legal status of mother		
	Undocumented	Legal immigrant	Native-born citizen
Total	100.0	100.0	100.0
Retarded two grades	12.2	3.3	1.2
Retarded one grade	34.9	29.5	24.6
Normal progress	47.7	59.5	64.6
Advanced one grade	5.2	7.8	9.6
Weighted number of cases	1,881	2,055	1,136

plus 5 was equal to 0, the relative progress was normal. If the current grade minus the child's age plus 5 was equal to -1, the child was retarded one grade. Finally, if the current grade minus the child's age plus 5 was equal to -2, I defined the child as being retarded two grades. Kindergarten was coded as grade 0 and nursery school as grade -1.) I then made separate tabulations for all children in the sample who were enrolled in school, including kindergarten and nursery school, at each single year of age from 5 through 17. In each tabulation, relative progress in school was cross-tabulated by the mother's legal status. I then summarized the data by computing for each of the three subgroups of children a measure of relative progress in school standardized for age (in which the age standard was the age composition of all of the enrolled children).

The results are shown in Table 7.26. As can be seen, children of undocumented mothers had a much higher percentage who were retarded one or more grades than children of native-born mothers. Children of legal immigrant mothers have an intermediate proportion retarded.

From all of the above, we must conclude that the children of undocumented mothers were clearly handicapped in educational attainment relative to the children of native-born mothers and somewhat disadvantaged relative to the children of mothers who were legal immigrants.

8. A comparison of the economic characteristics of undocumented immigrants, legal immigrants, and U.S. natives of Mexican origin

In this chapter we explore the extent to which undocumented Mexican immigrants, a legal underclass, also constituted an economic underclass. In summary of the most important findings, undocumented persons had low occupational status and very inferior income, but at least for males, the unemployment rate was not high. Although they made substantial use of entitlement programs, it was apparently only for their American-born children.

The survey findings relate to economic status at a single point in time. Thus they can provide no direct data either on the persistence of poverty or on intergenerational transmission of poverty. Nevertheless, the substantial difference shown here between the economic status of the undocumented and of U.S. natives of Mexican origin should give a hint as to how frequently the American-born children of the undocumented will be able to better the status of their parents.

The chapter discusses, for the three subgroups mentioned in the chapter title, the following characteristics: employment status and weeks worked in 1979; occupation, industry, and class of worker of those employed; income; participation in entitlement programs; and taxation. For each, data from this study are compared with data from other studies if such a comparison is warranted. Of course, one cannot presume that results found for Los Angeles County will necessarily be the same as for the nation as a whole.

Data on couple income are presented for all married couples. All other data pertain only to persons of Mexican origin. Table 7.1 presented the percentage distribution by Mexican origin for all mothers and fathers of the study sample subdivided by legal status.

For some but not all characteristics I include data concerning the unmarried brothers and childless sisters of respondents of Mexican origin. The former were defined as those brothers 18 to 44 years of age living in Los Angeles County who were not married with wife present and the latter as those sisters 18 to 39 years old living in Los Angeles County who had never born a child.

All tables in this chapter describe characteristics of the surveyed persons based on weighted data. For further information concerning the weights and the effects of using weighted rather than unweighted data, see the beginning of Chapter 7.

Employment status and weeks worked in 1979

Employment status

Table 8.1 presents data on the employment status of mothers, fathers, unmarried brothers, and childless sisters of Mexican origin subdivided by legal status.

A rather high proportion of the mothers were in the labor force despite the fact that all of them had just had a baby. The unemployment rate among undocumented and legal immigrant mothers appears to have been considerably higher than among the native-born. This unemployment may be related in part to the lack of English-speaking ability among those born outside the United States.

For fathers, legal status apparently made little difference with respect to employment status. That the unemployment rate for undocumented fathers was only 8.9 percent indicates that most of them did not find it difficult to find work despite the handicap of their legal state. A later section of this chapter reports on mother's labor force participation as a function of her legal status and her eligibility for means-tested entitlements.

Weeks worked in 1979 and hours worked per week

Table 8.2 presents, for mothers and fathers of Mexican origin subdivided by legal status, the percentage who worked at least one week in 1979, and for those who worked at least one week in 1979 the percentage distribution by number of weeks worked in that year. Few differences by legal status are apparent.

A larger proportion of American-born mothers apparently worked at least one week in 1979 than did undocumented mothers or legal immigrant mothers (52.0 percent). For fathers working at least one week in 1979, the proportion who worked 49 weeks or more was apparently less among the undocumented than among either the legal immigrants or the native-born.

For mothers and fathers of Mexican origin who worked at least one week in 1979, tabulations were also made of the percentage distribution by number of hours usually worked per week in that year. No differences by legal status appeared for either mothers or fathers.

Tabulations were also made of the percentage distribution by number of hours worked in the week preceding the interview for mothers and fathers of Mexican origin who worked that week. Again no substantial differences by legal status appeared. A more complete multivariate analysis of the determinants of the annual number of hours worked in 1979 appears in Chapter 10.

Table 8.1. *Percentage distribution by employment status of mothers, fathers, unmarried brothers, and childless sisters of Mexican origin subdivided by legal status*

Employment status	Mother's legal status			Father's legal status			Brother's legal status			Sister's legal status		
	Un-docu-ment-ed	Legal immi-grant	Native-born citizen	Un-docu-ment-ed	Legal immi-grant	Native-born citizen	Un-docu-ment-ed	Legal immi-grant	Native-born citizen	Un-docu-ment-ed	Legal immi-grant	Native-born citizen
Total	100.0	100.0	100.0	100.0	100.0	100.0	100.0	100.0	100.0	100.0	100.0	100.0
Employed	22.0	27.8	31.5	89.7	91.5	86.6	87.1	83.7	71.4	73.4	57.5	72.1
Unemployed	7.6	5.4	1.4	8.8	5.0	6.9	5.4	7.7	21.2	10.5	7.3	10.8
Not in labor force	70.4	66.9	67.1	1.5	3.5	6.5	7.6	8.7	7.5	16.1	35.3	17.2
Percentage of labor force unemployed	25.8	16.2	4.3	8.9	5.1	7.4	5.8	8.4	22.9	12.5	11.3	13.1
Weighted number of cases	3,298	1,711	1,831	2,752	1,655	1,320	965	416	936	466	329	598

Table 8.2. *Percentage who worked one week or more in 1979 and percentage distribution by number of weeks worked in 1979 among those working one or more weeks for mothers and fathers of Mexican origin who lived 12 months in the United States in 1979 subdivided by legal status*

	Mother's legal status			Father's legal status		
Weeks worked in 1979	Un-docu-ment-ed	Legal immi-grant	Native-born citizen	Un-docu-ment-ed	Legal immi-grant	Native-born citizen
Percentage who worked one week or more	50.0	52.0	59.9	98.8	97.1	95.3
Weighted number of cases	2,911	1,649	1,807	2,562	1,605	1,286
Working one week or more						
Total	100.0	100.0	100.0	100.0	100.0	100.0
1–26 weeks	26.1	32.3	29.2	5.0	4.4	7.0
27–48 weeks	21.3	18.4	24.9	16.9	12.6	9.5
49 weeks or more	52.6	49.2	45.9	78.1	83.0	83.4
Weighted number of cases working one week or more	1,456	857	1,082	2,532	1,559	1,226

Occupation, industry, and class of worker

Occupation

Table 8.3 presents the percentage distribution by occupational group for employed Mexican-origin mothers subdivided by legal status. The table also presents the percentage distribution by occupational group for all employed females and all employed females of Hispanic origin in Los Angeles County according to the 1980 Census.[1] The occupational groups shown in Table 8.3 were purposely selected to include greater detail for occupations that were overrepresented in the sample of mothers than for those that were underrepresented.

A striking feature of the table is the very high proportions of undocumented and legal immigrant mothers who were sewing machine operators. Also noteworthy is the relatively high percentage of the undocumented women who were private household workers, a figure considerably higher than the proportions for the other two groups of mothers or for female workers in Los Angeles County as a whole. Another striking feature of the table is the much higher proportions of native-born than of immigrant women found in sales or administrative support occupations.

Table 8.3. *Percentage distribution by occupational group for (1) all employed women in Los Angeles County, 1980, (2) employed women of Hispanic origin in Los Angeles County, 1980, and (3) employed mothers of Mexican origin subdivided by legal status*

	All employed women	Employed women of Hispanic origin	Mother's legal status		
			Un-documented	Legal immigrant	Native-born citizen
Total	100.0	100.0	100.0	100.0	100.0
Executive, administrative, and managerial occupations	9.5	4.6	0.0	0.0	0.0
Health professionals	3.3	1.1	0.0	0.0	0.0
Teachers	5.2	2.4	0.0	0.0	5.7
Other professionals	4.4	1.8	0.6	2.5	2.6
Technicians and related support occupations	2.8	1.4	0.0	0.0	2.1
Sales occupations	10.7	7.6	2.5	4.6	8.9
Administrative support occupations, including clerical	34.5	26.6	1.4	13.9	50.7
Private household occupations	1.7	4.3	7.1	0.8	0.0
Other service occupations	13.0	14.9	6.5	14.3	14.6
Farm, forestry, and fishing occupations; transportation and material moving occupations; handlers, equipment cleaners, helpers, and laborers	3.0	6.1	11.6	9.7	5.7
Precision production, craft, and repair occupations	3.2	5.6	7.6	8.4	3.1
Textile sewing machine operators	2.4	7.9	29.4	27.4	1.0
Other machine operators, assemblers, and inspectors	6.3	15.7	33.2	18.3	5.6
Weighted number of cases			708	475	576

Source: For 1980 Census data, U.S. Bureau of the Census *1980 Census of Population*, PC80-1-D6, (Washington, D.C.: Government Printing Office, 1983), pp. 712–21.

Table 8.4. *Percentage distribution by occupational group for (1) all employed men in Los Angeles County, 1980, (2) employed men of Hispanic origin in Los Angeles County, 1980, and (3) employed fathers of Mexican origin subdivided by legal status*

	All employed men	Employed men of Hispanic origin	Father's legal status		
			Un-documented	Legal immigrant	Native-born citizen
Total	100.0	100.0	100.0	100.0	100.0
Executive, administrative, and managerial occupations	13.5	5.2	0.0	1.0	2.9
Professional specialty occupations	12.8	3.8	0.0	3.1	7.4
Technicians and related support occupations	3.3	1.6	0.0	0.9	8.2
Sales occupations	9.5	4.8	2.0	4.2	5.4
Administrative support occupations, including clerical	8.6	7.3	1.3	4.3	8.3
Service occupations	9.7	13.3	13.4	6.5	5.3
Farming, forestry, and fishing occupations	1.7	3.0	4.3	1.1	0.5
Mechanics and repairers	5.8	6.2	4.9	5.8	15.0
Construction trades	6.0	6.3	7.4	5.6	9.8
Other precision production, craft and repair occupations	7.2	9.2	9.7	16.0	6.3
Machine operators, assemblers, and inspectors	10.7	23.0	38.3	31.9	20.6
Transportation and material moving occupations	5.7	6.7	1.9	10.5	3.9
Handlers, equipment cleaners, helpers, and laborers	5.7	9.8	16.9	9.1	6.3
Weighted number of cases			2,441	1,509	1,143

Source: For 1980 Census data, same as for Table 8.3.

Tabulations of the percentage distribution by occupational group for employed childless sisters subdivided by legal status showed no large differences from the percentage distribution for mothers.

Table 8.4 presents the percentage distribution by occupational group for employed Mexican-origin fathers subdivided by legal status. The table presents also the percentage distribution by occupational group for all employed males and all employed males of Hispanic origin in Los Angeles County.[2] The occupational groups are presented in more detail for those occupations in which the largest number of fathers were found.

As can be seen from the table, undocumented fathers were substantially overrepresented as machine operators and as handlers, equipment cleaners, helpers, and laborers.

Additional tabulations of the percentage distribution by occupational group for employed unmarried brothers subdivided by legal status showed a pattern very similar to that for the fathers.

The data in Tables 8.3 and 8.4 may be compared with the data on current occupation reported by Van Arsdol et al. concerning undocumented clients of the One-Stop Immigration Service in Los Angeles. Comparability of the two data sets is impaired because the data gathered by Van Arsdol et al. were coded according to the categories of the 1970 Census; in many respects this coding scheme is quite different from that used in the 1980 Census and in the Los Angeles County Parents Survey. Nevertheless, both studies show the great majority of both men and women to be in blue-collar nonfarm occupations.[3]

Industry

Table 8.5 presents the percentage distribution by industry for employed mothers of Mexican origin subdivided by legal status together with comparable data for all employed females and all employed females of Spanish origin in Los Angeles County according to the 1980 Census.[4] The more detailed industry groups chosen for special emphasis were those containing the largest number of sampled mothers.

The most striking finding is the relative concentration of undocumented mothers in the apparel industry. Additional tabulations of the percentage distribution by industry for employed childless sisters subdivided by legal status showed a pattern very similar to that for the undocumented mothers.

Table 8.6 presents the percentage distribution by industry for employed fathers of Mexican origin subdivided by legal status together with 1980 Census data for all employed males and all employed males of Hispanic origin.[5] Industries that employed a high number of sampled fathers have been singled out for special attention.

As might be expected from what we have seen from the previous tables, undocumented fathers were very much underrepresented in such industries as transport, communications, and public utilities, other retail trade, finance, insurance real

Table 8.5. *Percentage distribution by industry for (1) employed women in Los Angeles County, 1980, (2) employed women of Hispanic origin in Los Angeles County, 1980, and (3) employed mothers of Mexican origin subdivided by legal status*

| | All employed women | Employed women of Hispanic origin | Mother's legal status | | |
			Un-documented	Legal immigrant	Native-born citizen
Total	100.0	100.0	100.0	100.0	100.0
Agriculture, forestry, and fisheries; mining; construction	1.6	1.4	0.6	0.0	0.0
Food-industries manufacturing	0.9	0.9	1.1	2.2	0.0
Apparel and other finished textile products	3.5	10.6	37.9	28.1	2.7
Other nondurable goods manufacturing	3.9	7.5	9.3	12.7	7.4
Electrical machinery, equipment, and supplies	2.7	4.3	6.2	7.3	1.4
Other durable goods manufacturing; not specified manufacturing industries	8.8	12.5	22.0	11.2	9.0
Transportation, communications, and other public utilities	5.3	3.6	2.3	2.2	4.8
Wholesale trade	3.6	3.4	1.7	3.9	0.0
General merchandise stores	3.4	3.2	0.0	1.3	1.6
Eating and drinking places	4.7	4.2	2.3	7.3	4.2
Other retail trade	8.2	6.3	4.5	2.2	15.2
Finance, insurance, and real estate	9.9	6.8	0.0	4.8	14.6
Business and repair services; Entertainment and recreation services	6.6	3.9	2.5	0.0	7.9
Private households	2.0	4.7	7.1	0.9	0.0
Other personal services	2.9	3.8	0.9	1.3	3.2
Health services	11.8	8.8	0.9	7.3	12.5
Educational services	11.0	8.2	0.0	7.3	8.5
Other professional services	5.9	3.4	0.0	0.0	1.4
Public administration	3.4	2.7	0.9	0.0	5.6
Weighted number of cases			708	463	567

Source: For 1980 Census data; U.S. Bureau of the Census, *1980 Census of Population,* PC80-1-D6, pp. 1423–5.

Table 8.6. *Percentage distribution by industry for (1) all employed men in Los Angeles County, 1980, (2) employed men of Hispanic origin in Los Angeles County, 1980, and (3) employed fathers of Mexican origin subdivided by legal status*

			Father's legal status		
	All employed men	Employed men of Hispanic origin	Un-docu-ment-ed	Legal immi-grant	Native-born citizen
Total	100.0	100.0	100.0	100.0	100.0
Agriculture, forestry, and fisheries	1.5	2.6	4.6	1.1	0.5
Mining: construction	7.4	7.6	12.5	7.9	10.0
Food-industries manufacturing	1.5	2.6	4.4	4.8	1.4
Apparel and other finished textile products	1.2	2.9	5.0	5.0	0.8
Other nondurable goods manufacturing	5.4	7.3	11.1	7.5	11.6
Furniture and fixtures manufacturing	1.3	3.6	4.6	4.2	1.7
Primary metal industries; fabricated metal industries	3.6	6.6	5.7	9.0	8.5
Machinery except electrical	3.4	3.9	2.8	5.5	4.3
Electrical machinery, equipment, and supplies	2.7	2.7	2.9	3.4	4.2
Aircraft, space vehicles, and parts	5.6	3.2	3.6	3.6	1.4
Other transportation equipment	1.5	2.5	3.6	2.3	0.8
Other durable goods manufacturing; not specified manufacturing industries	3.6	5.8	12.3	12.2	6.8
Transportation, communications, and other public utilities	8.6	6.5	2.1	4.5	9.8
Wholesale trade	5.7	5.3	3.0	2.6	0.0
Eating and drinking places	3.9	6.4	8.9	3.6	2.4
Other retail trade	10.8	9.4	5.1	10.3	8.3
Finance, insurance, and real estate; professional and related services	17.4	8.8	0.7	5.0	10.7
Business and repair services	6.7	6.4	5.6	4.9	7.3
Personal services; entertainment and recreation services	4.7	3.8	1.7	1.2	1.6
Public administration	3.6	2.1	0.0	1.5	7.9
Weighted number of cases			2,437	1,461	1,113

Source: For 1980 Census data, same as for Table 8.5.

Table 8.7. *Percentage distribution by class of workers for employed mothers and fathers of Mexican origin subdivided by legal status*

	Mother's legal status			Father's legal status		
	Un-docu-ment-ed	Legal immi-grant	Native-born citizen	Un-docu-ment-ed	Legal immi-grant	Native-born citizen
Total	100.0	100.0	100.0	100.0	100.0	100.0
Private wage and salary workers	96.9	92.0	73.8	97.0	89.0	81.1
Government workers	0.9	7.2	22.1	0.2	6.9	16.2
Self-employed workers	2.3	0.8	0.0	2.9	4.2	3.8
Unpaid family workers	0.0	0.0	4.2	0.0	0.0	0.0
Weighted number of cases	708	475	576	2,469	1,515	1,143

estate, and professional services, personal, entertainment, and recreation services, and in public administration.

They were overrepresented in most manufacturing industries with the exception of aircraft and machinery, except electrical. However, I am also struck with the fact that the undocumented fathers were not concentrated in just a few manufacturing industries. With the exception of the "white-collar" industries, the undocumented fathers sampled appear to be employed in a wide range of different types of industry.

Tabulations of the percentage distribution by industry for employed unmarried brothers subdivided by legal status are very similar to the data for fathers. However, a higher proportion of the unmarried brothers than of the fathers appear to have had jobs in agriculture or in eating and drinking places.

Class of worker

Table 8.7 presents the percentage distribution by class of workers for employed Mexican-origin mothers and fathers subdivided by legal status. The most salient feature of the table is the much higher proportion of native-born mothers and fathers found in government employment. This difference is undoubtedly due to the fact that most government employment demands not only a knowledge of English but also U.S. citizenship.

Table 8.8. *Percentage distribution by total personal income in 1979 for mothers and fathers of Mexican origin who lived twelve months in the United States in 1979 subdivided by legal status (Part A) and mean 1979 income of males and females in Los Angeles County 15 years old and over with income in 1979 by race and ethnicity (Part B)*

Part A

Income in 1979	Mother's legal status			Father's legal status		
	Undocu-mented	Legal immi-grant	Native-born citizen	Undocu-mented	Legal immi-grant	Native-born citizen
Total	100.0	100.0	100.0	100.0	100.0	100.0
None	47.5	46.7	29.7	3.1	4.8	7.5
$100–$2,900	13.5	12.0	15.2	4.0	0.9	2.3
$3,000–$5,900	20.4	12.5	16.0	12.0	4.5	5.6
$6,000–$9,900	18.2	23.4	25.1	54.4	31.3	17.9
$10,000–$14,900	0.3	4.7	11.5	20.6	37.9	33.1
$15,000 and over	0.0	0.7	2.5	5.8	20.7	33.6
Mean income of all persons	$2,507	$3,135	$4,562	$8,222	$11,472	$12,200
Weighted number of cases	2,917	1,649	1,816	2,578	1,635	1,286
Mean income of persons with income	$4,774	$5,881	$6,492	$8,485	$12,047	$13,185
Weighted number of cases	1,532	879	1,276	2,498	1,557	1,190

Part B

Mean 1979 income of persons in Los Angeles County 15 years old and over with income in 1979	Total	Black	Hispanic origin
Males	$16,875	$11,614	$11,098
Females	$8,438	$7,755	$6,483

Source: For data in Part B, U.S. Bureau of the Census, *1980 Census of Population,* PC80-1-D6, pp. 1903–4.

Income

Methodological remarks

The items dealing with income on the questionnaire were almost identical to those of the 1980 Census. However, income received while residing outside the United States was tallied separately from income received while residing in the United States. In all, ten different classes of income were recorded, and each of these was tallied separately dependent upon whether it was received while the person was in the United States or outside the United States. The questions on income were asked separately for mothers and for fathers. The sum of these two incomes was recorded as couple income.

Individual income

Part A of Table 8.8 presents data on the percentage distribution by income in 1979 of mothers and fathers of Mexican origin who lived 12 months in the United States in 1979. Presented also are figures on mean income both for all such persons and for those persons with income.

As shown in Part A, for both mothers and fathers, income was highest for those born in the United States, intermediate for those who were legal immigrants, and lowest for the undocumented.

The data from Part A on mean income for those persons with income can be compared with 1980 Census data for Los Angeles County, shown in Part B of Table 8.8.[6] The mean income of undocumented fathers with income ($8,485) from the survey was little more than one-half the census figure for all males with income, and less than three-quarters that of black males with income. Conversely, from the survey, both the mean income of legal-immigrant fathers ($12,047) and that of native-born fathers of Mexican descent ($13,185) exceed that from the census for all black males.

The mean income of undocumented mothers with income was $4,774, less than three-fifths that for all females with income and little more than three-fifths that for all black females with income. The survey figures for legal-immigrant mothers and for native-born mothers of Mexican descent were also somewhat lower than for black females. One must keep in mind that all of the survey figures for females pertain to recent mothers, many of whom may have worked fewer weeks in 1979 than the average for all females in the county.

Table 8.9. *Percentage distribution by couple income for legally and consensually married couples in which both husband and wife were in the United States twelve months in 1979 subdivided by legal status of mother and father*

Income in 1979	Mother's legal status			Father's legal status		
	Undocu-mented	Legal immi-grant	Native-born citizen	Undocu-mented	Legal immi-grant	Native-born citizen
Total	100.0	100.0	100.0	100.0	100.0	100.0
Under $6,000	11.9	6.6	5.2	11.3	5.8	7.2
$6,000–$9,900	39.4	17.9	14.0	37.8	21.5	13.1
$10,000–$14,900	30.3	34.2	21.6	31.7	29.8	23.8
$15,000–$19,900	14.4	18.3	27.1	14.7	22.7	21.4
$20,000 and over	4.0	23.1	32.2	4.5	20.1	34.5
Mean income	$10,475	$14,858	$17,338	$10,727	$14,557	$17,189
Weighted number of cases	2,501	1,574	1,453	2,450	1,676	1,402

Couple income

Table 8.9 presents data on couple income for couples in which both husband and wife had been in the United States for 12 months during 1979. The table includes both legally and consensually married couples providing the two considered each other husband and wife. Data are presented separately according to the legal status of the mother and according to the legal status of the father.

It is evident that the highest couple income occurred for couples in which the mother (or the father) was native-born, and the lowest for couples in which the mother (or the father) was undocumented.

Hourly wage in relation to the minimum wage

The questions on total earnings in 1979, total weeks worked in 1979, and usual number of hours worked per week in 1979 were used to compute an average hourly wage. This wage could also be compared with the legal minimum wage in 1979, which was $2.90. Table 8.10 presents the percentage distribution by whether the actual wage in 1979 was or was not below the minimum legal wage for mothers and fathers of Mexican origin subdivided by legal status. As can be seen, 13 percent of the undocumented fathers were reported to have received a wage below the legal

Table 8.10. *Percentage distribution by whether average hourly wage in 1979 was below the minimum wage for mothers and fathers of Mexican origin who were in the United States 12 months in 1979 and earned a wage subdivided by legal status*

Wage in 1979 relative to minimum wage	Mother's legal status			Father's legal status		
	Un-docu-mented	Legal immi-grant	Native-born citizen	Un-docu-mented	Legal immi-grant	Native-born citizen
Total	100.0	100.0	100.0	100.0	100.0	100.0
Below minimum wage	54.0	15.8	15.0	12.9	3.1	1.8
Minimum wage or more	46.0	84.2	85.0	87.2	96.9	98.2
Weighted number of cases	1,414	841	1,055	2,474	1,533	1,157

minimum as compared to 3 percent of the legal immigrant fathers and 2 percent of the native-born fathers. The proportions of mothers reporting that they received a wage below the legal minimum were considerably higher than among fathers; among undocumented mothers it was 54 percent, among legal immigrant mothers 16 percent, and among the native-born 15 percent.

The data on Table 8.10 can be compared with the data from North and Houstoun's study of apprehended illegal aliens who had worked in the United States for at least two weeks. They reported that among the 766 respondents who gave full information, 23.8 percent received below the minimum wage.[7] The reader may recall that 61 percent of their total sample of 793 was from Mexico and that 90.8 percent were male. A more complete multivariate analysis of the determinants of 1979 earnings and the 1979 average wage is found in Chapter 10.

Participation in entitlement programs

In general, undocumented persons in the United States are not allowed access to benefits from entitlement programs. Specifically, they may not receive funds from the Food Stamp Program, Aid to Families with Dependent Children (AFDC), the Medicaid program (called Medi-Cal in California), public housing, the Comprehensive Employment Training Administration (CETA) program, or unemployment insurance. Nevertheless, the American-born children of undocumented parents are in all cases native-born citizens of the United States and are fully eligible to all benefits from entitlement programs. This provision of the law is extremely important with respect to AFDC, food stamps, and Medicaid. American-born children of undocumented parents are fully eligible for each of these programs.

At the time the Los Angeles County Parents Survey was conducted, the legal provisions forbidding access to entitlement programs for the undocumented were well enforced with respect to all programs administered by the Los Angeles County Department of Public Social Services (DPSS): namely, food stamps, AFDC, general assistance, and Medi-Cal. According to DPSS procedure, all applicants for benefits who could not show that they were either U.S. citizens or permanent legal residents were told that their names would be submitted to the Immigration and Naturalization Service for verification as to their legal status. As a result of this procedure, there were in 1980 19,088 original applicants for benefits in the county who withdrew their request rather than give their names and addresses to the INS.[8]

In contrast to the rigorous screening procedure of the Los Angeles County DPSS has been the "honor system" used to screen applicants for unemployment insurance benefits by the State of California Employment Development Department. Applicants for unemployment benefits must certify that they are either citizens or permanent legal residents, but no verification procedure is used.[9] North conducted a five-year follow-up study of 192 illegal aliens apprehended in California by the INS in February 1975 and forced to leave the United States. All of these persons had a valid social security number. Seventy-seven percent of this group were found to have worked in California at some time during the five years following their deportation. Furthermore, of those who did work in California following their deportation, fully 35 percent received unemployment insurance at some time during the follow-up period.[10]

The questions on access to entitlement programs in my survey used the respondent's family (which in every case included at least one American-born child) as the unit of reference for receipt of benefits from entitlement programs such as food stamps, Medi-Cal, and public housing. Payments from the AFDC program to mothers directly or to mothers on behalf of their American-born children were included as part of the income for mothers. Payments under the AFDC program for unemployed fathers were included as part of the father's income.

Food stamps

Table 8.11 presents data concerning current monthly income from food stamps according to the legal status of the mother. Almost 19 percent of all families in which the mother was of Mexican origin and undocumented received some food stamp income. This percentage was almost the same as that receiving some food stamp income among the other two groups of mothers. However, among families receiving food stamps, the median and mean amounts received were substantially less for the families where the mother was undocumented than for families where either the mother was a legal immigrant or native-born. These results lend credence

Table 8.11. *Percentage distribution of current monthly income from food stamps for families of mothers of Mexican origin subdivided by legal status*

	Legal status of mother		
Food stamp income	Undocumented	Legal immigrant	Native-born citizen
Total	100.0	100.0	100.00
None	81.13	84.15	80.72
$1–$24	1.04	1.30	1.80
$25–$49	9.75	2.72	1.97
$50–$74	3.28	3.19	3.93
$75–$99	1.78	3.31	4.59
$100–$149	2.33	2.96	4.21
$150–$199	0.37	2.37	1.97
$200–$299	0.31	0.00	0.82
Weighted number of cases	3,260	1,691	1,831
Among families receiving payments			
Median amount	$42.00	$78.00	$83.00
Mean amount	$60.82	$83.50	$92.58

to the hypothesis that families where the mother was undocumented probably received only what they were entitled to by law: namely, food stamps for their American-born children.

Aid to families with dependent children

Table 8.12 presents data concerning (1) the proportion of all mothers of Mexican origin receiving AFDC income in 1979 (reported either as her own income or that of her husband), and (2) the proportion receiving AFDC income in 1979 for that subgroup of mothers of Mexican origin that was most likely to be eligible for such benefits: mothers who were not legally married at the time of interview, lived in the United States for 12 months in 1979, and had one or more children aged 2 or older born in the United States at the time of interview.

Table 8.12 shows that for this restricted group of mothers about 19 percent of those who were undocumented received AFDC benefits as compared to 21 percent of those who were legal immigrants and 46 percent of those born in the United States. The corresponding figures for the three classes of mothers in the total sample are considerably less: 2 percent for undocumented mothers, 3 percent for legal immigrant mothers, and 13 percent for mothers born in the United States.

Table 8.12 also shows the median and mean amounts of AFDC income received

Table 8.12. *Percentage distribution by receipt of income in 1979 from aid to families with dependent children for (1) all families with a Mexican-origin mother subdivided by legal status of the mother, and (2) families with a Mexican-origin mother who was not legally married at time of interview, lived in the United States for twelve months in 1979, and had one or more children aged 2 or older born in the United States at time of interview subdivided by legal status of the mother; and median and mean amounts of AFDC income received by all families where the mother was of Mexican origin and lived in the United States for twelve months in 1979 subdivided by legal status of the mother*

	Legal status of mother		
1979 AFDC Income	Undocumented	Legal immigrant	Native-born citizen
All Mexican-origin mothers			
Total	100.0	100.0	100.0
None	98.1	97.1	87.4
$1 or more	1.9	2.9	12.6
Weighted number of cases	3,298	1,711	1,831
Subgroup of mothers most likely to be eligible			
Total	100.0	100.0	100.0
None	81.3	79.1	54.1
$1 or more	18.7	20.9	45.9
Weighted number of cases	299	134	281
Among families receiving benefits			
Median Amount	$2,800	$3,600	$5,700
Mean Amount	$3,290	$3,750	$5,697
Weighted number of cases	62	44	230

in 1979 by the legal status of all mothers of Mexican origin residing in the United States for 12 months in 1979 and receiving some AFDC income (reported either as her own income or that of her husband). Congruent with what was evident with respect to food stamp income, the median and mean amounts received by the undocumented mothers appear to be considerably less than those received by mothers born in the United States and somewhat less than those received by mothers who were legal immigrants to the United States. However, these medians and means are based on small numbers; only 35 women in the sample received AFDC income, and of these only 6 were legal immigrants.

Table 8.13. *Percentage of all AFDC cases in which there were one or more illegal aliens in the household, by type of AFDC case, for California and five regions thereof, July 1979, January 1981, and July 1983, and percentage of all AFDC cases in which there were one or more illegal aliens who were parents of an assisted child, by type of AFDC Case, for California and five regions thereof, January 1981 and July 1983*

	Percentage with illegal alien in the household			Percentage with illegal alien parent in the household	
	July 1979	Jan. 1981	July 1983	Jan. 1981	July 1983
Family group cases					
California	2.5	4.4	7.2	3.5	6.6
Region 1	0.0	0.0	2.5	0.0	1.3
Region 2	0.0	3.0	4.1	1.0	4.1
Region 3	0.0	1.0	5.6	1.0	5.6
Region 4	0.0	0.7	4.5	0.7	4.5
Region 5	6.1	9.0	11.6	7.8	10.3
Size of California sample	588	658	595	658	595
Unemployed cases					
California	2.6	4.5	7.3	4.1	6.9
Region 1	1.3	1.9	1.1	1.9	1.1
Region 2	0.9	2.1	0.7	1.4	0.7
Region 3	3.8	1.1	4.1	1.1	4.1
Region 4	1.0	3.0	1.6	3.0	1.6
Region 5	5.1	10.2	21.1	9.2	19.7
Size of California sample	540	714	523	714	523

Note: Region 1–Alpine, Amador, Butte, Calaveras, Del Norte, El Dorado, Glenn, Humboldt, Inyo, Lake, Lassen, Mariposa, Mendocino, Modoc, Mono, Napa, Nevada, Placer, Plumas, Shasta, Sierra, Siskiyou, Sonoma, Sutter, Tehama, Trinity, Tuolomne, and Yuba counties; Region 2–Colusa, Fresno, Kings, Madera, Merced, Sacramento, San Joaquin, Solano, Stanislaus, Tulare, and Yolo Counties; Region 3–Alameda, Contra Costa, Marin, Monterey, San Benito, San Francisco, San Mateo, Santa Clara, and Santa Cruz Counties; Region 4–Imperial, Kern, Orange, Riverside, San Bernardino, San Diego, San Luis Obispo, Santa Barbara, and Ventura Counties; Region 5–Los Angeles County.

Sources: California State Department of Social Services, *Aid to Families with Dependent Children: Social and Economic Characteristics of Families Receiving Aid during July 1979; Aid to Families with Dependent Children: Social and Economic Characteristics of Families Receiving Aid during January 1981;* and *Aid to Families with Dependent Children: Social and Economic Characteristics of Families Receiving Aid during July 1983* (Sacramento: California DSS, 1981, 1982, and 1985).

It is appropriate to mention at this point some very interesting results concerning the proportion of AFDC cases in California in which one or more illegal aliens were living in the same household as the assisted persons. These results are contained in the publications of the California Department of Social Services mentioned in Chapter 4.[11] As was mentioned in that chapter, the department takes periodic surveys of the characteristics of persons in AFDC recipient cases. The department defines a case as the group of assisted persons living in the same household. Separate random samples are taken of cases in the "family group" type (i.e., with an absent father) and in the "unemployed" type (i.e., with an unemployed parent usually the father). These surveys sample a minimum of 500 cases in each type. The surveys conducted in July 1979, January 1981, and July 1983 inquired concerning the number of illegal aliens who were members of the same household as the assisted persons in the given case. Moreover, the surveys of January 1981 and July 1983 asked whether the illegal aliens present in the household were a parent of an assisted child, a child, or an adult who was not a parent of an assisted child.

A recapitulation of some of the published results from these three surveys is found in Table 8.13. For California and each of five Californian regions, the table presents, in the left-hand columns, the percentage of cases in which there were one or more illegal aliens in the household; the right-hand columns present the percentage of cases in which one or more illegal aliens in the household were parents of an aided child.

By July 1983 for the state as a whole and for Region 5 (Los Angeles County) in particular, a substantial proportion of both "family group" cases and of "unemployed" cases contained in the household at least one illegal alien who was a parent of an assisted child. In that year 6.6 percent of family group cases in California and 10.3 percent of family group cases in Los Angeles county contained in the household at least one illegal alien who was the parent of an assisted child. Among the unemployed cases the corresponding proportions were 6.9 percent and 19.7 percent. Moreover, in the two years for which data are available, a very high proportion of all cases having one or more illegal aliens in the household also contained an illegal alien who was a parent of an assisted child.

Table 8.13 also shows substantial increases from July 1979 to July 1983 in the proportion of cases with an illegal alien in the household. For the state as a whole, this four-year change is statistically significant both for the family group cases and for the unemployed cases. For Region 5 (Los Angeles County), it is statistically significant at the .01 level for the unemployed cases and at the .05 level for the family group cases.

Accordingly, it may be of some interest to estimate the increase in the number of AFDC cases, by type, that contained at least one illegal alien in the household and that contained at least one illegal alien who was a parent of an assisted child.

Table 8.14. *Estimated number of AFDC cases in which there were one or more illegal aliens in the household, by type of AFDC case, for California and Los Angeles County, July 1979, January 1981, and July 1983 and estimated number of AFDC cases in which there was an illegal alien who was a parent of the assisted child, by type of AFDC case, for California and Los Angeles County, January 1981 and July 1983*

| | Number with illegal alien in the household | | | Number with illegal alien parent in the household | |
	July 1979	Jan. 1981	July 1983	Jan. 1981	July 1983
Family group cases					
California	10,244	19,530	32,878	15,535	30,138
Los Angeles County	9,963	14,963	20,619	12,968	18,308
Unemployed cases					
California	850	2,830	6,134	2,579	5,798
Los Angeles County	459	1,843	4,905	1,662	4,580

Sources: Same as for Table 8.13 and the following publications of the California State Department of Social Services: *Public Welfare in California, July 1979; Public Welfare in California, January 1981;* and *Public Welfare in California, July 1983.*

This estimate has been done both for California as a whole and for Los Angeles County by multiplying the percentage from Table 8.13 by the total number of AFDC cases, by type, as reported by the California State Department of Social Services in another publication.[12] The results are shown in Table 8.14.

Although the results must be treated cautiously because of the sampling error involved, there does appear to have been both for California and for Los Angeles County an astounding increase in a very short period in the number of AFDC cases in which an illegal alien was reported as the parent of an assisted child. It is possible that this increase can be explained entirely by a very rapid growth of undocumented persons in the state. However, in my opinion, it is more likely that the increased number of cases was caused not only by an increase in the number of undocumented persons but also by an increased tendency among the undocumented to apply for AFDC benefits on behalf of their American-born children.

Unemployment insurance

Table 8.15 presents data for Mexican-origin mothers and fathers who worked 1 to 49 weeks in the United States in 1979 concerning whether they received unem-

Table 8.15. *Percentage distribution by whether received unemployment insurance benefits in 1979 for mothers and fathers of Mexican origin who worked 1 to 49 weeks in the United States in 1979 subdivided by legal status*

Receipt of benefits	Mother's legal status			Father's legal status		
	Un-docu-ment-ed	Legal immi-grant	Native-born citizen	Un-docu-ment-ed	Legal immi-grant	Native-born citizen
Total	100.0	100.0	100.0	100.0	100.0	100.0
Yes	3.7	7.8	4.0	13.7	18.8	7.4
No	96.3	92.2	96.0	86.3	81.2	92.6
Weighted number of cases	694	437	594	577	309	242

ployment insurance benefits. Only 3.8 percent of undocumented mothers received unemployment benefits versus 4.0 percent of the legal immigrants and 7.8 percent of the native-born. However, 13.7 percent of the undocumented fathers received unemployment benefits as contrasted with 19 percent of the legal immigrant fathers and 7 percent of the native-born fathers. The findings shown in this table corroborate the previously mentioned findings of David North that undocumented persons in California apparently experienced little difficulty in collecting unemployment benefits even though they were not legally allowed them.

Medi-Cal program

A continuing source of controversy in Los Angeles County has concerned the provision of medical services to indigent undocumented aliens. In March 1981, the Los Angeles County Board of Supervisors voted to require all applicants for nonemergency medical care who could not pay for such care to seek enrollment in the Medi-Cal program. This policy in effect meant that such persons would become liable to deportation because their names would be sent to the INS to verify their legal status. However, this action by the County Board of Supervisors was challenged in court by the County Health Alliance; on May 12, 1981, the Superior Court for Los Angeles County granted the County Health Alliance a preliminary injunction prohibiting the county from enforcing the new law. This injunction is still in effect.[13] In 1982 the chief administrative officer of Los Angeles County estimated that the annual cost to the county of health benefits for undocumented aliens was $76.5 million. Within this sum he further estimated that $1.9 million

Table 8.16. *Percentage distribution by whether the family was enrolled in the Medi-Cal program for mothers of Mexican origin subdivided by legal status*

Enrollment in Medi-Cal	Legal status of mother		
	Undocumented	Legal immigrant	Native-born citizen
Total	100.0	100.0	100.0
Yes	19.8	19.6	41.4
Only the baby	4.2	0.0	1.6
No	76.0	80.4	57.0
Weighted number of cases	3,298	1,711	1,831

was spent for unreimbursed costs of childbirth at county hospitals.[14] With respect to childbirth, the law allows the hospital expenses following birth of an American-born child of undocumented indigent parents to be paid for by Medi-Cal; however, the actual expenses for child delivery of an undocumented parent cannot be paid from Medi-Cal funding and are paid by the county if no other source of payment is forthcoming.

Table 8.16 presents data on the use of the Medi-Cal program. Respondents were asked, "Is your family registered in the Medi-Cal program?" Perhaps the wording should have been "Is any member of your family registered . . .?" because in families where the parents were undocumented, only the American-born children were legally eligible for the program. Some respondents answered the question with the statement "Only the baby." Others no doubt answered the question affirmatively when only their American-born children were registered. The table shows that someone in the family was enrolled in Medi-Cal among 24 percent of the families where the mother was undocumented, among 20 percent of the cases where the mother was a legal immigrant, and among 43 percent of the cases where the mother was born in the United States.

Public housing

Table 8.17 presents data for mothers of Mexican origin by legal status concerning whether she and her family were living in public or publicly subsidized housing. Approximately 1 percent of the undocumented mothers said they were living in such housing as contrasted with 3 percent of the legal immigrants and 6 percent of the native-born. Thus undocumented families do not appear to be living in housing from which they are legally barred.

Table 8.17. *Percentage distribution by whether the family was living in public or publicly subsidized housing for mothers of Mexican origin subdivided by legal status*

Residence in public or publicly subsidized housing	Legal status of mother		
	Undocumented	Legal immigrant	Native-born citizen
Total	100.0	100.0	100.0
Yes	1.2	3.3	6.5
No	97.4	96.1	93.5
Don't know	1.5	0.6	0.0
Weighted number of cases	3,298	1,711	1,804

Other entitlement programs

We have yet to consider certain other entitlement programs from which information was collected concerning benefits received. These include social security and railroad retirement, available to the elderly and to survivors of insured workers; Supplemental Security Income (SSI), which is available to the disabled; and other public assistance or welfare payments. To what extent can undocumented persons legally receive benefits from any of these programs?

With respect to social security benefits, no law prevents an undocumented person from receiving benefits provided he has a valid social security card. Since April 1974 it has been illegal for an undocumented person to be issued a social security card; in 1978 the barriers against undocumented persons receiving a card were heightened by a new regulation that demanded a personal interview of all applicants for a card who were age 18 or older. However, due to the laxness of earlier regulations, many undocumented workers do have valid social security cards.[15]

Supplemental Security Income is not legally available to undocumented persons. Finally, within the state of California general assistance is not legally available to undocumented persons, and screening practices identical to those used for the food stamp program or the AFDC program are used to deny benefits to the undocumented.[16] However, undocumented aliens in California and elsewhere are eligible to receive benefits from private welfare agencies.

But what benefits from these programs did undocumented persons actually receive? Tabulations were prepared concerning whether any benefits were received from social security and railroad retirement, SSI, or other public assistance or welfare payments. The proportion of either undocumented mothers or undocumented fathers receiving benefits from any of these programs was less than 2 percent. On the other hand, the percentage of either the legal immigrant or native-born mothers or fathers receiving such benefits was equally low.

Eligibility for entitlements and female labor force participation

Paula Hancock used the data from the Los Angeles County Parents Survey to conduct an interesting analysis of the relationship for mothers between eligibility for means-tested entitlements, type of legal status, and labor force participation.[17] Previously published data concerning women receiving AFDC benefits in California had shown that few of them were in the labor force. Hancock hypothesized that the likelihood of being eligible for AFDC and other means-tested benefits would have an important negative impact on labor force participation. Among citizens or legal-immigrant mothers, the likelihood of eligibility for such benefits would be largest among the unmarried, much less likely among women married to lower-income husbands, and least likely among women married to higher-income husbands. No undocumented mothers would be eligible (although their American-born children might be eligible). Thus, Hancock hypothesized that after controls for other relevant factors had been established, the positive impact of being undocumented rather than native-born or a legal immigrant on labor force participation would be largest for unmarried women, intermediate for married women with lower-income husbands, and least for married women with higher-income husbands.

Hancock tested this hypothesis on a sample excluding those women reporting themselves as permanent legal residents but who failed to show an alien registration card. When attention was focused only on the rank order of the coefficients, her hypothesis was sustained. Surprisingly, Hancock also found that being undocumented rather than native-born or a legal immigrant had a statistically significant negative impact on labor force participation among married women with higher-income husbands. A possible interpretation of this finding is that undocumented mothers of small children perceived that their chances of being deported were much greater if they worked outside the home than if they did not. Other things being equal, they may have had a greater aversion to labor force participation than either legal immigrants or the native-born. Being married to a husband with a reasonable income, they were free to express this aversion.

Taxation

I collected only limited information concerning taxation. I asked whether income tax had been deducted from the pay that year and finally whether social security (FICA) payments had been deducted. Tabulations were made for mothers and for

Table 8.18. *Percentage distribution by whether federal income tax was deducted from the paycheck for mothers and fathers of Mexican origin with earnings in 1979 subdivided by legal status*

	Mother's legal status			Father's legal status		
Federal income tax deduction	Undocu-mented	Legal immi-grant	Native-born citizen	Undocu-mented	Legal immi-grant	Native-born citizen
All persons with 1979 earnings						
Total	100.0	100.0	100.0	100.0	100.0	100.0
Yes	88.4	99.5	99.2	96.2	98.2	96.3
No	11.6	0.5	0.8	3.8	2.0	3.7
Weighted number of persons	1,402	841	1,049	2,453	1,513	1,1142
Persons receiving less than the minimum wage						
Total	100.0	100.0	100.0	100.0	100.0	100.0
Yes	83.2	100.0	100.0	90.6	75.0	100.0
No	16.8	0.0	0.0	9.4	25.0	0.0
Weighted number of cases	752	133	158	318	48	12
Persons receiving the minimum wage or more						
Total	100.0	100.0	100.0	100.0	100.0	100.0
Yes	94.5	99.4	99.1	97.1	98.8	96.3
No	5.5	0.6	0.9	2.9	1.2	3.7
Weighted number of cases	650	708	891	2,135	1,465	1,130

fathers of Mexican origin who had resided 12 months in the United States in 1979 and had worked for pay at least one week that year. Respondents were subdivided not only by legal status but also by whether their 1979 wage was or was not below the legal minimum wage.

Table 8.18 presents the data with respect to whether income taxes were deducted. Ignoring the very few legal immigrant fathers paid below the minimum wage, the data indicate that the only subgroup to have had a high proportion of earners with no income taxes deducted was that of the undocumented females receiving less than minimum wage, 17 percent of whom had no taxes deducted.

Additional tabulations were made with respect to whether social security taxes were deducted. For the undocumented the picture was very similar to that shown in Table 8.18. However, a higher proportion of the native-born had no social security taxes deducted than had no income taxes deducted. This difference probably reflects persons who worked for the federal government or other entity exempt from the FICA tax requirement.

The data shown in Table 8.18 for undocumented fathers show smaller proportions with no tax deductions than found in previous studies. In the North–Houstoun study of apprehended illegal immigrants who had worked in the United States for two weeks or more, 22.7 percent had no FICA deduction and 26.8 percent had no federal income-tax deduction. In Villalpando's study of apprehended illegal aliens in San Diego County, 19 percent had not had social security and federal income tax deducted from their pay.[18] The smaller proportions paid in cash or not having tax deductions among the undocumented fathers of this sample is probably due to the small proportions working in agriculture as compared to the North–Houstoun and Villalpando samples. According to law, agricultural employers, employers of household labor, and employers of casual labor involving payment of $50 or less in a 24-day period are not required to withhold the federal income tax.[19]

An important question is whether tax withholdings for undocumented persons are larger than their tax liability. I have no data from this survey concerning whether anyone filed an income tax and, if so, what refund they received or extra tax they paid. However, data on this topic have been collected by David North in the previously mentioned study in which he conducted a five-year followup of 192 illegal aliens apprehended in California by the INS in February 1975.[20]

According to North's findings, those who filed an income tax paid less than would have been the case if no return had been filed. In essence, filing allowed them to receive a refund on the taxes already deducted from their earnings. However, from these data it is not possible to say definitively whether the undocumented pay more federal income tax than they should. To make a definitive statement, one would have to have data on the income tax liability of those who did not file a return.

9. Characteristics of one individual compared to characteristics of another family member

Of what importance are the data of this chapter? Let me illustrate. U.S. immigration law places great weight on family ties. Within the quota for any one nation, the second preference is given to the admission of a spouse of a permanent legal resident and the fifth preference to the admission of siblings of U.S. citizens 21 years old and over. However, the waiting list for quota admission to the United States from Mexico is large and the waiting time lengthy. For example, as of 1979, for Mexicans there was a nine-year wait for entrance under the second preference.[1] How well does family preference work in the context of a lengthy waiting time? To answer this question, one must examine the joint distribution of legal status types for husbands and wives and also for respondents and their siblings.

Quite contrary to the emphasis on family reunification in the regular immigration law, the provisions for legalization of status embodied in the Immigration Reform and Control Act of 1986 make no provision for keeping families intact. The sole criterion is individual length of stay. In fact, as detailed in Chapter 11, an important objection already voiced to the Act is that it will not guarantee the legalization of all members of an immediate family. Therefore, data on the distribution of undocumented husbands and wives by the husband-wife difference in length of stay is of significance.

Legal status of the individual compared to legal status of the spouse

The universe for this analysis consists of the 759 interviews where data for both the father and the mother of the baby were collected. Table 9.1 shows the percentage distribution by five categories of legal status of spouses for all husbands and wives subdivided by five categories of their own legal status.

It is evident that there was indeed a substantial proportion of legal immigrants whose spouse was undocumented. Among husbands who were legal immigrants, 15.4 percent had a wife who was undocumented; among wives who were legal

169

Table 9.1. *Percentage distribution by legal status of spouse for wives and husbands subdivided by own legal status*

| | Un-docu-men-ted | Legal immigrant | | | | |
		Total	Natu-ral-ized	Showed card	Did not show card	Native-born citizen
Wives by legal status of Husband						
Total	100.0	100.0	100.0	100.0	100.0	100.0
Undocumented	88.0	9.8	13.9	8.6	10.4	7.3
Legal immigrant, total	9.3	76.3	62.6	78.8	75.9	14.1
Naturalized citizen	0.8	4.0	17.4	3.2	2.8	5.9
Permanent legal resident:						
Showed card	1.5	24.1	5.2	45.0	7.1	2.2
Did not show card	7.0	48.2	40.0	30.6	66.0	5.9
Native-born citizen	2.7	13.9	23.5	12.6	13.7	78.7
Weighted number of cases	2,880	1,650	115	746	789	1,516
Husbands by legal status of wife						
Total	100.0	100.0	100.0	100.0	100.0	100.0
Undocumented	90.3	15.4	12.4	9.2	18.6	5.2
Legal immigrant, total	5.8	72.4	37.3	83.6	73.1	15.3
Naturalized citizen	0.6	4.1	11.3	1.3	4.2	1.8
Permanent legal resident:						
Showed card	2.3	33.8	13.6	70.6	21.0	6.3
Did not show card	2.9	34.4	12.4	11.8	47.9	7.2
Native-born citizen	3.9	12.2	50.3	7.1	8.3	79.5
Weighted number of cases	2,806	1,740	177	476	1,087	1,500

immigrants, 9.8 percent had an undocumented husband. Furthermore, among American-born husbands, 7.3 percent had an undocumented wife; among American-born wives, 5.2 percent had an undocumented husband. These last results are surprising because spouses of native-born U.S. citizens may become legal immigrants without respect to any quota. On the other hand, 90.3 percent of all undocumented husbands had an undocumented wife and 88.0 percent of all undocumented wives had an undocumented husband.

Table 9.2. *Percentage distribution by legal status of unmarried brother and of childless sister for female and male respondents of Mexican origin subdivided by own legal status*

Legal status of other person	Female respondent's own legal status			Male respondent's own legal status		
	Un-docu-mented	Legal immi-grant	Native-born citizen	Un-docu-mented	Legal immi-grant	Native-born citizen
Unmarried brother						
Total	100.0	100.0	100.0	100.0	100.0	100.0
Undocumented	92.4	28.5	0.0	82.0	40.9	0.0
Legal immigrant	7.6	56.7	0.0	18.0	40.9	0.0
Native-born citizen	0.0	14.8	100.0	0.0	18.2	100.0
Weighted number of cases	661	582	859	222	88	92
Childless sister						
Total	100.0	100.0	100.0	100.0	100.0	100.0
Undocumented	87.4	21.2	0.0	90.5	0.0	0.0
Legal immigrant	11.2	75.6	4.0	9.5	78.7	0.0
Native-born citizen	1.4	3.2	96.0	0.0	21.3	100.0
Weighted number of cases	436	311	576	63	47	99

Legal status of the individual compared to legal status of the sibling

Recollect that respondents to the survey could be either male or female and that survey respondents of Mexican origin provided information concerning an unmarried adult brother (if any) or a childless adult sister (if any) living in Los Angeles County. The vast majority of all of the respondents were female. Hence the vast majority of the unmarried brothers and childless sisters were siblings of the mother. Data are available on the legal status of 161 unmarried brothers of female respondents and on the legal status of 114 childless sisters of female respondents. However, data are available on the legal status of only 33 unmarried brothers of a male respondent and of only 17 childless sisters of a male respondent. Thus the data concerning the legal status of fathers by the legal status of their brothers or sisters should not be considered very reliable.

Table 9.2 presents data on the legal status of the respondent's unmarried brother and childless sister for female and male respondents subdivided by their own legal status.

Table 9.3. *Percentage distribution by difference in years between husband's and wife's length of stay in the United States for wives and husbands of Mexican origin born outside the United States and with spouse born outside the United States*

Difference in stay	Wives		Husbands	
	Un-docu-mented	Legal immigrant	Un-docu-mented	Legal immigrant
Total	100.0	100.0	100.0	100.0
Wife's stay 5 or more years longer	2.6	10.3	4.0	6.8
Wife's stay 1 to 4 years longer	11.0	14.7	11.4	14.4
Wife's stay equal to husband's	21.8	30.7	23.8	25.2
Husband's stay 1 to 4 years longer	41.8	29.8	43.4	29.2
Husband's stay 5 or more years longer	22.9	14.5	17.4	24.4
Mean difference between husband's and wife's length of stay (in years)	3.04	3.24	2.70	3.85
Weighted number of cases	2,701	1,336	2,618	1,445

It can be seen that among female or male legal immigrant respondents, a substantial proportion had brothers or sisters who were undocumented, and another substantial proportion had brothers or sisters who were native-born. On the other hand, if the female or male respondent was undocumented, it was very likely that the unmarried brother or childless sister was undocumented. Moreover, if the female or male respondent was born in the United States, it was almost entirely certain that the unmarried brother or childless sister would also be born in the United States.

Difference between husband's and wife's length of stay by own legal status

Chapter 7 showed that the average year of first arrival in the United States was later for female immigrants than for male. Table 9.3 examines the difference in years between the length of the husband's stay in the United States and the length of the wife's stay in the United States. The tabulation is made for wives and husbands of Mexican origin with both members of the couple born outside the United States; both husbands and wives are subdivided by their own legal status.

Table 9.4. *Percentage distribution by year of arrival of self and year of arrival of spouse for undocumented husbands of Mexican origin with undocumented wives and for undocumented wives of Mexican origin with undocumented husbands*

Husbands	
Total	100.0
Arrived 1975 or earlier	69.5
With wife arriving 1975 or earlier	43.8
With wife arriving 1976 or later	25.6
Arrived 1976 or later	30.5
Weighted number of cases	2,472
Wives	
Total	100.0
Arrived 1975 or earlier	47.2
With husband arriving 1975 or earlier	42.7
With husband arriving 1976 or later	4.5
Arrived 1976 or later	52.8
Weighted number of cases	2,439

What is perhaps most surprising about the table are the small proportions of couples for whom the length of stay was equal. The range in these four proportions is from 21.8 percent where the mother was undocumented to 30.7 percent where the mother was a legal immigrant. The mean difference in length of stay varies from 3.85 years where the husband was a legal immigrant to 2.70 years where the husband was undocumented. Apparently, in many cases husbands enter the United States before their wives to establish themselves economically. On the other hand, many wives had been in the United States longer than their husbands. For example, among legal immigrant wives this proportion was 25.0 percent. Many of these wives who have been in the United States longer than their husbands may have been brought to the United States as children and then, upon reaching adulthood, married a newly arrived immigrant.

The data shown in Table 9.3 imply that many undocumented individuals securing legalization of status under the Immigration Reform and Control Act of 1986 will not be able to secure legal status for their spouse. We can be more specific concerning the exact proportion. Let us assume that the proportion who had a spouse arriving in 1982 or later, among all of the undocumented individuals in November 1986 (the date the Act was enacted) who had arrived in the United States before 1982, was approximately the same as the proportion who had a spouse arriving in 1976 or later among all of the undocumented individuals to November 1980 (close to the midpoint of the interviewing for the survey) who had arrived in the United States before 1976. Given this not improbable assumption, one can approximate the number of husbands or wives legalized under the 1986 Act who will still have an illegal spouse.

Table 9.4 provides the relevant data. The data shown in this table refer to all undocumented wives of Mexican origin with an undocumented husband and to all undocumented husbands of Mexican origin with an undocumented wife. According to the table, 69.5 percent of all undocumented husbands would be able to legalize their status. However, among those able to secure their own legalization, about 37 percent would not be able to attain the legalization of their wives. Among undocumented wives, on the other hand, only 47.2 percent would be able to legalize their status; approximately 90 percent of these would see their husbands legalized.

10. A multivariate analysis of the impact of legal status on the hourly wage, hours worked per year, and annual earnings

Are the earnings of undocumented Mexican immigrants lower than those of legal immigrants from Mexico merely because they lack legal status? There have been little hard data concerning this question; almost all existing studies of undocumented persons have been based on very special samples, and almost no studies were able directly to compare undocumented workers with legal immigrants.

Lower earnings for undocumented workers could come about because of their lower levels of skill or because, at given levels of skill, their undocumented status caused them to earn less than other workers. There are good reasons for believing that, given the same skill level, undocumented workers should have earned less than other workers. First, they were not personally legally eligible for many entitlement programs and thus may have been forced to take jobs that other workers might be able to refuse because they had the alternative of relying on income from such entitlement programs. Second, they were subject to employer-instigated deportation if they complained that the wage offered to them was below the minimum wage. Therefore, it is probable that employers able exclusively to hire undocumented persons were able to pay some or all of their workers less than the minimum wage without much fear of being detected. Third, the fact that they were always at risk of deportation (other than employer-instigated) meant that they could not be counted on to show up for work every day. In turn, this lack of reliability, by reducing the value of the undocumented person's worth to his employer, should have resulted in the employer's paying a lower wage.

The extent to which the lack of documentation has directly impeded earnings is, however, controversial. Barry Chiswick contended that undocumented workers would earn only 2 percent less than legal migrants from Mexico if they had the same characteristics as the legals.[1] Others have seen the lack of legal status as having a more substantial effect on earnings.[2]

The basis for Chiswick's contention that legal status had only a very small impact on wages was derived from comparing the earnings and characteristics of a sample of apprehended undocumented Mexican males studied by North and Houstoun[3] to a model of the determinants of earnings among all males born in Mexico enumerated in the 1970 Census of the United States. He assumed that all the Mexican-born

175

males enumerated in the 1970 census were legal residents. He determined the regression of various characteristics on the natural log of the average hourly wage for all Mexican-born males and then estimated the increase in the average wage that would have been received by the apprehended undocumented workers in the North and Houstoun sample if they were to have the mean level of each characteristic of all Mexican-born males.

The undocumented males in the North and Houstoun sample had received an average hourly wage of $2.34; the average hourly wage of all Mexican-born males was $4.33. However, if the undocumented males in the North and Houston sample had had the same characteristics as the average Mexican-born male, they would have received, according to Chiswick's estimate, $4.25 an hour. In Chiswick's model, by far the most important variable was length of residence in the United States. According to Chiswick's model, the effect of the difference between the actual mean length of residence of the apprehended undocumented males and all Mexican-born males was to contribute $1.52 to the difference in wage between the two groups. However, the validity of Chiswick's results rests on the assumption that the Mexican-born males enumerated in the 1970 Census excluded undocumented persons. If undocumented persons have been in the United States for a substantially shorter period, on the average, than legal residents, and if undocumented persons were included in the 1970 Census, Chiswick's results with respect to the impact of length of U.S. residence may be biased.

Details of the methodology

Universe

The results shown in this chapter relate to the weighted numbers of fathers and mothers of Mexican birth who had resided in the United States throughout 1979, had worked for pay for at least one week in that year, and had no missing values for any relevant variables. Both members and fathers were subdivided by their legal status into the two groups: either undocumented or legal immigrant (permanent legal resident or naturalized citizen).

Dependent and independent variables

Three dependent variables were employed: (1) the natural log of annual earnings in hundreds of dollars in 1979, (2) total hours worked in 1979, and (3) the natural log of the average hourly wage in dollars in 1979. Annual earnings were derived by summing the amounts received in answer to separate questions concerning salaries and wages, income from a nonfarm business, and income from a farm. The total hours worked in 1979 were derived by taking the product of weeks worked in 1979 and average hours worked per week in that year. The average hourly wage was derived by dividing annual earnings by the total hours worked in 1979.

The equations shown in Tables 10.1 through 10.3 were computed separately by sex for all Mexican-born persons, undocumented immigrants, and legal immigrants. The independent variables used for each of these eighteen equations differed somewhat depending on legal status. The following variables were used in the various equations:

Whether undocumented immigrant. This variable was used in the equations for all persons of Mexican birth of given sex.

Age in single years. The mean ages of the undocumented and legal immigrant fathers were 29.1 and 30.9 years, and of the same two classes of mothers 26.1 and 27.3 years.

Difficulty with English. This variable was coded into four categories ranging from fluently (coded 1) to not at all (coded 4) and was treated as an interval scale. The means on this variable for the undocumented and legal immigrant fathers were 3.0 and 2.3, and for the same two classes of mothers 3.4 and 2.4.

School years completed. The means on this variable for the undocumented and legal immigrant fathers were 5.8 and 8.2, and for the same two classes of mothers 5.8 and 8.6.

School years/U.S. school interaction. This variable was defined as the product of number of school years completed times a dummy variable coded 1 when the respondent had completed school in the United States. The theoretical rationale for including this variable was that persons completing any given level of schooling in Mexico were likely to be of higher ability than persons completing that level of schooling in the United States. This rationale was hypothesized because the mean educational attainment in Mexico is about one-half of that in the United States. Moreover, in large parts of rural Mexico it is impossible to obtain more than six years of school without leaving one's native village. The means on this variable for the undocumented and legal immigrant fathers were 0.2 and 3.0, and for the same two classes of mothers 0.7 and 4.5.

Length of stay in the United States. This variable was defined as the number of years the respondent had lived in the United States counting only those years in which he or she had lived at least six months. The means on this variable for the undocumented and legal immigrant fathers were 7.1 and 12.0, and for the same two classes of mothers 6.2 and 11.6.

Table 10.1. *Unstandardized regression coefficients for equations predicting natural log of 1979 average hourly wage, total number of hours worked in 1979 and natural log of 1979 earnings in hundreds of dollars for Mexican-born fathers and mothers*

| | Hourly wage | | Total hours | | 1979 earnings | |
	Father	Mother	Father	Mother	Father	Mother
Intercept	1.34	.882	1,859.3	1,276.0	4.25	3.26
	(11.6)	(5.13)	(12.6)	(3.75)	(26.3)	(8.15)
Age	.002	.005	−.066	9.01	.003	.010
	(0.83)	(1.23)	(0.18)	(1.17)	(0.62)	(1.14)
Difficulty with	−.071	−.026	−11.5	21.2	−.089	−.017
English	(3.36)	(0.78)	(0.42)	(0.33)	(2.97)	(0.22)
School years	.021	.015	9.77	7.90	.023	.028
completed	(3.62)	(1.70)	(1.32)	(0.46)	(2.82)	(1.36)
Schooling/U.S. school	−.014	−.003	−.130	−1.47	−.021	−.017
interaction	(2.37)	(0.41)	(1.77)	(0.10)	(2.61)	(1.01)
Legal immigrant	.187	.155	−6.90	−166.3	.195	−.061
	(5.42)	(3.27)	(0.16)	(1.78)	(4.01)	(0.55)
Length of U.S. stay	.013	.009	15.4	−1.96	.022	.015
	(3.05)	(1.52)	(2.82)	(0.17)	(3.70)	(1.06)
Unweighted number						
of cases	517	303	517	303	519	306
Mean	1.520	1.161	1,997.1	1,572.6	4.482	3.756
R-square	.260	.176	.030	.023	.206	.023

Note: t values are in parentheses; values of 2.59 or more are significant at the 0.01 level; values of 1.97 or more at the 0.05 level.

Model

The model used for all eighteen equations was ordinary-least-squares regression. The SAS program that was employed allowed for the use of weighted number of cases that were then divided by the average weight so that the measures of statistical significance could refer to the unweighted number of cases while bias due to use of unweighted cases could be avoided.

Results

The results of the eighteen equations are shown in Tables 10.1–10.3. Table 10.1 presents results for Mexican-born fathers and mothers. Table 10.2 presents results for undocumented fathers and mothers and Table 10.3 results for legal-immigrant fathers and mothers. In the discussion of the results, I define statistical significance as significance at the 0.05 level in a two-tailed test. Findings that do not meet this level of significance will be termed apparent. Because the number of male respondents is substantially larger than the number of female respondents, it will be much easier to find statistically significant coefficients for fathers than for mothers.

Fathers and mothers born in Mexico

Table 10.1 presents the results for fathers and mothers born in Mexico. The most important finding is that being a legal immigrant does have an independent effect on the hourly wage. Other findings are usually congruent with the theory that the level of skill has a positive impact on the hourly wage and annual earnings.

For fathers, being a legal immigrant rather than undocumented had a statistically significant positive effect on both the hourly wage and annual earnings and an apparent negative effect on total hours worked. For mothers, being a legal immigrant had a statistically significant positive impact on the hourly wage; however, there was an apparent negative effect on annual earnings and the negative effect on total hours worked approached statistical significance.

For both fathers and mothers, age had only apparent positive impacts on the hourly wage and on annual earnings; its apparent impact on total hours worked was negative for fathers and positive for mothers.

For fathers, difficulty with English had a statistically significant negative impact on both the hourly wage and on annual earnings but only an apparent negative effect on total hours worked. For mothers, difficulty with English had a negative effect on hourly wage and on annual earnings and a positive effect on total hours worked, but none of the coefficients were statistically significant.

For fathers, school years completed had a statistically significant positive effect on both the hourly wage and annual earnings and an apparent positive impact on total hours worked. For mothers, school years completed was only apparently positively related to the three dependent variables.

For fathers, the schooling/U.S. school interaction had a statistically significant negative impact on both hourly wage and annual earnings and a negative impact on total hours worked that approaches statistical significance. For mothers, the schooling/U.S. school interaction had an apparent negative impact on all three dependent variables. (See further discussion concerning the negative impact of this variable at the end of this chapter.)

For fathers, length of stay in the United States had a statistically significant positive effect on all three dependent variables. For mothers, length of stay apparently was positively related to both the hourly wage and annual earnings but negatively related to total hours worked.

Table 10.2. *Unstandardized regression coefficients for equations predicting natural log of 1979 average hourly wage, total number of hours worked in 1979 and natural log of 1979 earnings in hundreds of dollars for undocumented fathers and mothers*

	Hourly wage		Total hours		1979 earnings	
	Father	Mother	Father	Mother	Father	Mother
Intercept	1.27	.849	1,948.0	1,131.0	4.25	3.20
	(9.53)	(3.92)	(9.82)	(2.76)	(20.5)	(7.62)
Age	.004	.001	−1.07	12.2	.003	.008
	(1.13)	(0.14)	(0.22)	(1.36)	(0.58)	(0.84)
Difficulty with English	−.085	−.011	−34.7	14.6	−.116	−.011
	(3.50)	(0.26)	(0.90)	(0.18)	(3.07)	(0.14)
School years completed	.024	.019	13.7	7.31	.027	.025
	(3.64)	(1.86)	(1.42)	(0.37)	(2.66)	(1.23)
Schooling/U.S. school interaction	−.035	−.011	−22.6	1.10	−.042	−.023
	(2.55)	(0.91)	(1.10)	(0.05)	(1.97)	(1.01)
Length of U.S. stay	.021	.020	11.2	11.9	.029	.035
	(3.79)	(2.28)	(1.33)	(0.72)	(3.31)	(2.04)
Unweighted number of cases	323	193	323	193	325	195
Mean	1.401	1.065	1,974.1	1,628.8	4.347	3.725
R-square	.172	.064	.022	.020	.123	.048

Note: t values are in parentheses; values of 2.60 or more are significant at the 0.01 level; values of 1.97 or more at the 0.05 level.

Undocumented fathers and mothers

Table 10.2 presents results for undocumented fathers and mothers. In general, the results are congruent with the "human capital" theory that wages and earnings are determined by the individual's level of skill.

For both fathers and mothers, age had only an apparent positive impact on the hourly wage and on annual earnings; its apparent impact on total hours worked was negative for fathers and positive for mothers.

For fathers, difficulty with English had a statistically significant negative impact on the hourly wage and on annual earnings but only an apparent negative impact on total hours worked. For mothers, difficulty with English has only apparent negative impacts on hourly wage and annual earnings and an apparent positive effect on total hours.

For fathers, school years completed had a statistically significant positive effect on the hourly wage and on annual earnings and an apparent positive effect on hours

Table 10.3. *Unstandardized regression coefficients for equations predicting natural log of 1979 average hourly wage, total number of hours worked in 1979 and natural log of 1979 earnings in hundreds of dollars for legal immigrant fathers and mothers*

	Hourly wage		Total hours		1979 earnings	
	Father	Mother	Father	Mother	Father	Mother
Intercept	1.63	1.03	1752.0	1217.8	4.44	3.08
	(7.31)	(3.51)	(7.77)	(1.95)	(16.2)	(3.59)
Age	−.000	.014	0.90	0.28	.002	.013
	(0.08)	(1.95)	(0.15)	(0.02)	(0.24)	(0.63)
Difficulty with English	−.047	−.046	19.5	63.2	−.041	.013
	(1.16)	(0.83)	(0.48)	(0.54)	(0.84)	(0.08)
School years completed	.017	.002	1.47	20.2	.017	.042
	(1.53)	(0.14)	(0.13)	(0.56)	(1.21)	(0.85)
Schooling/U.S. school	−.005	.009	−6.87	−3.50	−.009	−.011
interaction	(0.61)	(0.84)	(0.79)	(0.15)	(0.89)	(0.33)
Length of U.S. stay	.007	−.003	17.9	−7.90	.017	.000
	(1.07)	(0.34)	(2.56)	(0.45)	(2.02)	(0.00)
Unweighted number of cases	194	110	194	110	194	111
Mean	1.718	1.331	2035.4	1474.1	4.708	3.811
R-square	.071	.083	.055	.014	.078	.014

Note: t values are in parentheses; values of 2.63 or more are significant at the 0.01 level; values of 1.98 or more at the 0.05 level.

worked. For mothers, completed school years apparently had a positive impact on all three dependent variables.

For fathers, the schooling/U.S. school interaction had a statistically significant negative effect on both hourly wage and annual earnings and an apparent negative effect on total hours worked. For mothers there was an apparent negative effect on hourly wage and annual earnings and an apparent positive effect on total hours worked.

For both fathers and mothers, length of stay in the United States had a statistically significant positive impact on hourly wage and annual earnings and only an apparent positive effect on total hours worked.

Legal immigrant fathers and mothers

Table 10.3 presents the results for fathers and mothers who were legal immigrants. In summary, as was the case for undocumented immigrants, wages and earnings appear to be related to the individual's level of skill.

Table 10.4. *Comparison of (1) actual mean hourly wage, mean total hours worked, and mean 1979 earnings of legal immigrant fathers and mothers, (2) actual mean hourly wage, mean total hours worked, and mean 1979 earnings of undocumented fathers and mothers, and (3) two sets of estimates of hypothetical mean hourly wage, total hours worked, and 1979 earnings of the undocumented if they had the mean characteristics of the legal immigrants*

	Hourly wage		Total hours		1979 earnings	
	Father	Mother	Father	Mother	Father	Mother
Legal immigrant, actual	5.56	3.78	2,035	1,474	11,158	4,521
Undocumented, actual	4.06	2.90	1,974	1,629	7,722	4,146
Difference	1.50	0.88	61	−155	3,336	375
Based on equations for all Mexican-born						
Undocumented hypothetical	4.60	3.23	2,039	1,612	9,261	4,599
Difference attributable to legal status	0.96	0.55	−4	−138	1,797	−78
Difference attributable to other characteristics	0.54	0.33	65	−17	1,539	453
Based on equations for undocumented only						
Undocumented hypothetical	4.68	3.30	2,014	1,703	9,184	4,974
Difference attributable to legal status	0.88	0.48	21	−229	1,875	−375
Difference attributable to other characteristics	0.62	0.40	40	74	1,462	828

For fathers, age had an apparent negative impact on the hourly wage but apparent positive impacts on total hours worked and on annual earnings. For mothers, the apparent effect of age was positive for all three dependent variables.

For fathers, difficulty with English had apparent negative effects on the hourly wage and on annual earnings and an apparent positive effect on total hours. For mothers, difficulty with English had an apparent negative effect on the hourly wage but apparent positive effects on the other two dependent variables.

For both fathers and mothers, completed school years had apparent positive effects on all three dependent variables.

For fathers, the schooling/U.S. school interaction had apparent negative effects on all three dependent variables. For mothers, its apparent effect on the hourly wage was positive, but its apparent effect on the other two dependent variables was negative.

For fathers, length of U.S. stay had a statistically significant positive impact on both total hours worked and annual earnings and an apparent positive impact on the hourly wage. For mothers, length of stay had apparent negative impacts on both the hourly wage and total hours worked and no effect on earnings.

The relative effect of legal status versus other variables

Table 10.4 presents a comparison for Mexican-born fathers and mothers of the relative effect of legal status vis-à-vis other characteristics on the hourly wage, total hours worked, and annual earnings. Shown in the table are the actual hourly wage, total hours worked, and annual earnings of both the legal and the undocumented immigrants. Shown also are two sets of estimates of the hourly wage, total hours worked, and annual earnings that the undocumented would have if they possessed the mean value held by legal immigrants on the characteristics other than legal status that were relevant to the three dependent variables. For each of these sets of estimates, the table shows the difference in hourly wage, total hours worked, and annual earnings between the legal immigrants and the undocumented that was attributable to legal status alone, and the difference in these matters that was attributable to differences between the legal immigrants and the undocumented in other characteristics.

The two sets of figures defining what the undocumented would have if they possessed the mean values on other characteristics held by the legal immigrants were obtained (1) by multiplying the mean values of legal immigrants for the various characteristics by the regression coefficients in each of the six equations for the Mexican-born, and (2) by multiplying these same mean values by the regression coefficients in each of the six equations for the undocumented. The hypothetical values based on the regression equations for all Mexican-born respondents are superior to those based on the equations for the undocumented if we assume that the coefficients for the two classes of Mexican-born are in fact identical because the coefficients for all Mexican born have a lower sampling error. However, if one believes that the coefficients for the undocumented are in fact different from those for legal immigrants, then the hypothetical figures based on the equations for the undocumented only are to be preferred.

Table 10.4 shows that legal-immigrant fathers had a higher hourly wage, worked more total hours, and had higher annual earnings than undocumented fathers. The table also shows that for fathers the direct effect of a legal-immigrant status had considerably greater impact on both the hourly wage and annual earnings than the differences in other relevant characteristics between the undocumented and legal immigrants. For example, the actual average hourly wage of the undocumented fathers was $4.06. Using the equation for all Mexican-born, the undocumented fathers would earn $4.60 if they had the same value on other characteristics as legal immigrants, whereas legal immigrant fathers themselves earned $5.56 an hour on the average. The difference attributable directly to legal immigrant status is thus $0.96, and the difference attributable to other characteristics $0.54. In contrast, for fathers, the direct impact of a legal status on hours worked depends on which equation is used; it was negative if the equation for all Mexican-born fathers is used and positive otherwise.

For the mothers, legal immigrants received a higher wage and had higher annual earnings than the undocumented but worked fewer total hours. Regardless of which equation is used, the results with respect to the hourly wage parallel those for the fathers; the positive difference attributable directly to a legalized status was more important than the positive difference attributable to other characteristics. However, the results on total hours worked and annual earnings for the mothers are different from those for the fathers. Regardless of the manner in which the results were calculated, the direct effect of a legalized status was to decrease the total hours worked. However, whether other characteristics differentiating the undocumented from the legal immigrants reduce or increase the total hours worked depends on which equation is used.

Moreover, for mothers, regardless of which equation is used, the direct effect of a legal-immigrant status is to reduce annual earnings, whereas the effect of the other characteristics differentiating the legal immigrants from the undocumented is to increase annual earnings. We would speculate that undocumented mothers work longer and thus earn more than legal-immigrant mothers with the same characteristics in large part because their husbands earn less than do legal immigrants.

Discussion

The effects of legal status on wages and earnings

The focus of this chapter has been on the relative importance of legal status, per se, versus other variables in explaining the differences in hourly wage, total hours worked, and annual earnings between undocumented immigrants from Mexico, legal immigrants from Mexico, and the U.S.-born of Mexican descent. Separate results have been presented for the fathers and mothers of our sample.

I have shown that among those born in Mexico, being a legal resident had a statistically significant positive impact on the hourly wage for both fathers and mothers after controls for length of stay in the United States and other relevant variables. For fathers, being a legal immigrant also had a statistically significant positive impact on annual earnings. However, for mothers, being a legal immigrant had no positive impact on annual earnings largely because undocumented mothers apparently worked more total hours than mothers who were legal immigrants.

My results with respect to the impact of legal status on the hourly wage of men born in Mexico are in direct contradiction to those of Chiswick. Chiswick assumed that all of the Mexican-born enumerated in the 1970 census were legal immigrants. Passel and Warren have estimated that approximately one-half of all Mexican-born persons counted in the 1980 Census of the United States were undocumented.[4] It is plausible, therefore, that some undocumented Mexicans were enumerated in the 1970 Census. Moreover, my own data reveal a strong correlation between legal status and length of stay in the United States. For the male respondents analyzed in this chapter, the mean length of stay for the undocumented was 7.1 years whereas that for legal immigrants was 12.0 years. I believe that Chiswick's results with respect to the impact of length of stay on the hourly wage may have been biased. Alternatively, it is possible that Chiswick's results are correct for 1970 and my own results correct for 1980.

However, I have not yet addressed an important question, namely the meaning of a difference in wage or earnings by legal status. In the beginning of this chapter I advanced three reasons why lower earnings for undocumented workers might come about. These reasons pertained to the situation of undocumented workers. However, an alternative hypothesis is plausible. According to this alternative hypothesis, wages and earnings were favorably affected by characteristics beyond those that I was able to enter into my equations. Furthermore, legal immigrants had more of these characteristics than undocumented workers. Therefore, they achieved a higher wage and earnings. This hypothesis is the more plausible because of the large number of legal immigrants who probably secured their legal status through marriage. Presumably, potential spouses would take earnings capacity into account in deciding whether to marry an undocumented person in order that that person could legalize his or her status. Moreover, legal immigrants receiving visas through the third and sixth preferences (for professional workers and skilled and unskilled workers in short supply) might also have earnings capabilities greater than what would be predicted given the other characteristics measured here. Therefore, I believe that the coefficients for legal status obtained in my equations reflect both the difference in external situation and an innate difference in earnings capacity. On the other hand, it is likely that not all of the workers who reported themselves as legal immigrants were in fact here legally. If so, the coefficients I obtained were smaller in magnitude than they would have been without this source of bias. It is possible that my obtained coefficients for legal status did represent fairly well the impact of the external situation alone. On the one hand, the actual coefficients were probably biased upward because they included a selectivity factor; however, they may have been biased downward because not all who reported themselves as legal immigrants were what they claimed to be.

The reported results pertain, of course, to the situation before the passage of the Immigration Reform and Control Act of 1986. One may speculate that, because the law imposes criminal sanctions on employers knowingly hiring illegal aliens, there may now be some additional wage reduction for undocumented workers.

The true effect of schooling

My results are also relevant to the controversy concerning the degree to which the apparent effect of educational attainment on earnings is due to the superior innate ability of those persons who go on to attain higher levels of education. My data show that, at least for Mexican-born fathers, there is a statistically significant negative impact of an interaction between number of school years completed and whether that schooling was completed in the United States. Unless we are prepared to believe that each year of school in Mexico gives much better preparation for high earnings than each year of school received in the United States, we must conclude that the apparent effect of educational attainment is confounded with the effect of natural ability. In short, that rare individual who completes only six years of schooling in the United States probably has natural abilities relevant to earnings that are decidedly below average. In contrast, in Mexico, where six years of schooling is the norm, that individual is likely to possess an average level of innate talent.

11. Policy options and their likely consequences

Policies are mechanisms designed to ensure that a value or series of values are achieved given constraints inherent in a real situation. It is relatively easy to formulate policy when there is only one value or even when there is more than one value provided that all of the values are mutually compatible. The dilemmas with respect to policy occur when there are several values that cannot be simultaneously maximized. In such a case the policy must be designed to advance the sum of all of the values as much as possible, or at least as much as is necessary to achieve majority support. In most cases policy succeeds in advancing some values only at the expense of other values. For that reason, it is important to begin any discussion of policy by discussing the values that are considered relevant by the parties concerned.

This chapter first outlines the values that may be most affected by possible policies to influence the stock and flow of undocumented Mexican immigrants in the United States. After an overview of history of legislation designed to curb undocumented immigration to the United States, we consider specific policy options. Finally, I propose a policy that I think best advances the various values at issue.

The values at stake

The standard of living

All of us would like to see policies adopted that would improve the standard of living for the average American. It is important to find out, if possible, therefore, how undocumented Mexican immigration affects this standard of living. However, none of us is just the "average" American. We are all members of particular groups. Policies that will improve the standard of living of one group may have negative impacts on the standard of living of other groups. Therefore, we also ought to know how undocumented Mexican immigration affects the standard of living of each group.

In much of the economic literature concerning the effects of immigration, three groups are distinguished: unskilled laborers, skilled laborers, and owners of land

187

and capital. This division is useful, but one should not forget that many, if not most, owners of land and capital are also workers, some even unskilled. Moreover, a time dimension needs to be added. The distinction between these three groups is crucial when we consider the short-term impact of changes in the stock and flow of Mexican immigrants. We also need to distinguish the short-term effects of immigration from the long-term effects. When we look at the long-term impact of Mexican immigration, we are looking at the effect of the immigrant's children on the children of the population who are not Mexican immigrants. With respect to the children from either of these two groups, many with unskilled parents will themselves be skilled, while some with skilled parents will be unskilled. Hence the differential impact on current skilled and unskilled workers will be much muted in later generations. To a certain extent the same can be said for the ownership of land and capital. Hence, I shall simply consider one additional group with a stake in immigration policy–namely, the stake of future generations of Americans.

Let us first consider a very oversimplified model that may be useful to initiate a discussion of how these various groups are affected by the flow of unskilled labor. Let us assume that there are only three factors of production: (1) land and capital, (2) skilled labor, and (3) unskilled labor. Let us assume also that all land and capital are owned by nonimmigrants, all immigrants are unskilled, the market is perfect, and there is no government with the power to tax and effect transfer payments. Under these circumstances, economic theory can show that in the short term a flow of immigrants will reduce the wage of unskilled workers but will enhance the wage of the skilled workers and also increase the rent and profits of the owners of land and capital. Moreover, it can also be shown that the average standard of living of the native population will be increased. This last occurs because the immigrant unskilled workers receive only their marginal product of labor rather than the average product.[1] The picture becomes considerably more complicated when the long term is considered or when we introduce a government with the power to tax and to distribute benefits. In these cases, it is by no means certain that the average income level of the nonimmigrant population is increased; it may even decline.

The empirical studies reviewed earlier in this book support the general conclusion that unskilled workers have born the brunt of the impact of undocumented Mexican immigration. In Los Angeles County and in California, their major response has been out-migration rather than unemployment. For those who have remained in Los Angeles County, there has also been some diminution of wages.

On the other hand, as has been emphasized by both the Urban Institute study and the Rand Corporation study, skilled labor and the owners of land and capital in California have enjoyed certain benefits from such immigration. Because of the availability of cheap labor, certain industries, such as the apparel industry, have enormously expanded, providing jobs for managers from the native population as well as unskilled jobs for the undocumented. Moreover, skilled manual workers and white-collar workers (whose earnings have not been threatened by the influx of undocumented Mexicans) have seen the cost of many of their goods and services decline. Within the native-born Mexican community, it is probable also that the economic interests of at least some persons in the skilled segment of the community have been enhanced at the same time as that of less skilled persons have been damaged. This disparity is because the influx of undocumented Mexicans has provided additional jobs for bilingual immigration lawyers, bilingual schoolteachers, bilingual social service workers, and bilingual factory foremen.

The large banks that have made major loans to the Mexican government are another major interest group in the United States with a vested interest in the continued flow of undocumented Mexican immigrants to the United States.

We have yet to consider how taxation and transfer payments affect the gains and losses to skilled and unskilled American workers provoked by undocumented immigration. As was pointed out in Chapter 3, Muller and Espenshade estimated that for each Mexican immigrant household in Los Angeles County, the average fiscal deficit for the state and local governments was more than $2,000.[2] The average fiscal deficit for each undocumented Mexican household may be similar. This fiscal deficit has to be made up by other Californian taxpayers. Much of the burden of meeting this deficit does fall on the possessors of skilled labor and on the owners of land and capital. With respect to the federal tax and federal benefits, our knowledge is much more limited. However, there is some reason to believe that there may be a reverse situation with undocumented Mexican immigrant households contributing more than they benefit. We shall discuss the contribution to the federal budget in a later section.

Nevertheless, the magnitude of the average fiscal deficit of undocumented Mexican households is not the crucial figure with respect to policy. What is relevant to policy is the difference between the aggregate fiscal deficit (or surplus) in the two following situations: (1) a situation with existing tax rates and existing benefits but also the presence of undocumented Mexicans and (2) a situation with existing tax rates and benefits but with no undocumented Mexicans.

In determining this difference for the state of California, we must reckon with the fact that the influx of undocumented Mexicans was accompanied by the out-migration of many working-class whites. Many of these whites who left California may also have received more in state and local benefits than they paid in state and local taxes. We must also consider the consequences that ensued because the inflow of undocumented Mexicans reduced the wage level of the unskilled workers with whom they have competed but also increased the profits of many of the businessmen who have hired the undocumented. The reduction in the wage level may induce a larger proportion of legally resident persons to apply for benefits from means-tested entitlement programs. If so, the state and local tax burden on the total California population, and particularly upon those who are skilled workers or owners of land and capital, has been increased. In addition, given lower wages, the taxes of unskilled workers will have been reduced. On the other hand, an increase in business profits means that more taxes will be collected from business firms and the aggregate state and local fiscal deficit thereby decreased.

In truth, we do not know what the effect of the influx of undocumented Mexicans has been on the aggregate fiscal deficit (or surplus) for the state of California.

Let us now consider the impact of Mexician immigration on the long-term standard of living in the United States. Here it is important to mention that the impact will depend both on the number of immigrants and on those innate characteristics of the immigrants that are relevant to economic productivity. One economist-demographer, Julian Simon, is of the opinion that any increase in population brings a higher standard of living because more people means more creative minds and more creative minds bring increased technological progress.[3] However, his opinion is not that of the majority. Perhaps the majority opinion was best expressed in the words of the Commission on Population Growth and the American Future, who declared, "no substantial benefits would result from continued growth of the nation's population" and further, "Recognizing that our population cannot grow indefinitely, and appreciating the advantages of moving now toward the stabilization of population, the commission recommends that the nation welcome and plan for population stabilization."[4] Thus, to the extent that undocumented Mexican immigration would cause the U.S. population to increase, it probably would adversely affect the standard of living of future generations. The situation is different if it is expected that because of below-replacement fertility the United States is in danger of population decline. If the U.S. population begins to decline, a very high proportion of the population will be beyond the age of retirement. In that case, a continuous influx of working-age Mexican immigrants who paid social security tax and bore lots of children might serve to stabilize the size of the U.S. population, balance its age distribution, and preserve the financial soundness of the social security system.

Equity

Conservatives and liberals have different notions of equity. Conservatives tend to believe that equity is achieved when each individual is rewarded in proportion to his economic contribution to society within a free market. Liberals believe that equity is achieved only when the gap between rich and poor is small. Thus liberals favor a policy of substantial income transfer from the rich to the poor by means of progressive taxation and means-tested entitlement programs. However, a believer in the liberal notion of equity has another dilemma in deciding the desirable level of immigration from Mexico. He must decide whether equity is best achieved by a policy that restores the status of the native-born poor at the expense of denying an opportunity to the much poorer potential immigrant from Mexico, or by a policy that does the opposite.

Among both conservatives and liberals there is probably a consensus that discrimination on the basis of race, ethnic origin, or sex is not compatible with equity.

There is probably also a consensus that any policy that involves a rapid curtailment of formerly held privileges is less desirable than one that provides for a slower rate of change.

Preservation of American culture

Perhaps the major objection to increased Mexican immigration on the part of the American public comes from the belief that such immigration threatens the preservation of American culture as it now exists. There is among native Americans a consensus that English ought to be the language used in ordinary and official discourse. Yet it is feared that if enough Mexican immigrants arrive, this consensus might be destroyed and the United States might institute both English and Spanish as official languages.

The fear that English could eventually become only one of two official languages of the nation might be obviated by enacting now a constitutional amendment stipulating English as the only official language of the federal government. The empirical evidence on the use of English among native-born persons of Mexican descent shown in the Los Angeles County Parents study ought to reduce the fear that Mexican Americans will never learn English. However, if there is a continuing influx of Mexican immigrants and if all Americans are to speak English freely, fiscally expensive programs to teach English as a second language must be carried out.

Many Protestants may fear that because almost all Mexican immigrants are Roman Catholic, the power of the Roman Catholic church in the United States will be enhanced by continued Mexican immigration. Such increased power might lead to an erosion of the traditionally defined separation of church and state and to various governmental actions corresponding more to the wishes of the Roman Catholic church than is now the case.

Civil liberties

Most Americans would concur that nothing should threaten their available civil liberties. Yet there are fears that legislation suggested to reduce the flow of undocumented immigrants into the United States might severely abridge the civil liberties

U.S. citizens have enjoyed up to now. I shall discuss these fears in more detail when I evaluate employer sanctions.

Ethnic conflict

Traditionally in the United States immigration has been associated with ethnic conflict as members of newly arrived immigrant groups have clashed with members of other ethnic groups that arrived earlier. The conflicts are often related (1) to the desires of the older ethnic groups to preserve their culture and to reduce economic competition from the members of the newer groups and (2) to the desires of the newer immigrant groups to preserve their culture and to avoid discrimination based on ethnic or immigrant status.

The power of the United States in international affairs

Obviously, most Americans value the fact that the power of the United States in international affairs is very large. They also wish the nation to maintain its present degree of power, particularly vis-à-vis the USSR.

Mexico has an extensive land frontier with the United States but a per capita income less than one-sixth as large as ours. These facts alone are sufficient to cause many Mexicans to be envious if not hostile to the United States. Add to these the fact that the United States fought a war with Mexico and took away almost one-half of its territory, and one can find an additional reason why many Mexicans are hostile to the United States.

Nevertheless, the friendship of Mexico is of strategic importance to the United States. As of 1981 Mexico's proven oil reserves of 72 billion barrels were the fourth largest in the world. Moreover, its production of petroleum was also the fourth largest, being smaller only than that of the Soviet Union, Saudi Arabia, and the United States.[5]

In recent years the Mexican economy has been in deep trouble. The current period of economic crisis follows upon a prior period of boom. The boom followed the announcement by President Lopez Portillo in 1978 that Mexico had discovered huge new deposits of petroleum.[6] Almost immediately after this announcement, because of war between Iran and Iraq, the worldwide price of petroleum more than doubled. In 1979 the price of Mexico's Maya heavy crude oil was slightly more than $15; by 1981 it had risen to more than $35.[7] During this period of boom, the Mexican government contracted a tremendous foreign indebtedness. Its total external public and private debt rose from about $50 billion in 1980 to $85 billion in 1983.[8]

However, the price of oil fell in 1982 from its previous level of more than $35 a barrel to about $26 a barrel.[9] In 1980 the interest payments on Mexico's public and private external debt had equaled only 23.1 percent of its exported goods and services. By 1983 this proportion had risen to 38 percent.[10] The price of oil was quite stable from 1982 through the fall of 1985. Then it plummeted again. By April 1986 Mexican oil sold for less than $10 a barrel.[11]

By the spring of 1986, Mexico was not able to meet the $10 billion interest payments on its $97 billion external debt without increasing that debt solely for the purpose of making the interest payments.[12]

If Mexico were to fail in its payments, there would be severe repercussions on the eight U.S. banks that have made large loans to Mexico (Citibank, Manufacturers Hanover Trust, Chase Manhattan, Chemical Bank, Bank of America, Morgan Guaranty Trust Company, Bankers Trust Company, and First National Bank of Chicago). These banks have lent the Mexican government a total of $10.5 billion.[13]

By 1987 Mexico's acute financial crisis of the spring of 1986 had been temporarily resolved. In the fall of 1986, the International Monetary Fund worked out a compromise agreement between the government of Mexico and its international lenders.[14] Moreover, a rise in the price of petroleum made the Mexican debt problem more tractable.

However, it is not likely that a long-term solution to the problem of Mexico's external debt will soon be reached. In this context of economic difficulties over the long term, the contribution to the Mexican economy of its undocumented workers in the United States should be considered. In a recent paper, Manuel García y Griego and Francisco Giner de los Ríos provide some valuable information in this regard.[15] First, they provide data showing the very high rate at which the Mexican labor force is currently expanding. With a low projection of size for the future labor force, the Mexican labor force during the 1984–88 period is presumed to be expanding at an annual rate of 3.6 percent; with a high projection, it is presumed to be expanding at a rate of 3.9 percent. García y Griego and Giner de los Ríos have also estimated that from 1980 to 1984 the number of person-years of economic activity among undocumented Mexican workers in the United States (both permanent and shuttle) increased by 360,000. During these same four years, the economically active population of Mexico increased according to the low projection by 2.95 million and according to the high projection by 3.5 million. Thus the 1980–84 increase in person-years of activity of undocumented workers in the United States was equal to between 10.2 and 12.2 percent of the increase in the economically active population in Mexico during the same time period. García y Griego and Giner de los Rios also estimated that in 1984 the total number of person-years of economic activity among undocumented Mexican workers in the United States was 1.4 million, which represented 5.9 to 6.4 percent of the economically active population of Mexico in that year. Moreover, they estimated that in 1984 the permanent and shuttle undocumented workers in the United States sent back remittances of $1.8 billion.

During the first 75 years of the twentieth century, the Mexican government held an ambivalent attitude concerning Mexican emigration to the United States. During the last decade, it has come to believe that such migration represents a safety valve and has expressed its opposition to U.S. legislation intended to restrict its flow.[16]

On December 8, 1983, the Mexican Senate passed a resolution concerning the Simpson–Mazzoli bill and addressed it to Thomas O'Neill, Speaker of the U.S. House of Representatives. This resolution declared,

That the Chamber expresses as a resolution our alarm and concern for the repercussions which will impact both countries if the Simpson–Mazzoli legislation is passed, since this transcendent matter should not be considered from a unilateral perspective, but rather should be treated from a bilateral and even multilateral perspective, taking into account the far-reaching migratory phenomenon of undocumented persons between our two countries.[17]

In an article published in 1984 in the prestigious American journal *Foreign Affairs*, the President of Mexico, Miguel de la Madrid, expressed the following thoughts:

Labor relations are also a matter of concern. The situation of Mexican migrant workers in the United States has been, and continues to be, of special interest. We have reiterated our support for the rights and interests of Mexican nationals abroad. We have no intention of meddling in the legislative processes of the United States. But we express our concern over measures such as the Simpson–Mazzoli bill which could affect the social, labor, and human rights of numerous Mexicans, whose daily work and efforts represent considerable benefit to the U.S. economy.[18]

It would be a severe blow to the United States if social turmoil in Mexico caused the transformation of Mexico into an ally of the Soviet Union. It is quite possible that if the United States were sharply to curtail the flow of undocumented Mexican immigrants, the consequences would be sufficient to instigate precisely this event.

Moreover, U.S.–Mexican relations are not the only consideration with respect to the relationship between the level of immigration to the United States and the power of the United States in international affairs. The French economist-demographer Alfred Sauvy contends that the population size that will maximize the military power of a nation is larger than that population size that will maximize per capita income.[19] Sauvy assumes that military power is maximized when the total gross national product minus that necessary for population subsistence is maximized. However, the population size that will maximize this amount is always larger than that which will maximize the average per capita income. Thus, according to Sauvy, one must choose between the value of maximizing the standard of living and the value of maximizing military power. Accordingly, although an increased flow of immigrants may reduce the average standard of living, it may also increase the power of the United States in world affairs.

Let us apply Sauvy's argument more specifically to the case of undocumented Mexican immigration to the United States. Currently almost one-third of the U.S. federal budget expenditures are devoted to national defense, international affairs, and veteran's benefits.[20] In addition, a large part of the interest on the national debt (equal to about 15 percent of federal expenditures) was incurred to meet past military expenditures.[21] About 27 percent of federal expenditures relate to social security and Medicare;[22] few undocumented Mexicans currently profit from either of these two programs. Thus, as of the moment, it would appear that the federal taxes now being paid by undocumented Mexican immigrants do help to pay for our national defense and international affairs expenditures.

Brief historical overview of proposals for legislative change

Before 1986 the last time the U.S. Congress had approved legislation affecting the inflow of undocumented aliens was in 1952. In that year it approved the so-called Texas proviso specifically stating it should not be considered unlawful for employers to hire persons with no legal right to work in the United States.

Beginning in the early 1970s, however, there were many attempts to enact legislation designed to reduce the number of undocumented aliens entering the nation. The first such legislation was the bill introduced by Representative Rodino of New Jersey and passed in the House of Representatives in 1973 that introduced employer sanctions for hiring undocumented workers. The bill did not, however, pass the Senate.

On August 5, 1977, President Jimmy Carter proposed legislation to Congress that would simultaneously reduce the inflow of illegal aliens, grant a legalization of status to many of the undocumented immigrants currently in the nation, and increase the legal quota for immigrants from Mexico. Congress did not act on these proposals but instead decided to appoint a Select Commission on Immigration and Refugee Policy. This commission's final report of March 1, 1981, made proposals very similar to those President Carter had advanced almost four years earlier. In July 1981 President Reagan announced a series of proposals with regard to illegal immigration that in rough outline were similar to those of President Carter.

The next spring Republican Senator Simpson from Wyoming and Democratic Congressman Mazzoli from Kentucky introduced a bill into Congress designed to provide a legalization of status for many existing illegal aliens and employer sanctions against the future hiring of illegal aliens. The Senate passed the bill in August 1982 by a vote of 81 to 18. However, the House of Representatives failed to act.

Bills were then reintroduced into both the Senate and House of Representatives in 1983. Amendments by relevant committees in the Senate and House of Representatives soon resulted in two quite different versions of the bill. The provisions for status legalization in the Senate bill were less liberal than those in the House bill, whereas the provisions for employer sanctions were more severe. In May 1983 the Senate by a vote of 76 to 18 passed its version of the bill. However, in October 1983 Speaker of the House O'Neill announced that he would not allow the House version of the bill to be voted upon because of opposition to the bill by Hispanics and his belief that there was no constituency for the legislation. Protest of the speaker's decision was widespread; in January 1984 O'Neill relented and decided to allow the House to vote on the bill. The House passed its version of the bill in June of that year by the narrow vote of 215 to 211. During the summer House and Senate conferees tried to reconcile the two quite different versions of the bill that had emerged from each chamber. In October 1984, shortly before Congress was scheduled to adjourn, the conferees admitted that they had not been able to reconcile their differences.

On September 19, 1985, the Senate passed a new version of the Simpson bill by a vote of 69 to 30. The major difference between the 1985 bill and the earlier bill that had passed the Senate in 1983 was the inclusion in the 1985 bill of a "guest workers" program for the growers of perishable crops that allowed 350,000 foreign workers at any one time. In early October 1986, after many observers thought the House of Representatives was too divided to act before adjournment, that body, by a vote of 230 to 166, passed an immigration reform bill not too dissimilar to the one that had already passed the Senate. After representatives of the Senate and House worked out a compromise, the House passed the compromise on a vote of 238 to 173. On October 17, 1986, the Senate gave its approval to the compromise bill by a vote of 63 to 24, and on November 6, 1986, President Reagan signed the Immigration Reform and Control Act of 1986 into law.

The main features of the 1986 legislation were (1) sanctions for the employment of undocumented workers, (2) a legalization program for many of the undocumented, (3) a limited program of "guest workers" for agriculture, (4) a provision that warrants must henceforth be obtained before INS officials could make raids in open agricultural fields, and (5) authorization for increased funding of the INS border patrol.

Evaluation of specific provisions enacted or proposed

Employer sanctions

The 1986 Immigration Reform and Control Act stipulates that it will be unlawful for an employer *knowingly* to hire an illegal alien. It also stipulates graduated civil fines and criminal penalties for convicted employers. However, the act also stipulates that if the General Accounting Office (GAO) finds that widespread discrimination in employment has resulted solely from employer sanctions, Congress must be informed by November 6, 1989. If the GAO reports such discrimination, Congress may, after December 6, 1989, consider a joint resolution (not subject to presidential approval) that would end employer sanctions.

The key clause here is that it shall be illegal for an employer knowingly to hire an illegal alien. What does "knowingly" imply? According to the act, if a new employee has shown the employer: (1) either a social security card or a birth certificate and (2) a driver's license from a U.S. state, the employer could not be accused of acting unlawfully. All experts agree that currently all three of these documents are easily available to undocumented workers, either genuine or counterfeit. Driver's licenses are easy to obtain simply by presenting a birth certificate, which either may be counterfeit or may belong to some other person. Genuine social security cards can be obtained in the same manner. An employer who wants to hire an undocumented employee can easily arrange matters so that there will be no proof that he did so unlawfully. With respect to employers who want to or feel they must employ undocumented persons, it is quite possible that they could be prosecuted only if an INS raid results in the location of an undocumented worker who had previously been located and deported by INS from the same workplace. Enforcement of employer sanctions is also made more difficult by virtue of the fact (shown in Chapter 4) that most undocumented workers are in workplaces with only a few employees. Hence the number of employers whose records must be inspected is very large. Without a better system of determining "knowing" employment, it is likely that employer sanctions will not substantially reduce the number of undocumented workers hired.

The Select Commission on Immigration and Refugee Policy also considered the question of the mechanisms for determining "knowing" employment. The members of the commission were sharply divided on this subject. Eight members voted in favor of a more secure identification system, and seven members voted against.[23] The staff report of the commission contains a discussion of various alternatives for a more secure identification system.[24]

David North has also written extensively on the subject and provides an even more thorough discussion than the staff report of the commission.[25] North proposes a variety of mechanisms, some more certain to detect undocumented persons than others. He notes that three threats must be avoided: (1) counterfeiting, (2) alteration, and (3) impersonation.

In my opinion, impersonation is the main problem. Impersonation can occur when an individual uses someone else's birth certificate to apply for a driver's license or social security card. Hence a foolproof system must begin with a foolproof birth certificate. The birth certificate must possess a thumbprint that can be matched to that of the individual who presents that birth certificate to obtain another document such as the social security card or driver's license. The social security card, if used as evidence of right for employment, must also contain that same thumb-print. It should also contain a photograph and, as suggested by North, some encrypted data (such as mother's maiden name). It is obvious, of course, that such a foolproof system would take many decades to put fully into effect.

A more secure system than presently available could be obtained by reissuing all social security cards in a noncounterfeit form and with both a photograph of the bearer and encrypted information.

The development of a fraudproof social security card (or other worker-identification card) is perceived by many persons as a grave invasion of civil liberties. Annelise Anderson has argued that once such a card had been created it would inevitably be used by government for purposes other than merely preventing the employment of undocumented workers. In her words, "No totalitarian government operates without one."[26] In my opinion, the American public's fear of a national identity card is so great that Congress will never institute a mechanism for identifying undocumented workers substantially more secure than that presented in the 1986 Immigration Reform and Control Act.

On the other hand, the mechanisms for determining "knowing" employment included in the 1986 Immigration Reform and Control Act create a problem additional to the fact that they are probably not very effective. The leaders of the Mexican-American community have become convinced that the mechanisms will lead to employment discrimination against Mexican-Americans who are either native-born or legal immigrants.[27] They believe that many employers, rather than taking a chance of being accused of hiring undocumented persons, will simply refrain from hiring any persons of Mexican descent. Whether their fear is well-founded can be ascertained only by later events. Nevertheless, the fear of such consequences was so great that the leading group to oppose the Mazzoli bill in the House of Representatives was the Hispanic caucus.[28] The Act's provision authorizing congressional review if sanctions do result in discrimination was included to reduce opposition by this caucus.

Legalization of status for the currently undocumented

The 1986 Immigration Reform and Control Act provided legalization of status for many of the undocumented persons in the United States. All persons residing continuously in the United States since January 1, 1972, were allowed to adjust their status to that of permanent legal resident. In addition, the Act created a new legal status called temporary residence status. All persons who had resided continuously in the United States in an unlawful status since before January 1, 1982 (or who had lived in the United States and worked for at least ninety days in agriculture during the year ending May 1, 1986), were to be granted the opportunity for achieving the status of temporary resident if they applied for such legalization between May 5, 1987, and May 5, 1988. All persons wishing to become temporary resident aliens would be required to pay a fee set by the U.S. attorney general (since established as $185 for adults and a maximum of $420 per family) and, in general, be admissible to the United States as an immigrant under established law.

As a temporary resident alien, an individual would be allowed to live and work in the United States but would not be allowed to receive benefits from federally funded means-tested entitlement programs. After one and one-half years as a temporary resident, an individual could apply to become a permanent legal resident upon demonstration that he or she had a minimal knowledge of the English language and of U.S. history and government or that he or she was pursuing a course of study in the English language and in the history and government of the United States. If accepted as a permanent resident alien, the individual would not be entitled to benefits from federally funded means-tested entitlement programs until a date five years following the date of becoming a temporary resident.

The Act makes no provisions for family reunification. For example, if a man entered the United States before January 1, 1982, but his wife and children entered after that date, only the husband could legalize his status. Moreover, even if his wife and children had entered the United States before July 1, 1982, but had not maintained continuous residence (with no absence greater than forty-five days), their status still could not be legalized. The Act's lack of regard for family unity aroused sharp opposition from Archbishop Roger Mahony of the Roman Catholic Church in Los Angeles. He called for new legislation to provide that if one family member were to qualify for legalization, other family members should also receive derivative eligibility.[29] As was shown in Chapter 9, it is likely that a high proportion of husbands who succeed in legalizing their status will have wives who have not been able to become legalized.

As of November 2, 1989, 2,059,600 persons of all nationalities had been approved as temporary residents among 3,031,166 who had applied for legalization and had received preliminary processing. Only 115,646 applications had been denied, 612 cases had been terminated, and 855,300 pending.[30]

What proportion of undocumented Mexicans will receive legal status? Warren and Passel estimated that 49 percent of all undocumented Mexicans counted in the 1980 Census had entered the United States in 1975 or later. I believe, as noted in Chapter 3, that the figure should be higher. If, in November 1986, about one-half of all undocumented Mexicans had also been in the United States for less than five years, a proper administration of the legalization procedures enacted should probably have excluded about one-half of all undocumented Mexicans who were not seasonal agricultural workers in 1986. Unless most of these persons left the United States due to the success of employer sanctions or were able to legalize their status through presentation of counterfeit documents (alleged to be widespread among applicants to the seasonal agricultural worker program[31]), there would continue to be a large number of undocumented Mexicans in the country among those present when the Immigration Reform and Control Act became law.

A feature of any legalization program that has been noted by the Select Commission on Immigration and Refugee Policy and by other writers is that it may promote future undocumented immigration.[32] Prospective immigrants, knowing that amnesty had been granted to one cohort of undocumented immigrants, might come to believe that it would be granted again. Hence the combination of weak provisions with respect to employer sanctions and generous provisions with respect to amnesty may actually encourage more undocumented immigration than would have occurred without passage of the 1986 Act.

What values does legalization of status serve? Let us compare first the undocumented alien before passage of the 1986 Act with the alien in the newly created status of temporary resident alien. From the employer's point of view, a worker who is a temporary resident alien is more valuable than was the undocumented worker because the employer does not have to fear that he will unexpectedly be deported. On the other hand, the employer can no longer threaten deportation if the worker demands a higher wage. It is probable that the employer will both pay a higher wage and receive higher productivity. Thus employers of legalized but formerly undocumented workers will probably neither gain nor lose. Nevertheless, if a higher wage is paid, then taxes collected will be higher and the general public stands to benefit. Moreover, as I pointed out in Chapter 8, a legalization of status is likely to induce a higher proportion of married mothers to enter the labor force for they would no longer have to fear deportation. This change would again increase the volume of taxes collected and would benefit the public in general.

Let us now compare the consequences of transforming persons into permanent resident alien status with access to all entitlement programs as compared to transforming them into temporary resident aliens. Here the tax consequences to the general public are not favorable. Access to entitlement programs will directly raise the tax burden on the general public and, as shown in Chapter 8, also reduce labor-force participation among those now eligible for entitlement programs. As a result the amount of taxes collected from the permanent resident aliens will be less than if they were aliens with temporary status. Moreover, the more that permanent residents withdraw from the labor force (because their reservation wage is higher than the wage that employers wish to pay), the more will the employer be tempted to hire undocumented workers.

The consequences for Mexico of a legalization program or its absence will depend on the success of the program for employer sanctions. Were employer sanctions completely successful in eliminating all undocumented persons in the United States, then the consequences for Mexico of the hypothetical absence of a legalization program would be quite severe. Probably around 2 million persons would suddenly return to Mexico where they might not find immediate employment. Moreover, the substantial volume of remittances of U.S. dollars would cease. A chief rationale for legalization, therefore, is to avoid repercussions in Mexico given the elimination of jobs for undocumented immigrants in the United States. If, as I suspect, about one-half of the undocumented Mexicans in the United States will be granted legal status, then the number who would return to Mexico, with the complete success of employer sanctions, would be only around 1 million. On the other hand, an employer sanction program that reduced the number of undocumented persons in the United States by only 25 percent would not affect Mexico as severely. Only around 500,000 would return without legalization, and the legalization program would reduce that number only to 250,000.

One further point: it should make relatively little difference to Mexico whether undocumented immigrants are transformed into legal immigrants with access to means-tested entitlement programs or whether they are transformed into legal immigrants without access to such programs.

Guest-worker programs

The Immigration Reform and Control Act of 1986 made rather complex provisions for the entry of agricultural guest workers. The secretaries of labor and agriculture were authorized to decide the numbers needed. However, for fiscal 1990 the number of entrants under the program could be no more than 95 percent of the number of agricultural workers who had been given temporary legal status. Moreover, the numbers in succeeding years would have to be even less than the number in 1990.

—The obvious rationale for the inclusion of the guest-worker program for growers of "perishable crops" in the 1986 Act was to placate those employers of agricultural laborers who have in the recent past relied very heavily upon undocumented labor.

However, guest-worker programs can be criticized on the grounds that they are not equitable and infringe on the civil liberties of both employers and employees. All guest-worker programs restrict the use of guest workers to those employers who have petitioned the government for their use, and they allow the government to decide which employers have the right to employ such workers.

Additional funds for enforcement

The 1986 Immigration Reform and Control Act authorized expenditures by INS for the border patrol such that the average level of personnel in each of fiscal 1987 and 1988 would be at least 50 percent higher than for fiscal 1986. This level implies a continuation of the trend toward more funding, which advanced from $349 million in fiscal 1980 to $576 million in fiscal 1985.[33]

No one knows the relative cost effectiveness of enforcing employer sanctions versus having an increased number of border patrol officers on duty at the border. Apart from that question, David North has made several suggestions that might greatly improve the efficiency of INS enforcement operations. One of these ideas is to increase the funding of the border patrol by making available to it revenues from new fees collected from persons passing through ports of entry and from the issuance of nonimmigrant visas. A second suggestion, to discourage visa abusers, is to require a nonrefundable return airline ticket for all nonimmigrants arriving in the United States by air. A third suggestion is that the existing fence along the border with Mexico be removed somewhat to the north of the actual border so that the border patrol can patrol both sides of it rather than only one side.[34]

Reduction in the level of entitlement benefits

One can make a strong case for the argument that a major cause for the presence of undocumented workers in the United States is that means-tested entitlement programs raise the reservation wage of legal residents to such an extent that employers are no longer interested in hiring them. If benefits from entitlement programs were lower, more legally resident persons would enter the work force and fewer undocumented persons would be hired. This argument has been made directly by Arthur Corwin.[35] Obliquely, the same argument has been made by Michael Piore and by Wayne Cornelius and his associates.[36] They argue that undocumented workers do not displace native-born Americans because they mostly take jobs Americans will not accept.

The plausibility of this argument is advanced by the empirical correlations reported in Chapter 3. There I showed that the highest of six correlations between economic-opportunity variables in six states and the proportion of the Mexican-origin population in those states that was undocumented in 1980 was the correlation with the average monthly AFDC payment in 1970.

The argument is therefore persuasive on both logical and empirical grounds. Nevertheless, it is extremely unlikely that such a means of curbing undocumented immigrants would be acceptable to the American people. In fall 1984 an initiative to reduce welfare spending (Proposition 41) appeared on the California ballot. At the time, AFDC and Medicaid benefits in California were close to being the highest in the nation. The initiative proposed that welfare payments in the state be no higher than the average figure paid by other states plus 10 percent. The initiative was opposed even by the Republican governor of California, George Deukmejian, and was overwhelmingly defeated with 63 percent of the electorate voting against it.[37]

Change in the constitutional requirement concerning citizenship

According to the Fourteenth Amendment to the U.S. Constitution, "All persons born or naturalized in the United States, and subject to the jurisdiction thereof, are citizens of the United States and of the State wherein they reside."[38] The Fourteenth Amendment is closely in accord with the principle of *jus soli*. Many other nations have quite different legislation.[39] In these nations, whose laws are in accordance with *jus sanguinis,* only the children of citizens are themselves citizens.

This constitutional requirement certainly enhances the attraction of the United States to undocumented immigrants because it gives them the expectation that their children will be able to attain more success in life than they themselves will have. Therefore, it probably acts to stimulate the volume of undocumented immigration to the United States.

On the other hand, the constitutional requirement serves a very valuable function in preventing ethnic conflict if one assumes that the future flow of undocumented immigrants cannot be eliminated. The reason is that it prevents the development of a permanent underclass. Currently Germany is experiencing considerable ethnic conflict between its citizens and its Turkish immigrants, and France has conflict between its citizens and its resident Arab population.[40] No doubt these conflicts are exacerbated by the fact that neither nation allows citizenship to the children of its immigrants.

The constitutional requirement also provides a greater safety net for certain undocumented families. Because of it, these families are able to obtain food stamps and AFDC assistance for their American-born children.

In a 1985 book, Peter Schuck and Rogers Smith advocated that Congress should pass a law denying American citizenship to persons born in the future in the United States to undocumented parents.[41] They believe that the Supreme Court should then uphold the constitutionality of such a law. Such a law would appear to be a patent violation of the clear words of the Fourteenth Amendment. Nevertheless, the authors argue that Congress, in submitting this amendment to the states just after the close of the Civil War, did not intend that it be used to protect the children of undocumented persons. Of course, at that time the United States had no undocumented persons because no laws restricted persons from entering the United States.

If the Supreme Court were to approve such a law on the aforementioned grounds, it would set a bad precedent. To extend this theory onto similar circumstances, if a future Congress were to pass a law depriving homosexuals of citizenship, the Supreme Court could approve it on the grounds that in the late 1860s AIDS did not exist. Moreover, if it had existed, Congress in the 1860s would have wanted to deny citizenship to all homosexuals. Similarly, suppose a future Congress were to pass a law depriving all Jews of citizenship. The Court could then approve it on the grounds that in the 1860s the State of Israel did not exist. The court could argue that if the State of Israel had existed in the 1860s, the Congress of that period would have believed that the existence of such a nation caused American Jews to have a double allegiance. Therefore, the Congress of the 1860s would not have intended that the Fourteenth Amendment be used to give citizenship to Jews.

On the other hand, suppose Congress and the states were to approve a revision of the Fourteenth Amendment by a new constitutional amendment specifically denying citizenship to the native-born children of undocumented persons. In this case, the damage to equity would be very much reduced. However, due to the general difficulties in passing any constitutional amendment, the likelihood of such a formal revision of the Fourteenth Amendment is extremely unlikely.

More vigorous enforcement of minimum wage and fair labor standards

Alejandro Portes has advocated more vigorous enforcement of minimum wage and fair labor standards legislation as a means of diminishing the attractiveness to employers of undocumented workers and thus of reducing the volume of undocumented immigration. He also urges more vigorous enforcement of these laws to lessen the impact of such immigration on the wages paid to native-born unskilled workers.[42]

Enforcement of these laws would be most likely to have an effect chiefly on the number of female undocumented Mexican workers. As was shown in Chapter 8, most undocumented male workers receive more than the minimum wage. However, a very high proportion of female workers were receiving less than the minimum wage. Many of those receiving less than the minimum wage were working in the apparel industry. If employers in the apparel industry were forced to pay their female workers more, it is likely that many would find that they could not afford to do so. Hence many jobs now held by undocumented Mexican females would be lost, and some of the displaced undocumented workers might return to Mexico. However, it is doubtful that enforcement of labor laws in the apparel industry would have much effect on the labor conditions of native-born unskilled workers. Figures from the 1980 Census tabulated by researchers in the Urban Institute study indicate that more than 89 percent of production workers in the apparel industry in Los Angeles County were immigrants.[43]

A major reason why it has been so difficult to enforce labor laws in the apparel industry is that the undocumented workers who suffer from violations of the law have not dared to complain. Hence, it is not likely that more stringent enforcement of labor standards, taken as an action in isolation from other measures, is a cost-effective means for reducing the flow of undocumented immigrants even in the apparel industry. Moreover, as was shown in Chapter 8, the majority of undocumented workers, particularly the men, work in jobs where they already receive the minimum wage. Enforcement of labor standards is not likely to affect the jobs held by these workers.

An open border

The idea of an open border has been advanced by certain Chicanos and also by the *Wall Street Journal*.[44] At least two separate policies are possible, each of which would contain no restrictions on the number of Mexican immigrants to the United States. The first policy would allow an unlimited number of Mexican immigrants to live and work in the United States but would not allow them access to means-tested entitlement programs, the privilege of eventually becoming a U.S. citizen, or the privilege of petitioning for relatives to become permanent legal residents. The second policy would treat any Mexican who wished to immigrate to the United States the same as any other permanent legal resident of the United States.

We have no way of estimating how many more Mexican immigrants would come to the United States under each of these two variants of an open-border policy than come to the United States at present. Nevertheless, because many undocumented Mexican immigrants now pay large sums to coyotes to guide them across the border and not all potential Mexican immigrants can afford such sums, it would appear that either version of an open border would substantially increase the flow of Mexican immigrants. Moreover, the second type of open-border policy would have the larger effect.

The first type of open border, in comparison with the second, would appear to have the least harmful effects on the U.S. taxpayer. But both types of open border substantially advance Mexican values at the possible expense of the values of United States residents. Even with respect to the interest of the United States in preventing a Mexican regime allied to the Soviet Union, an open-border policy may present too much of a concession to the interests of Mexico.

Personal policy preference

It should be evident from what has been said earlier that I do not concur with those who see major benefits to the United States from the continued flow of undocumented Mexican immigration. On the other hand, I do not concur with those other experts who see such migration as an unmitigated harm. I believe such migration will probably have, on balance, detrimental effects on the U.S. standard of living, particularly in the long term, unless it serves only to stabilize rather than increase our population size. But because the volume of this immigration is not likely to be very high, this negative effect, if any, will not be of major importance. Employer sanctions, as enacted in the Immigration Reform and Control Act of 1986, are not likely to affect the volume of undocumented immigration substantially. Furthermore, the American public would never tolerate the type of national identification card that would be necessary to make employer sanctions really effective. Finally, Mexican-American spokepersons have cogently argued that employer sanctions without the presence of a foolproof national identification card will cause at least some employers to discriminate against legally resident persons of Mexican descent.

It is unlikely that continued immigration from Mexico at its current level presents a significant threat to the preservation of American culture. There seems to be clear evidence that almost all U.S.-born persons of Mexican descent speak English well. Moreover, the fertility of native-born persons of Mexican descent is not high.

The United States should consider the political consequences in Mexico that might be occasioned by a policy severely restricting the present flow of undocumented immigrants. It is important to remember that the net annual flow of undocumented Mexican immigrants is rather small relative to the size of the population of the United States but is much larger relative to the population of Mexico. This is because the U.S. population is about three times that of Mexico. There is a real danger that Mexico could undergo a political change that would transform it into an ally of the Soviet Union. The continued flow of Mexican immigrants into the United States at close to its present volume will help prevent that possibility from occurring.

Being undocumented is the cause of many worries and unhappy events. Not only that, but the U.S. taxpayer will benefit if deportations and the fear of deportation cease. This benefit would occur because deportations reduce the productivity of undocumented workers. Moreover, Paula Hancock's data (see Chapter 8) indicate that fear of deportation reduces the probability that married undocumented women will work. As a result, fewer taxes can be collected from undocumented persons.

Specific proposals

The proposals I shall now set forth are by no means entirely original. In making them, I draw heavily upon ideas and policies previously advanced by many other persons.[45]

Legalization of status

Despite the legalization procedures of the 1986 Immigration Reform and Control Act, there are no doubt many undocumented persons remaining in the United States. For a fee of $200 per individual, I would allow all undocumented persons from any nation who had resided unlawfully for at least the last year in the United States to transform their status into that of legal entrant. Legal entrants would have the right to reside and work in the United States for the rest of their lifetimes. They would not have the rights to mean-tested entitlement programs or to the benefits of the Medicare program of the social security system nor the right to become a permanent legal resident unless they qualified on the same grounds as any other alien. They would, however, have rights to the old-age, survivors, and disability insurance programs of the social security system, to unemployment benefits, and to a public education. Their native-born children would continue to have all of the rights of U.S. citizens.

For the future, I would propose that all citizens of the two nations that border the United States, Mexico and Canada, should have the lifetime privilege of becoming a legal entrant under an annual quota of 150,000 persons for both nations combined. A fee would be charged to each entrant based on the price that would clear the market given the quota number.

It might seem better to have confined this privilege to Mexicans only. However, a special favoritism to Mexico should be avoided in favor of a policy providing equal benefits to the citizens of both nations with whom the United States shares a common border.

How much more money would future legal entrants have to pay for their permit than the $200 required of persons who in the base period had lived in the United States for at least one year? One cannot be certain. Nevertheless, the market price in the near term would probably be no more than two or three times higher than that charged to persons already in the United States.

Moreover, for all Mexicans and Canadians, I would allow the legal entry permit to be marketable. Any individual who sold his permit back to the U.S. government would be allowed to assume that it was valid for fifty years from date of issue. For example, if he sold it five years after issue, it would be good for forty-five additional years and he would be given a refund equal to 90 percent of the current market price. A marketable system is of great importance for Mexicans given the fact that many of them do not wish to remain in the United States permanently. A stipulation could be added stating that the entry permit could be sold back to the U.S. government by a Mexican only at an American consulate in Mexico and by a Canadian only at an American consulate in Canada. In this way, it would not be possible for an individual to sell his permit and then remain surreptitiously in the United States. The U.S. government would piece together remaining years from the permits sold back to it and would issue one new permit for each fifty years of nonuse from previously issued permits. In order to prevent persons with expired permits from staying in the United States after their permits had expired, I would not want the government to sell permits for less than a lifetime.

Among those prospective entrants who did not have all of the money needed to pay for the permit, many could use personal property or land as collateral and b..rrow sufficient funds to pay the remainder. Others could probably obtain a loan from relatives or friends already in the United States. The necessity for paying the lifetime fee should result in immigration of individuals with a higher probability of economic success than would be likely given some other rationing mechanism.

Given the size of the quota and the marketability of the permit, I believe that paying for the permit would represent a good bargain. Accordingly, there would henceforth be relatively few persons from either Mexico or Canada desirous of entering the United States as undocumented persons.

What would be the consequences of this proposal for the number of legal entrants in the United States? I think it plausible, given the adoption of this proposal in 1989, that at least 1 million persons, other than those already legalized under the 1986 Act, would qualify and be willing to pay the $200 fee chargeable to persons already in the United States for at least one year. Thereafter, presuming the marketability of the permits, one could expect the number of Mexicans and Canadians with permits to increase by almost 150,000 per year for the first twenty-five years (the actual number would be equal to 150,000 minus any deaths). After fifty years the total number of living entrants who had paid the market price for a permit would be somewhat less than 7.5 million. How many would be Mexican and how many Canadian is not certain. After about the first fifty years, the number of entrants in the United States with marketable permits could not substantially increase because the number of persons with permits who died each year would just about equal the number of new permits sold.

It is probable that after fifty years Mexico would no longer be confronted with rapid increase in the size of its labor force. This prediction will be true if Mexico were able within the next thirty years to end the rapid annual increase in the number of births that has characterized its past history. However, currently Mexico's labor force is expanding at an annual rate of almost 4 percent, and it is improbable that there will be much diminution in this rate of expansion during the next decade.

My final stipulation with respect to the permits for legal entry would be that a large share of the proceeds from their sale must be devoted to increasing the funding of immigration law enforcement.

Immigration law enforcement

I do not propose any system of employer sanctions. However, I would favor spending at least as much money to enforce immigration control as does the Immigration Reform and Control Act of 1986.

During the summer of 1984, I had occasion to observe the means used to secure the Olympic Village set up on the University of Southern California campus for the athletes participating in the various events. I noticed that the athletes were protected by two parallel lines of high barbed-wire fences. Anyone attempting to penetrate into the village would not only have to climb up and down two fences but would also be subject to repulse by guards patrolling the territory between the two fences. It seems to me such a system of fences would be ideal for the U.S. – Mexican border. The single fence precisely at the border, now existing across from Tijuana, Mexicali, and other Mexican-border cities, is full of holes that have been cut by persons from the Mexican side. Once an immigrant has gone through one of these holes, it is relatively easy to escape further into the United States. With two parallel fences, the potential undocumented immigrant would have to cut both. Neither of the parallel fences should be immediately at the border. Thus, the INS border patrol could exert a constant presence not only in the corridor between the two fences but on the side of the first fence closest to Mexico.

Reform of the system for admitting permanent legal residents

The current system that imposes a maximum quota of 20,000 immigrants from any one nation is not fair. It discriminates too much against the citizens of nations with large populations or with large numbers of persons desiring to become immigrants to the United States. I believe that it should be abolished in favor of one worldwide quota.

Moreover, I favor even more radical reform in the system for admitting permanent legal residents. As has been previously pointed out by Jagdish Bhagwati, under the current system of preferences in the United States, the very limited number of immigrants who meet the requirements for admission enjoy a large economic windfall, particularly if they come from a less developed nation where their earnings would be much less than in the United States.[46] A system should be instituted in which the United States government authorizes the sale of 350,000 new nonrefugee admissions per year. The proposed system would thus discard the present system of preferences. I further propose that the market set the price. A 50 percent rebate should be given to those persons (spouses and children of U.S. citizens and parents of U.S. citizens aged 21 or older) who currently can come into the United States without quota. Relatives of U.S. citizens should have some preference in entering the United States. But charging a fee to such persons should reduce the extent of fraud currently encountered.

I would allow a permanent legal resident who had paid a market fee for admittance the right to sell his permit unless he had lived in the United States for five years or more. Such a sale could occur only in a U.S. consulate in his own country of origin. If the individual had received a 50 percent rebate in the original purchase, he would have to pay back to the U.S. government one-half of the price he received in the sale. The marketability of the permits would ensure that the net flow of legal immigrants would be almost as large as the quota (the difference being immigrants of five or more year's duration of residence who later emigrated). Moreover, it would also mean that the total number of permits on the market would always be considerably larger than the 350,000 new permits sold by the U.S. government each year.

I believe this reform in the system for admitting permanent legal residents would be more equitable than the current system and would also provide, on the average, for more economically productive immigrants. Moreover, in contrast to the current system, it provides a cap on nonrefugee admissions.

Results of proposed reforms

All of the reforms I have proposed would, in all probability, not increase the net number of immigrants, both legal and undocumented, entering the United States in future years. In making its current population estimates, the U.S. Bureau of the Census now assumes that the net annual flow of undocumented immigrants into the United States is 200,000 and that the annual outflow of foreign-born legal immigrants is 133,000.[47] In fiscal 1986 the number of legal immigrants to the United States who were not refugees was 497,325.[48] Adding together these 497,325 legal immigrants with the 200,000 net undocumented immigrants and subtracting the 133,000 legal immigrants who annually emigrate, we obtain the sum of 564,325 net foreign-born immigrants. Under current law, this sum is bound to increase in future years if only because there is no limit on the number of admissions of persons who are close relatives of U.S. citizens.

I propose the admission of 350,000 permanent immigrants and 150,000 legal entrants. This sums to only 500,000. The net flow of legal immigrants and entrants would be somewhat less than this due to the emigration of some immigrants who had lived in the United States five years or more. I believe that there would still be some flow of undocumented immigrants, particularly from Western Hemisphere nations other than Mexico and Canada. However, elimination of national quotas and increased funding of the INS border patrol (coupled with better ideas for border control) should drastically reduce the net flow of such persons.

The conversion of undocumented Mexicans into legal entrants would reduce their marked concentration in Los Angeles County. A principal reason for the concentration of such immigrants there at the present time is that the county is close to the Mexican border. This fact is very important because in the event the undocumented Mexican is apprehended by the INS and deported to the nearest Mexican border city, he needs to travel only a short distance to get back to Los Angeles.

The net tax consequences of my proposal would probably differ little from the net tax consequences of current policy. Unemployment benefits are now commonly received by undocumented persons even though such persons are not legally allowed to receive them. The Supreme Court has already ruled that undocumented children must be given a free public education. Finally, under current law, undocumented persons with a valid social security card are entitled to social security benefits. Government expenditures for immigrants would rise, but not substantially. On the positive side, government receipts would be enhanced by the fees charged for the legal-entry permits. Moreover, removal of the fear of deportation would also imply that immigrants would work more weeks and that therefore more taxes would be collected.

The new immigration category, legal entrant, created by my proposal would certainly contain a package of rights much more generous than that now granted to undocumented Mexican immigrants. Moreover, my proposal would also reform the system of admitting individuals to the category of permanent legal resident. Accordingly, it would be much easier for Mexicans in the category of legal entrant to elevate their status than it is under current law for newly entering undocumented Mexican immigrants.

Would my proposal eliminate the existence of undocumented immigrants, who now enjoy the fewest legal privileges in the nation? As I have already stated, the answer cannot be unequivocally positive. But the number of undocumented immigrants is largely a function of the fact that U.S. immigration law supplies national quotas for legal immigration that bear little relation to the demand generated within each nation. My proposal would significantly adjust supply to meet demand. Thus, I believe it would drastically reduce the number of such less-privileged individuals.

Notes

Chapter 1

1 David M. Heer, "USC Neighborhood Changes," unpublished paper, 1982.
2 Peter H. Schuck and Rogers M. Smith, *Citizenship without Consent: Illegal Aliens in the American Polity* (New Haven, Conn.: Yale University Press, 1985), p. 29.
3 "Mexicans Try to Identify Boxcar Victims," *Los Angeles Times,* July 5, 1987.
4 Schuck and Smith, *Citizenship without Consent,* pp. 163–4.
5 U.S. Immigration and Naturalization Service, *1974 Annual Report* (Washington, D.C.: Government Printing Office, 1974), p. iii; L. Meyer, "Aliens Hard to Count," *Washington Post,* February 2, 1975.
6 Robert Warren and Jeffrey S. Passel, "A Count of the Uncountable: Estimates of Undocumented Aliens Counted in the 1980 United States Census," *Demography 24,* no. 3 (1987): 375–93.
7 U.S. Immigration and Naturalization Service, "Provisional Legalization Application Statistics, November 2, 1989."
8 David M. Heer and Jeffrey S. Passel, "Comparison of Two Methods for Computing the Number of Undocumented Mexican Adults in Los Angeles County," *International Migration Review 21,* no. 4 (1987): 1446–73.

Chapter 2

1 U.S. Bureau of the Census, *Statistical Abstract of the United States, 1985* (Washington, D.C.: Government Printing Office, 1985), p. 86; U.S. Bureau of the Census, *Historical Statistics of the United States Colonial Times to 1970* (Washington, D.C.: Government Printing Office, 1975), Part 1, pp. 107–8.
2 U.S. Bureau of the Census, *1980 Census of Population,* Vol. 1, Characteristics of the Population, PC-80-D1 (Washington, D.C.: Government Printing Office, 1984), p. 9.
3 Everett S. Lee, "A Theory of Migration," *Demography 3* (1966): 47–57.
4 David M. Heer, *Society and Population* (Englewood Cliffs, N.J.: Prentice-Hall, 1975), pp. 94–6.
5 Population Reference Bureau, *1985 World Population Data Sheet* (Washington, D.C.: Population Reference Bureau, 1985).
6 Edward W. Fernandez and Arthur R. Cresce, "Social and Economic Status of the Hispanic Foreign-born: The Assimilation Experience," unpublished paper presented at the Annual Meeting of the Population Association of America, Boston, March 28–30, 1985.
7 Heer, *Society and Population,* p. 95.
8 James W. Wilkie and Adam Perkal, eds., *Statistical Abstract of Latin America,* Vol. 23 (Los Angeles: UCLA Latin American Center Publications, University of California, 1984), p. 358.
9 Secretaría de Programación y Presupuesto, *Anuario Estadístico de los Estados Unidos Mexicanos, 1980* (Mexico City: Secretaría de Programación y Presupuesto, 1982), p. 59.

10 Vernon M. Briggs, Jr., *Immigration Policy and the American Labor Force* (Baltimore: The Johns Hopkins University Press, 1984), p. 27.

11 David Carliner, "The Legal Framework," unpublished paper prepared for Professors World Peace Academy conference, Crossing the Border, San Diego, California, February 2, 1985.

12 Briggs, *Immigration Policy*, p. 38.

13 Arthur F. Corwin, "A Story of Ad Hoc Exemptions: American Immigration Policy toward Mexico," in Arthur F. Corwin, ed., *Immigrants–and Immigrants: Perspectives on Mexican Labor Migration to the United States* (Westport, Conn.: Greenwood Press, 1978), p. 144; Julian Samora, *Los Mojados: The Wetback Story* (Notre Dame, Ind.: University of Notre Dame Press, 1971), p. 40.

14 Corwin, "Story of Ad Hoc Exemptions."

15 Corwin, ibid., p. 146.

16 Arthur F. Corwin and Johnny M. McCain, "Wetbackism since 1964: A Catalogue of Factors," in Arthur F. Corwin, ed., *Immigrants–and Immigrants: Perspectives on Mexican Labor Migration to the United States* (Westport, Conn.: Greenwood Press, 1978), p. 87.

17 Briggs, *Immigration Policy*, p. 99. See also Manuel García y Griego, "The Importation of Mexican Contract Laborers to the United States, 1942–64: Antecedents, Operation, and Legacy," in Peter G. Brown and Henry Shue, eds., *The Border That Joins: Mexican Migrants and U.S. Responsibility* (Totowa, N.J.: Rowman and Littlefield, 1983), pp. 49–98.

18 U.S. Immigration and Naturalization Service, *Guide to Immigration Benefits, Rev. Ed., 1982* (Washington, D.C.: Government Printing Office, 1982), p. 49.

19 Gary Abrams, "Silva Letter Holder in an Immigration Limbo," *Los Angeles Times,* March 17, 1985.

20 Briggs, *Immigration Policy,* p. 87.

21 John Crewdson, *The Tarnished Door: The New Immigrants and the Transformation of America* (New York: Times Books, 1983); Pablo Cruz, *Pablo Cruz and the American Dream,* compiled by Eugene Nelson (Salt Lake City, Utah: Peregrine Smith, 1975); Grace Halsell, *The Illegals* (New York: Stein and Day, 1978); Edwin Harwood, *In Liberty's Shadow* (Stanford, Calif.: Hoover Institution Press, 1986); Samora, *Los Mojados.*

22 Briggs, *Immigration Policy,* p. 132.

23 U.S. Bureau of the Census, *Statistical Abstract of the United States, 1985* (Washington, D.C.: Government Printing Office, 1985), p. 91; U.S. Bureau of the Census, *Statistical Abstract of the United States, 1989* (Washington, D.C.: Government Printing Office, 1989), p. 175; U.S. Immigration and Naturalization Service, *1988 Statistical Yearbook of the Immigration and Naturalization Service* (Washington, D.C.: INS 1989), p. 110.

24 Unpublished data from the INS.

25 U.S. Immigration and Naturalization Service, *1981 Statistical Yearbook of the Immigration and Naturalization Service* (Washington, D.C.: U.S. INS, 1984), pp. 122–3.

26 U.S. Immigration and Naturalization Service, *1980 Statistical Yearbook of the Immigration and Naturalization Service* (Washington, D.C.: U.S. INS, 1983), p. 121.

27 Robert Warren and Jeffrey S. Passel, "A Count of the Uncountable: Estimates of Undocumented Aliens Counted in the 1980 Census," *Demography* 24, no. 3 (1987):375–93.

28 Memorandum of August 16, 1985 from Jeffrey S. Passel to Roger Herriot, Chief, Population Division, U.S. Bureau of the Census (personal communication from Jeffrey S. Passel).

29 U.S. Immigration and Naturalization Service, *1980 Statistical Yearbook of the Immigration and Naturalization Service* (Washington, D.C.: U.S. INS, 1983), pp. 121–2.

30 Carlos H. Zazueta and César Zazueta, *En las Puertas del Paraíso* (Mexico City: Centro Nacional de Información y Estadísticas del Trabajo, 1980), p. 62.

31 Harwood, *In Liberty's Shadow,* pp. 77–124.

32 U.S. Immigration and Naturalization Service, *1986 Yearbook of the Immigration and Naturalization Service* (Washington, D.C.: 1987), p. 95.

33 Harwood, *In Liberty's Shadow*, pp. 177–80.
34 W. Tim Dagodag, "Source Regions and Composition of Illegal Mexican Immigration to California," *International Migration Review 9*, no. 4 (1975): 499–511.
35 Samora, *Los Mojados*, pp. 64–65.
36 Zazueta and Zazueta, *En las Puertas del Paraíso*.
37 Corwin and McCain, "Wetbackism since 1964," p. 75.
38 Zazueta and Zazueta, *En las Puertas del Paraíso*, p. 70.
39 Richard Mines, *Developing a Community Tradition of Migration to the United States: A Field Study in Rural Zacatecas, Mexico, and California Settlement Areas*, Monographs in U.S.–Mexican Studies, 3 (La Jolla: Program in United States–Mexican Studies, University of California, San Diego, 1981), pp. 65–73.
40 Arthur Golden, "Sham Nuptials Worry Immigration Officials," *San Diego Union*, September 10, 1985.
41 Harwood, *In Liberty's Shadow*, p. 158.
42 Charles Hirschman, "Prior U.S. Residence among Mexican Immigrants," *Social Forces 56*, no. 4 (1978): 1179–1201.
43 Lisa Kubiske, "A Survey of Immigrant Visa Applicants Handled by the Mexico City Consular District," *FAIR/Information Exchange*, October 15, 1985.
44 Andrea Tyree and Katherine Donato, "The Sex Composition of Legal Immigrants to the United States," *Sociology and Social Research 69*, no. 4 (July 1985): 577–85.
45 Wayne A. Cornelius, *The Future of Mexican Immigrants in California: A New Perspective for Public Policy*, Working Papers in U.S.–Mexican Studies, 6 (La Jolla: Program in United States–Mexican Studies, University of California, San Diego, 1981), p. 61.
46 For an interesting account of the factors determining the migration to the United States from Mexico during these decades, see Douglas Massey, Rafael Alarcon, Jorge Durand, and Humberto Gonzalez, *Return to Aztlan: The Social Process of International Migration from Western Mexico* (Berkeley: University of California Press, 1987), pp. 39–44.
47 Abraham Hoffman, "Mexican Repatriation during the Great Depression: A Reappraisal," in Arthur F. Corwin, ed., *Immigrants–and Immigrants: Perspectives on Mexican Labor Migration to the United States* (Westport, Conn.: Greenwood Press, 1978), pp. 225–47; Carey McWilliams, "Getting Rid of the Mexican," *American Mercury 28* (1933): 322–324.
48 Hoffman, ibid., pp. 227–34.
49 Briggs, *Immigration Policy*, p. 132.
50 Ibid, p. 100.
51 U.S. Bureau of the Census, *1980 Census of Population*, Vol. 1, Characteristics of the Population, PC80-1-D1-A (Washington, D.C.: Government Printing Office, 1984), Table 254.
52 U.S. Bureau of the Census, *1970 Census of Population*, Vol. 1, Characteristics of the Population, Part 1, Section 2 (Washington, D.C.: Government Printing Office, 1973), p. 598.
53 U.S. Commission on Civil Rights, *Counting the Forgotten: The 1970 Census Count of Persons of Spanish Speaking Background in the United States* (Washington, D.C.: U.S. Commission on Civil Rights, 1974), p. 45.
54 Maurice D. Van Arsdol, Jr., Joan W. Moore, David M. Heer, and Susan Paulvir Haynie, *Non-apprehended and Apprehended Undocumented Residents in the Los Angeles Labor Market: An Exploratory Study*, Final Report of Contract No. 20-06-77-16 to the Employment and Training Administration, U.S. Department of Labor (Los Angeles Population Research Laboratory, University of Southern California, 1979; available from the National Technical Information Service, Springfield, Va.), p. 120.
55 Arthur F. Corwin, "The Numbers Game: Estimates of Illegal Aliens in the United States, 1970–81," *Law and Contemporary Problems 45*, no. 2 (1982), pp. 273–6; Crewdson, *The Tarnished Door*, pp. 108–11; Jeffrey S. Passel and Karen A. Woodrow, "Geographic Distribution of Undocumented

Immigrants: Estimates of Undocumented Aliens Counted in the 1980 Census by State," *International Migration Review 18*, no. 3 (1984), p. 644.

Chapter 3

1 L. H. Whittemore, "Can We Stop the Invasion of Illegal Aliens?," *South Bend Tribune*, February 29, 1976.
2 U.S. Immigration and Naturalization Service, *1974 Annual Report* (Washington, D.C.: Government Printing Office, 1974), p. iii.
3 L. Meyer, "Aliens Hard to Count," *Washington Post*, February 2, 1975.
4 Lesko Associates, "Final Report: Basic Data and Guidance Required to Implement a Major Illegal Alien Study," prepared for the U.S. Immigration and Naturalization Service, Washington, D.C., October 1975.
5 Howard Goldberg, "Estimates of Emigration from Mexico and Illegal Entry into the United States, 1960–70, by the Residual Method," Final Research Paper, Georgetown University Center for Population Research, 1975.
6 Lesko Associates, "Final Report."
7 Goldberg, "Estimates of Emigration."
8 Letter of December 23, 1975 from Vincent P. Barabba to Congressman Herman Badillo, cited in Jorge A. Bustamante, "Immigration from Mexico: The Silent Invasion Issue" in Roy Bryce-Laporte, ed., *Sourcebook on the New Immigration: Implications for the United States and the International Community* (New Brunswick, N.J.: Transaction Books, 1980), pp. 139–44.
9 Bustamante, "Immigration from Mexico."
10 "Marshall Warns on Illegal Aliens," *Los Angeles Times*, September 23, 1977.
11 "Rising Tide," *Wall Street Journal*, September 19, 1977.
12 Maurice D. Van Arsdol, Jr., Joan W. Moore, David M. Heer, and Susan Paulvir Haynie, *Non-apprehended and Apprehended Undocumented Residents in the Los Angeles Labor Market: An Exploratory Study*, Final Report of Contract No. 20-06-77-16 to the Employment and Training Administration, U.S. Department of Labor (Los Angeles, Population Research Laboratory, University of Southern California, 1979; available from National Technical Information Service, Springfield, Va. 22151)
13 Charles B. Keely and Eleanor P. Kraly, "Recent Net Alien Immigration to the United States: Its Impact on Population Growth and Native Fertility," *Demography 15* (1978): 267–83.
14 Van Arsdol et al., *Non-apprehended and Apprehended Undocumented Residents*, pp. 103–27.
15 David M. Heer, "What Is the Annual Net Flow of Undocumented Mexican Immigrants to the United States?," *Demography 16*, no. 3 (1979): 417–23.
16 Clarice Lancaster and Frederick J. Scheuren, "Counting the Uncountable Illegals: Some Initial Statistical Speculations Employing Capture-recapture Techniques," in *1977 Proceedings of the Social Statistical Section of the American Statistical Association* (Washington, D.C.: American Statistical Association), pp. 530–6.
17 Van Arsdol et al., *Non-apprehended and Apprehended Undocumented Residents*, p. 124.
18 J. Gregory Robinson, "Estimating the Approximate Size of the Illegal Alien Population in the United States by the Comparative Trend Analysis of Age-specific Death Rates," *Demography 17*, no. 2 (1980): 159–176.
19 Juan Diez-Cañedo, "A New View of Mexican Migration to the United States," unpublished Ph.D. dissertation, Massachusetts Institute of Technology, 1980. The results of the same research are also contained in Juan Diez-Cañedo Ruiz, *La Migración Indocumentada de Mexico a los Estados Unidos* (Mexico City: Fondo de Cultura Económica, 1984).
20 Manuel García y Griego, *El Volumen de la Migración de Mexicanos no Documentados a los Estados*

Unidos (Nuevas Hypotesis) (Mexico City: Centro Nacional de Información y Estadísticas del Trabajo, 1980).

21 Frank D. Bean, Allan G. King, and Jeffrey S. Passel, "The Number of Illegal Migrants of Mexican Origin in the United States: Sex Ratio–Based Estimates for 1980," *Demography 20*, no. 1 (1983): 99–109.

22 Charles B. Keely, "Counting the Uncountable: Estimates of Undocumented Aliens in the United States," *Population and Development Review 3*, no. 4 (1977): 473–81.

23 Kenneth Roberts, Michael E. Conroy, Allan G. King, and Jorge Rizo-Patrón, "The Mexican Migration Numbers Game," Research report, Bureau of Business Research, University of Texas at Austin, 1978.

24 Jacob S. Siegel, Jeffrey S. Passel, and J. Gregory Robinson, "Preliminary Review of Existing Studies of the Number of Illegal Residents in the United States," paper prepared at the request of the Select Commission on Immigration and Refugee Policy, U.S. Bureau of the Census, Washington, D.C., 1980.

25 Joshua S. Reichert and Douglas S. Massey, "Patterns of U.S. Migration from a Mexican Sending Community: A Comparison of Legal and Illegal Migrants," *International Migration Review 13*, no. 4 (1979): 599–623.

26 Manuel García y Griego and Leobardo Estrada, "Research on the Magnitude of Mexican Undocumented Immigration to the U.S.: A Summary," in *Mexican Immigrant Workers in the U.S.*, Antonio Rios-Bustamante, ed. (Los Angeles: Chicano Studies Research Center, University of California at Los Angeles, 1981), pp. 51–70.

27 Kenneth Hill, "Illegal Aliens: An Assessment," in Daniel B. Levine, Kenneth Hill, and Robert Warren, eds., *Immigration Statistics: A Story of Neglect* (Washington, D.C.: National Academy Press, 1985), pp. 225–50.

28 Robert Warren and Jeffrey S. Passel, "A Count of the Uncountable: Estimates of Undocumented Aliens Counted in the 1980 Census," *Demography 24*, no. 3 (August 1987): 375–93.

29 García y Griego and Estrada, "Magnitude of Mexican Undocumented Immigration."

30 U.S. Bureau of the Census, *1980 Census of Population*, Vol. 1, Characteristics of the Population, PC-80-1-B1 (Washington, D.C.: Government Printing Office, 1983), p. C-1.

31 Centro Nacional de Información y Estadísticas del Trabajo (CENIET), *Los Trabajadores Mexicanos en Estados Unidos: Resultados de la Encuesta Nacional de Emigración a la Frontera Norte del País y a los Estados Unidos* (Mexico City, CENIET, 1982). Earlier preliminary figures were substantially smaller; 405,000 for absent workers and 371,000 for returned workers. These preliminary figures were cited in García y Griego and Estrada, "Magnitude of Mexican Undocumented Immigration."

32 Vernon M. Briggs, Jr., *Immigration Policy and the American Labor Force* (Baltimore: Johns Hopkins University Press, 1984), pp. 234–5.

33 Arthur F. Corwin, "A Story of Ad Hoc Exemptions: American Immigration Policy toward Mexico," in Arthur F. Corwin, ed., *Immigrants–and Immigrants: Perspectives on Mexican Labor Immigration to the United States* (Westport, Conn.: Greenwood Press, 1978), p. 139.

34 Richard Mines and Douglas S. Massey, "Patterns of Migration to the United States from Two Mexican Communities," *Latin American Research Review 20*, no. 2 (1985): 104–23.

35 David S. North and Marion F. Houstoun, *The Characteristics and Role of Illegal Aliens in the U.S. Labor Market: An Exploratory Study* (Washington, D.C.: New TransCentury Foundation, 1976), p. A-9.

36 Patricia Morales, *Indocumentados Mexicanos* (Mexico City: Editorial Grijalbo, 1981), p. 178.

37 CENIET, *Los Trabajadores Mexicanos*, p. 76.

38 David M. Heer and Jeffrey S. Passel, "Comparison of Two Methods for Estimating the Number of Undocumented Mexican Adults in Los Angeles County," *International Migration Review 21*, no. 4 (1987): 1446–73.

39 Richard Mines, *Developing a Community Tradition of Migration: A Field Study in Rural Zacatecas, Mexico, and California Settlement Areas* (La Jolla: Program in U.S.–Mexican Studies, University of California, San Diego, 1981), pp. 96–99; James Stuart and Michael Kearney, *Causes and Effects of*

Agricultural Labor Migration from the Mixteca of Oaxaca to California (La Jolla: Program in U.S.–Mexican Studies, University of California, San Diego, 1981), pp. 7–9; Joshua S. Reichert and Douglas S. Massey, "Patterns of Migration from a Mexican Sending Community: A Comparison of Legal and Illegal Migrants," *International Migration Review 13*, no. 4 (1979): 599–623; Wayne A. Cornelius, *Mexican Migration to the United States: Causes, Consequences, and U.S. Responses* (Cambridge, Mass.: Center for International Studies, Massachusetts Institute of Technology, 1978), p. 19.

40 Heer and Passel, "Estimating the Number of Undocumented Mexican Adults."

41 U.S. Bureau of the Census, *1980 Census of Population*, Vol. 1, Characteristics of the Population, PC-80-1-C1, pp. E1–E13.

42 Jeffrey S. Passel and Karen A. Woodrow, "Geographic Distribution of Undocumented Immigrants: Estimates of Undocumented Aliens Counted in the 1980 Census by State," *International Migration Review 18*, no. 3 (1984): 642–71.

43 John Crewdson, *The Tarnished Door: The New Immigrants and the Transformation of America* (New York: Times Books, 1983), p. 108; Arthur F. Corwin, "The Numbers Game: Estimates of Illegal Aliens in the United States, 1970–81," *Law and Contemporary Problems, 45*, no. 2 (1982): 274–6.

44 Crewdson, *The Tarnished Door.*

45 Cornelius, *Mexican Migration*, p. 26.

46 Miguel Cervera, *Tabla de Estancia en los Estados Unidos para Trabajadores Mexicanos Indocumentados* (Mexico City: Centro Nacional de Información y Estadistícas del Trabajo, 1979), p. 27.

47 Passel and Woodrow, "Geographic Distribution of Undocumented Aliens."

48 Memorandum of August 16, 1985 from Jeffrey S. Passel to Roger Herriot, Chief, Population Division, U.S. Bureau of the Census (personal communication from Jeffrey S. Passel).

49 Recently released data on applicants for legalization from all nations under the Immigration Reform and Control Act of 1986 show a geographic concentration similar to that shown in Table 3.4. As of June 24, 1988, there had been 1,731,683 applications for legalization (excluding those of seasonal agricultural workers). Of these, 54.9 percent were filed from California and 33.8 percent from Los Angeles County. See U.S. Immigration and Naturalization Service, "Provisional Legalization Application Statistics, June 24, 1988."

50 North and Houstoun, *Characteristics and Role of Illegal Aliens*, pp. A7–8.

51 Ibid., p. A9.

52 Carlos Zazueta and Rodolfo Corona, *Los Trabajadores Mexicanos en los Estados Unidos: Primeros Resultados de la Encuesta Nacional de Emigración* (Mexico City: Centro Nacional de Información y Estadísticas del Trabajo, 1979).

53 U.S. Bureau of the Census, *1980 Census of Population*, Supplementary Report, PC80-S7 (Washington, D.C.: Government Printing Office, 1982), pp. 14–17.

54 U.S. Bureau of the Census, *1980 Census of Population*, Vol. 1, Characteristics of the Population, PC80-1-C45, Table 57.

55 U.S. Bureau of the Census, *1980 Census of Population*, Vol. 1, Characteristics of the Population, PC80-1-C1, pp. B22–B23.

56 Ibid., Table 97.

57 Passel and Woodrow, "Geographic Distribution of Undocumented Immigrants," Table 10.

58 Published findings from the Urban Institute study include Thomas Muller, *The Fourth Wave: California's Newest Immigrants: A Summary* (Washington, D.C.: The Urban Institute Press, 1984); Thomas J. Espenshade and Tracy Ann Goodis, "Recent Immigrants to Los Angeles: Characteristics and Labor Market Impacts," Policy Discussion Paper, The Urban Institute, May 1985; Donald M. Manson, Thomas J. Espenshade, and Thomas Muller, "Mexican Immigration to Southern California: Issues of Job Competition and Worker Mobility," Policy Discussion Paper, The Urban Institute, August 1985; and Thomas Muller and Thomas J. Espenshade, *The Fourth Wave: California's Newest Immigrants* (Washington, D.C.: The Urban Institute Press, 1985). The findings of the study by the Southern California Association of Governments are in *Southern California: A Region in Transition*, Vol. 1–3 (Los

Angeles: SCAG, December 1984). Published findings from the Rand study are in Kevin F. McCarthy and R. Burciaga Valdez, *Current and Future Effects of Mexican Immigration in California* (Santa Monica, Calif.: Rand Corporation, 1985).

59 Heer and Passel, "Estimating the Number of Undocumented Mexican Adults."
60 U.S. Bureau of the Census, *1980 Census of Population,* Vol. 1, Characteristics of the Population, PC80-1-D6, Table 195.
61 Heer and Passel, "Estimating the Number of Undocumented Mexican Adults."
62 Muller, *The Fourth Wave,* p. 18.
63 Manson, Espenshade, and Muller, "Mexican Immigration to Southern California," p. 20.
64 U.S. Bureau of the Census, *1980 Census of Population,* Vol. 2, Subject Reports, PC80-2-2A (Washington, D.C.: Government Printing Office, 1985), Table 22.
65 Manson, Espenshade, and Muller, "Mexican Immigration," p. 23.
66 U.S. Bureau of the Census, *1980 Census of Population,* Vol. 2, Subject Reports, PC80-2-2A, Table 28.
67 Manson, Espenshade, and Muller, "Mexican Immigration," p. 18.
68 Ibid., p. 25.
69 U.S. Bureau of the Census, *1980 Census of Population,* Vol. 2, Subject Reports, PC80-2-2A, Table 11.
70 Philip L. Martin, "Illegal Immigration and the Colonization of the American Labor Market," *CIS Paper,* No. 1 (Washington, D.C.: Center for Immigration Studies, 1986).
71 Southern California Association of Governments, *Southern California,* Vol. 2: Impacts of Present and Future Immigration, pp. IV-1-IV-6.
72 Espenshade and Goodis, "Recent Immigrants," p. 25.
73 Ibid., p. 26.
74 Ibid., pp. 19–21.
75 Ibid., pp. 26–27.
76 Ibid., p. 27.
77 McCarthy and Valdez, *Effects of Mexican Immigration,* p. 21.
78 Muller and Espenshade, *The Fourth Wave,* p. 143.
79 Muller, *The Fourth Wave,* p. 17.
80 Ibid., p. 22.
81 Ibid., p. 16.
82 Ibid., pp. 22–3.
83 Ibid., p. 23.

Chapter 4

1 James E. Pearce and Jeffery W. Gunther, "Immigration from Mexico: Effects on the Texas Economy," *Economic Review,* Federal Reserve Bank of Dallas, September 1985, pp. 1–14; Frank D. Bean, Harley L. Browning, and W. Parker Frisbie, "The Sociodemographic Characteristics of Mexican Immigrant Status Groups: Implications for Studying Undocumented Mexicans," *International Migration Review* 18, no. 3 (1984): 672–91.
2 Bob Williams, "Alien Survey: What Caused Breakdown," *Los Angeles Times,* February 13, 1979; William J. Eaton, "Illegal Aliens Survey Expected to Resume," *Los Angeles Times,* June 23, 1979; Arthur F. Corwin, "The Numbers Game: Estimates of Illegal Aliens in the United States, 1970–81," *Law and Contemporary Problems 45,* no. 2 (1982): 223–97.
3 Maurice D. Van Arsdol, Jr., Joan W. Moore, David M. Heer, and Susan Paulvir Haynie, *Nonapprehended and Apprehended Undocumented Residents in the Los Angeles Labor Market: An Exploratory Study,* Final Report of Contract No. 20-06-77-16 to the Employment and Training Administration, U.S. Department of Labor (Los Angeles: Population Research Laboratory, University

of Southern California, 1979; available from the National Technical Information Service, Springfield, Va. 22151); Richard C. Jones, "Changing Patterns of Undocumented Mexican Migration to South Texas," *Social Science Quarterly 65,* no. 2 (1984): 465–81; Estevan T. Flores, "Research on Undocumented Immigrants and Public Policy: A Study of the Texas School Case," *International Migration Review 18,* no. 3 (1984): 505–23.

4 Jorge A. Bustamante, "Undocumented Immigration from Mexico: Research Report," *International Migration Review 11,* no. 2 (1977) 149–77; Jorge A. Bustamante and Geronimo G. Martinez, "Undocumented Immigration from Mexico: Beyond Borders but within Systems," *Journal of International Affairs 33,* no. 2 (1979): 265–84; Centro Nacional de Información y Estadísticas del Trabajo (CENIET), *Análisis de Algunos Resultados de la Primera Encuesta a Trabajadores no Documentados Devueltos de los Estados Unidos,* Octubre 23–Noviembre 13 de 1977 (Mexico City: CENIET, 1979); W. Tim Dagodag, "Source Regions and Composition of Illegal Mexican Immigration to California," *International Migration Review 9,* no. 4 (1975): 499–511; David S. North and Marion F. Houstoun, *The Characteristics and Role of Illegal Aliens in the U.S. Labor Market* (Washington, D.C.: New TransCentury Foundation, 1976); Julian Samora, *Los Mojados: The Wetback Story* (Notre Dame, Ind.: University of Notre Dame Press, 1971); M. Vic Villalpondo, *A Study of the Socioeconomic Impact of Illegal Aliens on the County of San Diego* (San Diego: County of San Diego Human Resources Agency, 1977).

5 North and Houstoun, *Characteristics and Role of Illegal Aliens,* pp. 69–72.

6 CENIET, *Análisis de Algunos Resultados.*

7 North and Houstoun, *Characteristics and Role of Illegal Aliens.*

8 Van Arsdol et al., *Non-apprehended and Apprehended Undocumented Residents.*

9 Wayne A. Cornelius, *Interviewing Undocumented Immigrants: Methodological Reflections Based on Fieldwork in Mexico and the United States,* Working Papers in U.S.–Mexican Studies, 2 (La Jolla: Program in United States–Mexican Studies, University of California, San Diego, 1981), p. 10.

10 Reynaldo Baca and Dexter Bryan, "Mexican Undocumented Workers in the Binational Community: A Research Note," *International Migration Review 15,* no. 4 (1981): 737–48.

11 Gilbert Cárdenas, "Manpower Impact and Problems of Mexican Illegal Aliens in an Urban Labor Market," unpublished Ph.D. dissertation, Sociology Department, University of Illinois at Urbana–Champaign, 1977.

12 Wayne A. Cornelius, *The Future of Mexican Immigrants in California: A New Perspective for Public Policy,* Working Papers in U.S.–Mexican Studies, 6 (La Jolla: Program in United States–Mexican Studies, University of California, San Diego, 1981).

13 Richard Mines, *Developing a Community Tradition of Migration to the United States: A Field Study in Rural Zacatecas, Mexico, and California Settlement Areas,* Monographs in U.S.–Mexican Studies, 3 (La Jolla: Program in United States–Mexican Studies, University of California, San Diego, 1981).

14 Joshua S. Reichert and Douglas S. Massey, "Patterns of U.S. Migration from a Mexican Sending Community: A Comparison of Legal and Illegal Migrants," *International Migration Review 13,* no. 4 (1979): 599–623.

15 Wayne A. Cornelius, *Mexican Migration to the United States: Causes, Consequences, and U.S. Responses* (Cambridge, Mass.: Migration and Development Study Group, Center for International Studies, Massachusetts Institute of Technology, 1978).

16 Mines, *Developing a Community Tradition.*

17 Sheldon L. Maram, *Hispanic Workers in the Garment and Restaurant Industries in Los Angeles County: A Social and Economic Profile,* Working Papers in U.S.–Mexican Studies, 12 (La Jolla: Program in United States–Mexican Studies, University of California at San Diego, 1980).

18 Lisa Kubiske, "A Survey of Immigrant Visa Applicants Handled by the Mexico City Consular District," *FAIR/Information Exchange,* October 15, 1985.

19 The results of these three surveys are found in the following three publications of the State of California Department of Social Services: *Aid to Families with Dependent Children: Social and Economic*

Characteristics of Families Receiving Aid during July 1979 (May 1981); *Aid to Families with Dependent Children: Social and Economic Characteristics of Families Receiving Aid during January 1981* (July 1982); and *Aid to Families with Dependent Children: Social and Economic Characteristics of Families Receiving Aid during July 1983* (March 1985).

20 Robert Warren and Jeffrey S. Passel, "A Count of the Uncountable: Estimates of Undocumented Aliens Counted in the 1980 Census," *Demography 24*, no. 3 (August 1987): 375–93.
21 CENIET, *Análisis de Algunos Resultados.*
22 North and Houstoun, *Characteristics and Role of Illegal Aliens.*
23 Samora, *Los Mojados.*
24 Reichert and Massey, "Patterns of U.S. Migration."
25 Van Arsdol et al., *Non-apprehended and Apprehended Undocumented Residents.*
26 Baca and Bryan, "Mexican Undocumented Workers."
27 Maram, *Hispanic Workers.*
28 Ibid.
29 North and Houstoun, *Characteristics and Role of Illegal Aliens*, p. 82.
30 Cornelius, *Mexican Migration*, p. 19.
31 Van Arsdol et al., *Non-apprehended and Apprehended Undocumented Residents*, pp. 37–44.
32 Baca and Bryan, "Mexican Undocumented Workers."
33 Maram, *Hispanic Workers*, pp. 19–24.
34 Ibid., pp. 80–83.
35 Cornelius, *Mexican Migration*, p. 26.
36 Maram, *Hispanic Workers*, pp. 14–19.
37 Ibid., pp. 75–80.
38 Mines, *Developing a Community Tradition*, pp. 187–188.
39 Bustamente, "Undocumented Immigration from Mexico"; Bustamente and Martinez, "Undocumented Immigration from Mexico"; Cárdenas, "Manpower Impact and Problems of Mexican Illegal Aliens in an Urban Labor Market," pp. 58–62; Dagodag, "Source Regions and Composition of Illegal Mexican Immigration to California"; Jones, "Changing Patterns of Undocumented Mexican Migration to South Texas"; North and Houstoun, *Characteristics and Role of Illegal Aliens*, pp. 52–54; Samora, *Los Mojados*, pp. 91–94; Van Arsdol et al., *Non-apprehended and Apprehended Undocumented Residents in the Los Angeles Labor Market*, pp. 28–31. For a summary of data from several studies see Patricia Morales, *Indocumentados Mexicanos* (Mexico City: Editorial Grijalbo, 1981), pp. 183–91, and Richard C. Jones, "Macro-Patterns of Undocumented Migration between Mexico and the U.S." in Richard C. Jones, ed., *Patterns of Undocumented Migration: Mexico and the United States* (Totowa, N.J.: Rowman and Allanheld, 1984), pp. 33–57.
40 Manuel García y Griego, "La Polemica sobre el Volumen de la Emigración a Estados Unidos," in Centro de Estudios Internacionales, *Indocumentados: Mitos y Realidades* (Mexico City: El Colegio de México, 1979), pp. 209–26.
41 Jones, "Macro-Patterns of Undocumented Migration," see note 37.
42 Van Arsdol et al., *Non-apprehended and Apprehended Undocumented Residents*, pp. 28–31.
43 Bustamante, "Undocumented Immigration from Mexico."
44 Cárdenas, "Manpower Impact," p. 61.
45 Morales, *Indocumentados Mexicanos*, pp. 186–88.
46 Bustamante, "Undocumented Immigration from Mexico."
47 North and Houstoun, *Characteristics and Role of Illegal Aliens*, p. 103.
48 Cornelius, *Mexican Migration*, p. 23.
49 Carlos H. Zazueta and César Zazueta, *En las Puertas del Paraiso* (Mexico City: Centro Nacional de Información y Estadísticas del Trabajo, 1980), p. 70.
50 Cornelius, *Mexican Migration*, p. 23.
51 Villalpando, *Socioeconomic Impact of Illegal Aliens*, p. 163.

52 Cárdenas, "Manpower Impact," pp. 78–80.
53 Van Arsdol et al. *Non-apprehended and Apprehended Undocumented Residents*, p. 27.
54 Cornelius, *Mexican Migration*, p. 24.
55 Ibid., pp. 45–46.
56 Wayne A. Cornelius, "La Nueva Mitologia de la Emigración Indocumentada Mexicana a los Estados Unidos," in Centro de Estudios Internacionales, *Indocumentados: Mitos y Realidades* (Mexico City: El Colegio de Mexico, 1979), pp. 111–35.
57 North and Houstoun, *Characteristics and Role of Illegal Aliens*, pp. 79–81.
58 Villalpando, *Socioeconomic Impact of Illegal Aliens*, p. 64.
59 Kubiske, "A Survey of Immigrant Visa Applicants," p. 7.
60 Maram, *Hispanic Workers*, pp. 27–29.
61 Ibid., pp. 86–89.
62 Carlos H. Zazueta and Fernando Mercado, "El Mercado de Trabajo Norteamericano y los Trabajadores Mexicanos: Algunos Elmentos Teóricos y Empíricos para su Discusion," unpublished paper presented at the Mexico–United States Seminar on Undocumented Migration sponsored by the University of New Mexico and the Centro de Estudios Economicos y Sociales del Tercer Mundo, Mexico City, September 1980.
63 Cornelius, *Mexican Migration*, p. 66.
64 Cornelius, *The Future of Mexican Immigrants*, p. 33.
65 Maram, *Hispanic Workers*, pp. 39–41.
66 Ibid., pp. 97–100.
67 North and Houstoun, *Characteristics and Role of Illegal Aliens*, pp. 138–39.
68 Cárdenas, "Manpower Impact," p. 101.
69 Cornelius, *The Future of Mexican Immigrants*, p. 62.
70 Kubiske, "A Survey of Immigrant Visa Applicants," p. 6.
71 Maram, *Hispanic Workers*, p. 44.
72 Ibid., p. 101.
73 U.S. Bureau of the Census, *Statistical Abstract of the United States, 1987* (Washington, D.C.: Government Printing Office, 1987), p. 408.
74 Ramón M. Salcido, "Undocumented Aliens: A Study of Mexican Families," *Social Work* 24, no. 4 (1979): 306–34.
75 Ramón M. Salcido, "Use of Services in Los Angeles County by Undocumented Families: Their Perceptions of Stress and Sources of Social Support," *California Sociologist 5*, no. 2 (1982): 119–31.

Chapter 5

1 James R. Abernathy, Bernard G. Greenberg, and Daniel G. Horvitz, "Estimates of Induced Abortion in North Carolina," *Demography* 7, no. 1 (Spring 1970): 19–29.
2 Joan W. Moore (with contributing authors), *Homeboys: Gangs, Drugs and Prison in the Barrios of Los Angeles* (Philadelphia: Temple University Press, 1979).

Chapter 6

1 Robert Warren and Jeffrey S. Passel, "A Count of the Uncountable: Estimates of Undocumented Aliens Counted in the 1980 United States Census," *Demography 21*, no. 4 (August 1987): 375–93.
2 U.S. Commission on Civil Rights, *The Tarnished Golden Door: Civil Rights Issues in Immigration* (Washington, D.C.: U.S. Commission on Civil Rights, 1980), p. 17.

Chapter 7

1 David M. Heer and Jeffrey S. Passel, "Comparison of Two Methods for Estimating the Number of Undocumented Mexican Adults in Los Angeles County," *International Migration Review 21*, no. 4 (Winter 1987): 1446–73; Robert Warren and Jeffrey S. Passel, "A Count of the Uncountable: Estimates of Undocumented Aliens Counted in the 1980 United States Census," *Demography 24*, no. 3 (August 1987): 375–93.
2 Heer and Passel, "Estimating the Number of Undocumented Mexican Adults."
3 Wayne A. Cornelius, *Mexican Migration to the United States: Causes, Consequences, and U.S. Responses* (Cambridge, Mass.: Migration and Development Study Group, Center for International Studies, Massachusetts Institute of Technology, 1978), p. 19.
4 Sheldon L. Maram, *Hispanic Workers in the Garment and Restaurant Industries in Los Angeles County: A Social and Economic Profile*, Working Papers in U.S.–Mexican Studies, 12 (La Jolla: Program in United States–Mexican Studies, University of California at San Diego, 1980), pp. 20–22 and pp. 81–82.
5 Kevin F. McCarthy and R. Burciaga Valdez, *Current and Future Effects of Mexican Immigration in California: Executive Summary* (Santa Monica, Calif.: Rand Corporation, 1985), p. 28.
6 Frank D. Bean, Harley L. Browning, and W. Parker Frisbie, "The Sociodemographic Characteristics of Mexican Immigrant Status Groups: Implications for Studying Undocumented Mexicans," *International Migration Review 18*, no. 3 (1984): 672–91.
7 Ibid.
8 U.S. Bureau of the Census, *1970 Census of Population*, Vol. 1, Characteristics of the Population, Part 6, Section 1 (Washington, D.C.: Government Printing Office, 1973) p. 430; U.S. Bureau of the Census, *1980 Census of Population*, Vol. 1, Characteristics of the Population, PC80-1-D6 (Washington, D.C.: Government Printing Office, 1983), p. 13.
9 Dee Falasco and David M. Heer, "Economic and Fertility Differences between Legal and Undocumented Migrant Mexican Families: Possible Effects of Immigration Policy Changes," *Social Science Quarterly 65*, no. 2 (1984): 495–504.
10 U.S. National Center for Health Statistics, *Health, United States, 1983* (Washington, D.C.: Government Printing Office, 1983), p. 172.
11 Heer and Passel, "Estimating the Number of Undocumented Mexican Adults."
12 Edwin Harwood, *In Liberty's Shadow* (Stanford, Calif.: Hoover Institution Press, 1986), p. 197.
13 Stephanie J. Ventura, "Births of Hispanic Parentage, 1980," *Monthly Vital Statistics Report*, Vol. 32, No. 6, Supplement (September 23, 1983), p. 10.
14 Frank Bean, Ruth M. Cullen, Elizabeth H. Stephen, and C. Gray Swicegood, "Generational Differences in Fertility among Mexican Americans: Implications for Assessing the Effects of Immigration," *Social Science Quarterly 65*, no. 2 (1984): 573–82; Frank D. Bean and Gray Swicegood, "Generation, Female Education and Mexican American Fertility," *Social Science Quarterly 63*, no. 1 (1982): 131–44.

Chapter 8

1 U.S. Bureau of the Census, *1980 Census of Population*, Vol. 1, Characteristics of the Population, PC80-1-D6 (Washington, D.C.: Government Printing Office, 1983), pp. 712–21.
2 Ibid.
3 Maurice D. Van Arsdol, Jr., Joan W. Moore, David M. Heer, and Susan Paulvir Haynie, *Nonapprehended and Apprehended Undocumented Residents in the Los Angeles Labor Market: An Exploratory Study*, Final Report of Contract No. 20-06-77-16 to the Employment and Training Administration, U.S. Department of Labor (Los Angeles: Population Research Laboratory, University

of Southern California, 1979; available from the National Technical Information Service, Springfield, Va. 22151), pp. 71–72.

4 U.S. Bureau of the Census, *1980 Census of Population,* Vol. 1, Characteristics of the Population, PC80-1-D6, pp. 1372–4.

5 Ibid.

6 Ibid., pp. 1903–4.

7 David S. North and Marion F. Houstoun, *The Characteristics and Role of Illegal Aliens in the U.S. Labor Market: An Exploratory Study* (Washington, D.C.: New TransCentury Foundation, 1976), p. 128.

8 David S. North, *Government Records: What They Tell Us about the Role of Illegal Immigrants in the Labor Market and in Income Transfer Programs* (Washington, D.C.: New TransCentury Foundation, 1981), p. 67.

9 David S. North, *Immigration and Income Transfer Policies in the United States: An Analysis of a Non-relationship* (Washington, D.C.: New TransCentury Foundation, 1982), p. 25.

10 North, *Government Records,* pp. 53–7.

11 See the following three publications of the State of California, Department of Social Services: *Aid to Families with Dependent Children: Social and Economic Characteristics of Families Receiving Aid during July 1979* (May 1981); *Aid to Families with Dependent Children: Social and Economic Characteristics of Families Receiving Aid during January 1981* (July 1982): and *Aid to Families with Dependent Children: Social and Economic Characteristics of Families Receiving Aid during July 1983* (March 1985).

12 See the issues of July 1979, January 1981, and July 1983 of State of California, Department of Social Services, *Public Welfare in California.*

13 Linda J. Wong, John E. Huerta, and Morris J. Baller, *The Rights of the Immigrant Poor* (Los Angeles: Mexican-American Legal Defense and Educational Fund, 1983), pp. 44–7.

14 Memorandum of April 2, 1982 from Harry L. Hufford, Chief Administrative Officer, County of Los Angeles to Deane Dana, Supervisor, Fourth Supervisorial District.

15 North, *Immigration and Income Transfer Policies in the United States,* p. 21.

16 Ibid., pp. 13–9.

17 Paula F. Hancock, "The Effect of Welfare Eligibility on the Labor Force Participation of Women of Mexican Origin in California," *Population Research and Policy Review 5,* no. 2 (1986): 163–85.

18 North, *Government Records,* p. 11.

19 Ibid., p. 9.

20 Ibid., pp. 63–6.

Chapter 9

1 U.S. Commission on Civil Rights, *The Tarnished Golden Door: Civil Rights Issues in Immigration* (Washington, D.C.: U.S. Commission on Civil Rights, 1980), p. 17.

Chapter 10

1 Barry R. Chiswick, "Immigrants and Immigration Policy," in William Fellner, ed., *Contemporary Economic Problems* (Washington, D.C.: American Enterprise Institute for Public Policy Research, 1978), pp. 285–322.

2 See Walter Fogel, *Mexican Illegal Alien Workers in the United States* (Los Angeles: Institute of Industrial Relations, University of California, Los Angeles, 1978) and Maurice D. Van Arsdol, Jr., Joan W. Moore, David M. Heer, and Susan Paulvir Haynie, *Non-apprehended and Apprehended Undocumented Residents in the Los Angeles Labor Market: An Exploratory Study,* Final Report of Contract No. 20-06-77-16 to the Employment and Training Administration, U.S. Department of Labor (Los

Angeles: Population Research Laboratory, University of Southern California, 1979; available from the National Technical Information Service, Springfield, VA 22151).

3 David S. North and Marion F. Houstoun, *The Characteristics and Role of Illegal Aliens in the U.S. Labor Market* (Washington, D.C.: New TransCentury Foundation, 1976).

4 Robert Warren and Jeffrey S. Passel, "A Count of the Uncountable: Estimates of Undocumented Aliens Counted in the 1980 United States Census," *Demography 24*, No. 3 (August 1987): 375–93.

Chapter 11

1 Barry R. Chiswick, "The Impact of Immigration on the Level and Distribution of Economic Well-Being," in Barry R. Chiswick, ed., *The Gateway: U.S. Immigration Issues and Policies* (Washington, D.C.: American Enterprise Institute for Public Policy Research, 1982), pp. 289–313.

2 Thomas Muller and Thomas J. Espenshade, *The Fourth Wave: California's Newest Immigrants* (Washington, D.C.: The Urban Institute Press, 1985), p. 143.

3 Julian L. Simon, *The Ultimate Resource* (Princeton, N.J.: Princeton University Press, 1981), pp. 196–215.

4 Commission on Population Growth and the American Future, *Population and the American Future* (Washington, D.C.: Government Printing Office, 1972), pp. 12 and 110.

5 Manuel R. Millor, *Mexico's Oil: Catalyst for a New Relationship with the U.S.?* (Boulder, Colo.: Westview Press, 1982), pp. 61–2.

6 Ibid., p. 60.

7 Patrick Oster, "Mexico's Struggle with Slipping Oil Prices," *San Jose Mercury News*, April 20, 1986.

8 James W. Wilkie and Adam Perkal, eds., *Statistical Abstract of Latin America*, Vol. 24 (Los Angeles: UCLA Latin American Center Publications, 1986), p. 616.

9 Oster, "Mexico's Struggle."

10 Wilkie and Perkal, *Statistical Abstract of Latin America*, p. 617.

11 Oster, "Mexico's Struggle."

12 Ibid.

13 S. Karene Witcher, "Lending Banks Fear Mexico May Need Billions More Interest-Rate Concessions," *Wall Street Journal*, February 10, 1986.

14 S. Karene Witcher, "Mexico Lenders Agree to Join Rescue Package," *Wall Street Journal*, October 1, 1986.

15 Manuel García y Griego and Francicso Giner de los Ríos, "Es Vulnerable la Economia Mexicana a la Aplicacion de Politicas Migratorias Estadunidenses?," unpublished paper, El Colegio de Mexico, 1985.

16 Arthur F. Corwin, "Mexican Policy and Ambivalence toward Labor Emigration to the United States," in Arthur F. Corwin, ed., *Immigrants–and Immigrants: Perspectives on Mexican Labor Migration to the United States* (Westport, Conn.: Greenwood Press, 1978), pp. 176–224.

17 Richard D. Lamm and Gary Imhoff, *The Immigration Time Bomb* (New York: Truman Talley Books/ E.P. Dutton, 1985), p. 219.

18 Miguel de la Madrid H., "Mexico: the New Challenges," *Foreign Affairs 63*, no. 1 (1984): 62–76.

19 Alfred Sauvy, *General Theory of Population* (New York: Basic Books, 1969), pp. 51–64.

20 U.S. Bureau of the Census, *Statistical Abstract of the United States*, 1987 (Washington, D.C.: Government Printing Office, 1987), pp. 293–4.

21 Ibid.

22 Ibid.

23 Select Commission on Immigration and Refugee Policy, *U.S. Immigration Policy and the National Interest: Final Report*, Washington, D.C., 1981, p. 61.

24 Select Commission on Immigration and Refugee Policy, *U.S. Immigration Policy and the National Interest: Staff Report*, Washington, D.C., 1981, pp. 584–624.

25 David S. North, *Enforcing the Immigration Law: A Review of the Options* (Washington, D.C.: New TransCentury Foundation, 1980), pp. 55–75.

26 Annelise Anderson, *Illegal Aliens and Employer Sanctions: Solving the Wrong Problem* (Stanford, Calif.: Hoover Institution, 1986).

27 Rodolfo O. de la Garza, "Mexican Americans, Mexican Immigrants, and Immigration Reform," in Nathan Glazer, ed., *Clamor at the Gates* (San Francisco: Institute for Contemporary Studies Press, 1985), pp. 93–105; Frank del Olmo, "Simpson–Mazzoli: Implications for the Latino Community," in Wayne A. Cornelius and Ricardo Anzaldua Montoya, eds., *America's New Immigration Law: Origins, Rationales and Potential Consequences* (La Jolla: Center for United States–Mexican Studies, University of California, San Diego, 1983), pp. 123–6.

28 Lamm and Imhoff, *The Immigration Time Bomb*, pp. 233–42.

29 Archbishop Roger Mahony, "Statement on Those Who Will Not Qualify for Legalization under the New Immigration Reform and Control Act of 1986," Archdiocese of Los Angeles, April 13, 1987.

30 U.S. Immigration and Naturalization Service, "Provisional Legalization Application Statistics, Nov. 2, 1983."

31 Marita Hernandez, "INS Reports 'Dramatic' Rise in Fake Work Papers," *Los Angeles Times*, November 17, 1988; Philip L. Martin, "Immigration Reform and California Agriculture," *FAIR/Information Exchange*, October 6, 1988.

32 Select Commission on Immigration and Refugee Policy, *U.S. Immigration Policy and the National Interest: Final Report*, Washington, D.C., 1981, p. 82; Pastora San Juan Cafferty, Barry R. Chiswick, Andrew M. Greeley, and Teresa Sullivan, *The Dilemma of American Immigration: Beyond the Golden Door* (New Brunswick, N.J.: Transaction Books, 1983), p. 188; Arthur F. Corwin, "A Human Rights Dilemma: Carter and 'Undocumented' Mexicans," in Arthur F. Corwin, ed., *Immigrants – and Immigrants: Perspectives on Mexican Labor Migration to the United States* (Westport, Conn.: Greenwood Press, 1978), p. 333.

33 Material from press conference by Alan C. Nelson, Commissioner, U.S. Immigration and Naturalization Service, February 20, 1986 distributed by Federation for American Immigration Reform.

34 North, *Enforcing the Immigration Law*.

35 Corwin, "A Human Rights Dilemma," p. 335.

36 Michael J. Piore, *Birds of Passage: Migrant Labor and Industrial Societies* (New York: Cambridge University Press, 1979); Wayne A. Cornelius, Leo R. Chavez, and Jorge G. Castro, *Mexican Immigrants and Southern California: A Summary of Current Knowledge* (La Jolla, Center for United States–Mexican Studies, University of California, San Diego, 1982), pp. 34–8.

37 See Richard Paddock, "Prop. 41 Forecast Sees $2.8-Billion Cut from Welfare," *Los Angeles Times*, September 14, 1984; William Endicott, "Deukmejian to Vote No on Lottery, Three Other Key Ballot Initiatives," *Los Angeles Times*, November 3, 1986; and "Complete Election Returns: California Initiatives," *Los Angeles Times*, November 8, 1984.

38 *World Almanac and Book of Facts*, 1986 (New York: Newspaper Enterprise Association, 1986), p. 449.

39 Peter H. Schuck and Rogers M. Smith, *Citizenship without Consent: Illegal Aliens in the American Polity* (New Haven, Conn.: Yale University Press, 1985), p. 119.

40 Rudolf Walter Leonhardt, "Europe's Racial Time Bomb," *World Press Review*, December 1985, p. 28–9.

41 Schuck and Smith, *Citizenship Without Consent*.

42 Alejandro Portes, "Of Borders and States: A Skeptical Note on the Legislative Control of Immigration," in Wayne A. Cornelius and Ricardo Anzaldua Montoya, eds., *America's New Immigration Law: Origins, Rationales and Potential Consequences* (La Jolla: Center for United States–Mexican Studies, University of California, San Diego, 1983), pp. 17–30.

43 Muller and Espenshade, *The Fourth Wave*, p. 58.

44 Arthur F. Corwin, "A Story of Ad Hoc Exemptions," in Corwin, ed., *Immigrants – and Immigrants:*

Perspectives on Mexican Labor Migration to the United States (Westport, Conn.: Greenwood Press, 1978), pp. 176–224, p. 160; "Review & Outlook: Simpson–Volstead–Mazzoli", *Wall Street Journal*, July 3, 1987.

45 Anderson, *Illegal Aliens and Employer Sanctions*; Frank D. Bean and Teresa A. Sullivan, "Confronting the Problem," *Society* (May/June 1985): 67–73; Jorge A. Bustamante, "Las Propuestas de Politica Migratoria en los Estados Unidos y sus Reprercusiones en México," in Centro de Estudios Internacionales, *Indocumentados: Mitos y Realidades* (Mexico City: El Colegio de Mexico, 1979), pp. 197–208; Chiswick, "The Impact of Immigration"; Wayne A. Cornelius, "Simpson–Mazzoli vs. the Realities of Mexican Immigration," in Wayne A. Cornelius and Ricardo Anzaldua Montoya, eds., *America's New Immigration Law: Origins, Rationales, and Potential Consequences*, pp. 139–49; Kingsley Davis, "Emerging Issues in International Migration," *International Population Conference, Manila, 1981* (Liege: International Union for the Scientific Study of Population, 1981), Vol. II, pp. 419–430; Ward E. Y. Elliott, chapter on immigration policy in forthcoming book on U.S. population policy; Edwin Harwood, "How Should We Enforce Immigration Law?," in Nathan Glazer, ed., *Clamor at the Gates* (San Francisco: Institute for Contemporary Studies Press, 1985), pp. 73–91; North, *Enforcing the Immigration Law*.

46 Jagdish M. Bhagwati, "Taxation and International Migration: Recent Policy Issues," in Barry R. Chiswick, ed., *The Gateway: U.S. Immigration Issues and Policies* (Washington, D.C.: American Enterprise Institute for Public Policy Research, 1982), pp. 86–103.

47 U.S. Bureau of the Census, *Current Population Reports*, Series P-25, No. 983; Memorandum of October 15, 1985 from Jeffrey S. Passel to Roger A. Herriot, Chief, Population Division, U.S. Bureau of the Census.

48 U.S. Immigration and Naturalization Service, *1986 Statistical Yearbook of the Immigration and Naturalization Service* (Washington, D.C.: U.S. INS, 1987), pp. 8–9.

Index

age by legal status, 112–3
agricultural guest workers, 201
agriculture, 32, 106, 152
Aid to Families of Dependent Children (AFDC),
  59, 60, 79, 115, 156, 157, 202, 203; by legal
  status, 158–62
Albuquerque, New Mexico, 58
amnesty, *see* legalization of status
Anaheim, California, 32–3, 54, 56, 58, 63, 65
Anderson, Annelise, 198
apprehension history, 83–4, 86–7
Arab immigrants in France, 203
Aristotle, 2
Arizona, 31–3, 54, 56, 58, 59, 60, 62–3
Austin, Texas, 57, 61

Baca, Reynaldo, 76, 80
Badillo, Herman, 36
Bakersfield, California, 54, 56
Barabba, Vincent, 36
Bean, Frank, 40, 47, 73, 122, 125, 140
births by legal status, 108–12
border fence, 208–9
border patrol, 10, 12, 18–19, 28, 201–2, 208–9;
  see also U.S. Immigration and Naturalization
  Service
bracero program, 14, 16, 25, 29
Brownsville, Texas, 54, 55, 57, 61, 82
Bryan, Dexter, 76, 80
Bustamante, Jorge, 36, 82–3

California, 31–3, 53–4, 56, 58, 59–60, 62,
  63–71, 77, 78, 83, 85, 188
California Department of Social Services, 160–2
California Employment Development
  Department, 157
Cárdenas, Gilbert, 77, 83, 85
Carter, President Jimmy, 195
CENIET survey, 43–5, 46, 47, 51–3, 57–8, 74,
  75, 80, 83, 85
Cervera, Miguel, 52
CETA, 156

chain migration, 9
Chapman, Leonard, 34, 35
Chicago, Illinois, 33, 54, 56, 58, 59, 85
Chicano Pinto Research Project, 90, 91, 93
Chihuahua, Mexico, 42, 82
Chiswick, Barry, 175, 185
Chula Vista, California, 83, 84
class of worker by legal status, 152
Coahuila, Mexico, 82
Colorado, 31–2, 54, 56, 58, 59, 60, 62–3
Commission on Population Growth and the
  American Future, 190
Conroy, Michael E., 41–2
Constitution of the U.S., Fourteenth Amendment,
  3–4, 203–4
Cornelius, Wayne A., 47–8, 52, 76, 77, 80, 81,
  83, 84, 85, 115, 202
Corpus Christi, Texas, 57, 61
Corwin, Arthur, 44, 52, 202
County Health Alliance, 163
coyote, 10, 20, 21, 83, 86
Crewdson, John, 16, 52

Dallas, Texas, 55, 57, 61
death and injury, to undocumented immigrants,
  2, 16
Del Rio, Texas, 19
Denver, Colorado, 56
determinants of Mexican immigration, 8–24
Deukmejian, Governor George, 202
Diez-Cañedo, Juan, 39, 42, 47
Donabedian, Martin, 92
Dred Scott v. Sanford, 3
Durango, Mexico, 82

economic characteristics by legal status, 143–68
economic growth, impact on, 70–1
educational attainment by legal status, 120–5
El Paso, Texas, 2, 23, 33, 55, 57, 61
El Salvador, 46
employer sanctions, 196–8
employment, size of place, 85, 87

employment status by legal status, 144–53
entitlement program participation by legal status, 156–66
Espenshade, Thomas J., 189
Estrada, Leobardo, 42

Falasco, Dee, 92–3, 134–5
family reunification, 169–74, 199
female labor force participation by legal status, 145–6
fertility by legal status, 133–40
food stamp program participation, 156; by legal status, 157–8
Fourteenth Amendment, *see* Constitution of the U.S., Fourteenth Amendment
France, 203
Fresno, California, 54, 56

García, Robert S., 90, 91, 92
García y Griego, Manuel, 39–40, 42, 47, 81–2, 193
garment industry, 69, 78, 80, 81, 84, 85, 115, 149, 188, 204
general assistance, 157; by legal status, 165–6
geographic distribution, 53–61; in Los Angeles County, by legal status, 125–33
geographic origin in Mexico, 81–3, 86
Germany, 203
Giner de los Ríos, Francisco, 193
Goldberg, Howard, 35–6, 38, 41, 42, 47
Guanajuato, Mexico, 42, 82
Gunther, Jeffrey, 73

Hancock, Paula, 166, 206
Harwood, Edwin, 21, 139
Hawaii, 68
Heer, David, 1, 36–7, 38, 42, 46, 47, 48–51, 52, 64, 65, 66, 78, 101–2, 135–6, 205–6
Hill, Kenneth, 42
Hirschman, Charles, 22–3, 40
Hoffman, Abraham, 28
Houston, Texas, 33, 55, 57, 61, 74
Houstoun, Marion F., 39, 75–6, 80, 83, 84, 156, 168, 175–6
human subjects constraints, 90–2

Illinois, 31–3, 54, 56, 58, 60, 62–3, 77, 85
immigration and citizenship laws, 3–5, 11–24 (*see also* Constitution of the U.S., Fourteenth Amendment); Alien Contract Labor Law of 1885, 11, 12; Immigration Act of 1882, 11, 12; Immigration Act of 1917, 11, 15–16; Immigration Act of 1924, 12, 24–5; Immigration Act of 1952, 12; Immigration Act of 1965, 12–13; Immigration Act of 1976,
13–14, 15; Immigration Reform and Control Act of 1986, 4–5, 16–17, 19, 74, 169, 173–4, 186, 196–202; of 1875, 11; of 1921, 12, 24–5; of 1925, 12; of 1929, 12; of 1978, 14
immigration history by legal status, 117–20
immigration policy options, 187–211
income, 58, 60–61; by legal status, 154–6
income of black families, impact on, 63–5, 69
income of U.S.-born Hispanic-origin families, impact on, 63–5, 69–70
income per capita, impact on, 70–1
industry in which employed, 69; by legal status, 149–52
INS, *see* U.S. Immigration and Naturalization Service; *see also* border patrol
Iran, 46

Jalisco, Mexico, 42, 47, 52, 77, 78, 80, 81, 82, 83, 84, 85, 115
Jones, Richard C., 74
jus sanguinis, 4, 203
jus soli, 4, 203

Kearney, Michael, 47
Keely, Charles B., 37, 41
King, Allan G., 40, 41–2, 47, 73
Kraly, Eleanor P., 37
Kubiske, Lisa, 23, 78, 84, 85

labor union membership, 85–6, 87
Lancaster, Clarice, 38, 41, 42, 47
Laredo, Texas, 23, 55, 57, 60
Lee, Everett, 8
legal aid, 24, 76
legal immigration from Mexico, 7, 22, 24–5
legal status, 3–5, 98–105, 169–74; impact on earnings, 175–86
legal underclass, 3, 106, 143
legalization of status (amnesty), 198–201, 206–8
Leighton, Alexander, 86
length of stay by legal status, 172–4
Lesko Associates, 35, 36, 39, 41, 47
Los Angeles, California (city), 1–2, 20, 76, 82, 83–4, 85–6
Los Angeles County, California, 5–6, 18–19, 32–3, 46, 48–9, 53, 54, 56, 59, 61, 63–71, 76, 78, 80, 84, 106, 188, 189, 210
Los Angeles County Board of Supervisors, 163
Los Angeles County Department of Charities, 28
Los Angeles County Department of Public Social Services, 157
Los Angeles County Parents Survey, 5–6, 48–9, 78–9, 88–97, 98– 105, 106–42, 143–68, 169–74, 175–86
Los Angeles Unified School District, 69

Louisiana, 68

McAllen, Texas, 33, 55, 57, 61
Madrid, Miguel de la, 194
Mahony, Archbishop Roger, 199
Maram, Sheldon, 78, 80–1, 84–5, 85–6, 115
marital and family status, 46–8, 80–1; by legal status, 112, 114–17
marketable permits, 207–8, 209–10
Marshall, Secretary of Labor Ray, 36, 40
Martin, Philip, 68
Massey, Douglas S., 42, 47, 77, 80
Matamoras, Mexico, 82
Medicaid/Medi-Cal, 156, 157, 163–4, 202
Mexican Labor Program, see bracero program
Mexican-born persons in U.S., 25–30
Mexico: economy of, 192–5; energy consumption per capita, 10–11; income per capita, 9, 10; population of, 11, 31
Mexico City, Mexico, 23, 78
Michoacán, Mexico, 42, 44, 47, 77, 80, 82
Mines, Richard, 21, 47, 77, 78, 81
minimum wage and fair labor standards, 204–5
Moore, Joan, 90, 93
Muller, Thomas, 70, 71, 189; see also Urban Institute

Nelson, Eugene, 16
New Mexico, 31–2, 54, 56, 58, 60, 62–3
New York, 85
nonresponse rate, 95–7
North, David S., 39, 75–6, 80, 83, 84, 85, 156, 157, 163, 168, 175–6, 197–8, 202
Norton, Arthur, 94
Nuevo León, Mexico, 82
number of immigrants, 4, 7, 18, 24–30, 34–53

Oaxaca, Mexico, 47
occupation by legal status, 146–9
One Stop Immigration Service Center, 24, 36, 74, 76, 80, 82, 83–4, 149
open border, 205
Operation Wetback, 29
Oxnard, California, 54, 56, 64

Passel, Jeffrey, 18, 40, 42, 43–4, 45–6, 47, 48–9, 51, 53–7, 64, 65–6, 73, 74, 79, 100, 102, 112, 135–6, 185, 199
Pearce, James, 73
Phoenix, Arizona, 54, 56
Piore, Michael, 202
Portes, Alejandro, 39–40, 204
Portillo, President Lopez, 192
poverty, 58, 60–1; impact on, 62–3, 70–1
prices, impact on, 61–3, 70

profits, impact on, 70
public housing, 156; by legal status, 164–5

quotas, 12–14, 207–8, 209

railroad retirement, 165–6
Rand Corporation, 63, 69–70, 122, 188
Reagan, President Ronald, 195
Refugee Act of 1980, 13, 14
Reichert, Joshua S., 42, 47, 77, 80
remittances, 39, 84, 87, 193
restaurant industry, 78, 80, 81, 84, 86, 115
Reyes and Associates, 74
Riverside, California, 33, 54, 56, 64
Rizo-Patrón, Jorge, 41–2
Roberts, Kenneth, 41–2
Robinson, J. Gregory, 38–9, 42, 47
Rodino bill, 195

Sacramento, California, 19, 54, 56
Salcido, Ramón, 86
Salinas, California, 54, 56
Samora, Julian, 20, 80
sample, 92–3
San Antonio, Texas, 55, 57, 59, 61, 74, 77, 82, 83, 85
San Clemente, California, 19
San Diego, California, 19, 21, 33, 54, 56, 83, 84
San Francisco–Oakland, California, 33, 54, 56
San Jose, California, 54, 56
San Luis Potosí, Mexico, 42, 82
Sauvy, Alfred, 194
Scheuren, Frederick J., 38, 41, 42, 47
school enrollment and progress by legal status, 140–2
schools, impact on, 63, 69
Schuck, Peter, 203
Select Commission on Immigration and Refugee Policy, 42, 195, 197, 200
settlement intention, 81
sex, 79–80, 106
Siegel, Jacob S., 42
Silva v. Levi, 14–15, 16
Simon, Julian, 190
Simpson–Mazzoli bill, 194, 195
Smith, Rogers, 203
social consequences, 61–71
social security, 165–6
Southern California, 15, 63–71
Southern California Association of Governments (SCAG), 63, 66–7, 69
Spengler, Joseph J., 8
standard of living, impact on, 187–90
Stockton, California, 56
stress, 86, 87

Stuart, James, 47
Supplemental Security Income (SSI), 165–6
survey methods, 72–87
Swicegood, Gray, 140

Tamaulipas, Mexico, 82
Taney, Chief Justice Roger, 3
taxes, impact on, 65, 70
taxes paid, by legal status, 166–8
Texas, 2, 19, 23, 31–3, 54, 55–7, 58, 59–60, 61, 62–3, 67, 82, 83
Texas proviso, 195; *see also* immigration and citizenship laws, Immigration Act of 1952
Tijuana, Mexico, 20, 21, 78
Tucson, Arizona, 56
Turkish immigrants in Germany, 203

underclass, 3, 143
unemployment, 9; by legal status, 144–6
unemployment, impact on, 63, 69
unemployment insurance, 156; by legal status, 162–3
U.S. Border Patrol, *see* border patrol
U.S. Commission on Civil Rights, 29

U.S. Immigration and Naturalization Service (INS), 4, 15, 16–22, 29, 30, 34–5, 36, 40, 44, 49, 55–7, 74, 75, 77, 83–4, 139, 157, 163, 196, 197, 201–2
Urban Institute, 63, 67–8, 69, 70, 71, 188, 204

validity of legal status responses, 100–5
Van Arsdol, Maurice D., Jr., 36, 37, 74, 76, 80, 82, 83–4, 149
Villalpando, M. Vic, 83, 84, 168
Visalia, California, 54, 56

wages: hourly, in relation to minimum wage, 155–6; impact on, 63, 69
Warren, Robert, 43–4, 45–7, 48–9, 51, 79, 100, 102, 185, 199
Washington State, 55, 68
"white flight," 63, 66–9
Woodrow, Karen A., 51–2, 53–5

Zacatecas, Mexico, 21, 42, 44, 47, 77, 78, 82
Zazueta, César, 19, 20, 83
Zazueta, Carlos H., 19, 20, 83

Other books in the Arnold and Carolyn Rose Monograph Series

J. Milton Yinger, Kiyoshi Ikeda, Frank Laycock, and Stephen J. Cutler: *Middle Start: An Experiment in the Educational Enrichment of Young Adolescents*

James A. Geschwender: *Class, Race, and Worker Insurgency: The League of Revolutionary Black Workers*

Paul Ritterband: *Education, Employment, and Migration: Israel in Comparative Perspective*

John Low-Beer: *Protest and Participation: The New Working Class in Italy*

Orin E. Klapp: *Opening and Closing: Strategies of Information Adaptation in Society*

Rita James Simon: *Continuity and Change: A Study of Two Ethnic Communities in Israel*

Marshall B. Clinard: *Cities with Little Crime: The Case of Switzerland**

Steven T. Bossert: *Tasks and Social Relationships in Classrooms: A Study of Instructional Organization and Its Consequences**

Richard E. Johnson: *Juvenile Delinquency and Its Origins: An Integrated Theoretical Approach**

David R. Heise: *Understanding Events: Affect and the Construction of Social Action*

Ida Harper Simpson: *From Student to Nurse: A Longitudinal Study of Socialization*

Stephen P. Turner: *Sociological Explanation as Translation*

Janet W. Salaff: *Working Daughters of Hong Kong: Filial Piety or Power in the Family?*

Joseph Chamie: *Religion and Fertility: Arab Christian–Muslim Differentials*

William Friedland, Amy Barton, Robert Thomas: *Manufacturing Green Gold: Capital Labor, and Technology in the Lettuce Industry*

Richard N. Adams: *Paradoxical Harvest: Energy and Explanation in British History, 1870–1914*

Mary F. Rogers: *Sociology, Ethnomethodology, and Experience: A Phenomenological Critique*

James R. Beniger: *Trafficking in Drug Users: Professional Exchange Networks in the Control of Deviance*

Andrew J. Weigert, J. Smith Teitge, and Dennis W. Teitge: *Society and Identity: Toward a Sociological Psychology*

Jon Miller: *Pathways in the Workplace: The Effects of Race and Gender on Access to Organizational Resources*

Michael A. Faia: *Dynamic Functionalism: Strategy and Tactics*

Joyce Rothschild and J. Allen Whitt: *The Co-operative Workplace: Potentials and Dilemmas of Organizational Democracy*

Russell Thornton: *We Shall Live Again: The 1870 and 1890 Ghost Dance Movements as Demographic Revitalization*

Severyn T. Bruyn: *The Field of Social Investment*

Guy E. Swanson: *Ego Defenses and the Legitimation of Behaviour*

Liah Greenfeld: *Different Worlds: A Sociological Study of Taste, Choice and Success in Art*

Thomas K. Rudel: *Situations and Strategies in American Land-Use Planning*

Percy C. Hintzen: *The Costs of Regime Survival: Racial Mobilization, Elite Domination and Control of the State in Guyana and Trinidad*

John T. Flint: *Historical Role Analysis in the Study of Religious Change: Mass Educational Development in Norway, 1740–1891*

Judith R. Blau: *The Shape of Culture: A Study of Cultural Patterns in the United States*
Fred C. Pampel and John B. Williamson: *Age, Class, Politics and the Welfare State*
Thomas J. Fararo: *The Meaning of General Theoretical Sociology: Tradition and Formalization*
Lewis F. Carter: *Control and Charisma in Rajneeshpuram: The Role of Shared Values in the Creation of a Community*
Kenneth Baugh: *The Methodology of Herbert Blumer*

*Available from the American Sociological Association, 1722 N Street, N.W., Washington, DC 20036.